Wittgenstein's Folly

I0092041

Wittgenstein's Folly: Philosophy, Psychoanalysis and Language Games presents a dialogue between the philosopher Ludwig Wittgenstein, the author Françoise Davoine and Davoine's patients with extreme lived experience.

This book begins with Davoine's seminar at the École des Hautes Études en Sciences Sociales in Paris, which is attended by Wittgenstein. He then accompanies Davoine on visits to colleagues at the Austen Riggs Center in Massachusetts, in California, on a Sioux reservation in South Dakota and at Freud's house in Vienna. The dialogic form of the book allows a performance centered on the psychotherapy of madness and trauma, in which Wittgenstein takes the floor. Davoine introduces us to a contemporary Feast of Fools and creates new language games with madness, enlarging the scope of psychoanalytic approaches to authors like Wittgenstein. The chapters of this book closely resemble short plays in which a conversation with living human beings or with characters from philosophy, literature, science and the arts encounter one another and begin to open new ways of speaking that can render the "mad" more familiar and more manageable.

Wittgenstein's Folly: Philosophy, Psychoanalysis and Language Games will be of great interest to psychoanalysts and to academics and students engaged in psychoanalytic studies, philosophy and trauma-related studies.

Françoise Davoine is a psychoanalyst based in France. She is a former professor at the Centre for the Study of Social Movements, École des Hautes Études en Sciences Sociales (EHESS) in Paris, where she and Jean-Max Gaudillière conducted a weekly seminar on Madness and the Social Link for 40 years. She presents internationally and is the author of many books and articles.

Wittgenstein's Folly

Philosophy, Psychoanalysis and Language Games
2

Françoise Davoine

Translation by William J. Hurst

Manuscript Preparation by
Lee Watroba

Routledge
Taylor & Francis Group

LONDON AND NEW YORK

Designed cover image: Sophie Gaudilliere, 2016

First published in English 2024 by Routledge
Second edition published 2024
by Routledge
4 Park Square, Milton Park, Abingdon, Oxon, OX14 4RN

and by Routledge
605 Third Avenue, New York, NY 10158

Routledge is an imprint of the Taylor & Francis Group, an informa business

First edition in French published as La Folie Wittgenstein, E.P.E.L,
Paris 1992

First Edition in English published as Wittgenstein's Folly, trad.
William Hurst YBK Publishers,

New York 2012

Second Edition in French published as La Folie Wittgenstein,
Éditions du Croquant,

Bellecombe-en-Bauges 2012

British Library Cataloguing-in-Publication Data
A catalogue record for this book is available from the British Library

ISBN: 9781032568683 (hbk)
ISBN: 9781032568676 (pbk)
ISBN: 9781003437451 (ebk)

DOI: 10.4324/9781003437451

Typeset in Times New Roman
by codeMantra

In memory of

Jean Max Gaudillière
Edmond Sanquier, Martin Cooperman, Jerry Mohatt

Contents

Preface to the Second French Edition

Playing Hooky

The preface to Ludwig Wittgenstein's *Philosophical Investigations* ends with these remarks:

I make them (these investigations) public with doubtful feelings. It is not impossible that it should fall to the lot of this work, in its poverty and in the darkness of this time, to bring light into one brain or another—but, of course, it is not likely. I should not like my writing to spare other people the trouble of thinking. But, if possible, to stimulate someone to thoughts of his own. I should have liked to produce a good book. This has not come about, but the time is past in which I could improve it. Cambridge, January 1945.[1]

Like the *Tractatus* (which Wittgenstein wrote while in Austrian uniform, on the Eastern front during the First World War), the first part of The *Philosophical Investigations* was written in numbered paragraphs, this time totaling 693. The second part consists of 14 short chapters. Reading this work stimulated not really thoughts of my own but rather thoughts that came to me in the course of my analytic work.

"Wittgenstein's Folly" was first an object of study in the seminar "Madness and the Social Link," which I led with Jean-Max Gaudillière at the *Ecole des Hautes Etudes en Sciences Sociales*. From 1985 to 1988, the seminar was devoted to Wittgenstein and his contemporary Harry Stack Sullivan.[2] They both seemed to intervene, in a kind of polyphony of voices, whenever the topic or a question about transference at the limits of psychoanalysis came up, as in cases of madness and trauma. This might be during sessions between the analyst and her patients, or while on a visit to the Austin Riggs Center in Massachusetts, or during the times we spent among the Sioux of South Dakota. My account of the intrusions by these two ghosts is presented in the context of a conversation with a friend, Paul, which took place at his house in the woods. This is how the conversation format of *Wittgenstein's Folly* took shape. After the fact, I asked myself about the liberty I had taken by giving Wittgenstein a voice, without seeking the approval of specialists. Then, I was reassured by reading the *Colloquia* of Erasmus, and his *Praise of Folly,*[3] as well as Lucien's *Dialogues of the Dead,* a major source about a time when folly itself was the object of passionate interest.

During the two years in which this book was seeking a publisher, Ray Monk published a biography with the title, *Ludwig Wittgenstein: The Duty of Genius*. It taught me, *a posteriori,* the importance of war and captivity for the philosopher's symptoms, leading to his decision to abandon philosophy during the ten years following his release from a prisoner-of-war camp in Monte Casino in August 1919. He had been captured while engaged in fighting on the Southern Front in the Alps on November 3, 1918. He finally returned to Cambridge in 1929. Today, this would qualify as PTSD (post-traumatic stress disorder) or according to the French designation, "post-traumatic syndrome," with suicidal features and with a sense of brutality. Like many former warriors, such as Apollinaire, about whom Annette Becker wrote "the biography of war," Wittgenstein refused to give up his old uniform, a serious and disturbing concern for those around him. During the first two decades of the twentieth century, three of his brothers killed themselves, and Paul, the pianist, for whom Ravel composed his *Concerto for the left hand,* had his right arm amputated while at the Front in Galicia and was then taken into captivity in Russia, from which he came back traumatized.

Ray Monk's biography provided me with a confirmation of which I had never even dared to dream. Wittgenstein had actually played the role of patients captured by madness that I had proposed for him. Having counseled one of his disciples, the Irishman Maurice O'C. Drury, to become a physician rather than a philosopher, he presented him, as a birthday gift in 1936, Freud's *Interpretation of Dreams* (Drury, p. 136)*,* insisting all the while that with respect to dreams, his own were the expressions of fears and not of desires (Drury, p. 154). During this period, Freud was again taking up the questions he had considered in his *Neurotica,* which he abandoned in 1897 along with the field of trauma, as he acknowledged in a letter to Fliess on the September 21, 1897 (Freud-Fliess, pp. 264–266). Afflicted with cancer, his daughter taken by the Spanish flu and a grandson dead three years later, he was raising questions in *Moses and Monotheism*—while his books were being burned in a Nazi auto-da-fé—about the effacement of traces and about an unconscious that is "not the result of repression," but is at work in the madness of war. He had already mentioned this unconscious in *The Gradiva* and in *The Uncanny.*

At the same time, in 1938, just after the Anschluss and during the dark years of Nazism in Austria, Wittgenstein visited Maurice O'C. Drury and made an unusual request of him. "During his visit to Dublin," writes Drury, "Wittgenstein asked me if I could arrange for him to have discussions with patients who were seriously mentally ill. He said that this would be a matter of great interest to him" (Drury, p. 140). After interviewing Wittgenstein, the Medical Superintendent at St. Patrick's Hospital agreed. The scene that followed could figure in *Wittgenstein's Folly:* "Wittgenstein then went two or three days a week and visited some of the long-stay patients who had few to visit them. He became particularly interested in one elderly man, of whom he said: 'This man is much more intelligent than his doctors'" (Drury, p. 140). As he wanted Drury to continue meeting with this patient, Wittgenstein introduced him to Drury, who remarked on this meeting: "I was fascinated to see how gently and helpfully Wittgenstein was able to discuss with him.

When at one point I tried to join in the discussion, Wittgenstein at once told me to 'shut-up'. Afterwards, when we were walking home, Wittgenstein (said): 'When you are playing ping-pong, you mustn't use a tennis racket'" (Drury, p. 140).

There is also this scene: After Britain mobilized for war, Drury was sent to North Africa, to Egypt and from there much later to the Normandy coast where he was one of the medical officers aboard a landing craft on D-Day (Drury, p. 148). After the Normandy landing, while stationed near Bayeux, Wittgenstein wrote to him telling him he was reading Plato's *Theaetetus*. Not long after that Wittgenstein sent him a copy of a translation of Plato's *Theaetetus,* which he "tried to read under the difficulties of camp life" (Drury, p. 149). When Drury returned after the war, he was "in a state of considerable emotional turmoil and indecision" (Drury, p. 151). It was at that time that he decided to become a psychiatrist. Wittgenstein encouraged him and following his principle that "madness need not be regarded as an illness" (Drury, p. 222, fn.38), he cautioned him on the subject of physical treatment in psychiatry recommended: ". . . don't ever think that all human problems can be solved in this way" (Drury, p. 152). He deplored the lack of imagination in physicians and added: "Always take a chair and sit down by the patient's bedside; don't stand at the end of the bed in a dictatorial attitude. Let your patients feel they have time to talk to you" (Drury, p. 154).

During the Second World War, Wittgenstein remained in London. Employed as a dispensary porter at Guy's Hospital (Drury, p. 145), where the wounded were streaming in, he would tell them not to take their "mind-numbing" medications. Then, he was called to Newcastle to participate in research on the physiology of shock. While there, even amid the experiments, he worried about how patients could escape their victimization.

Since the first edition of *Wittgenstein's Folly (La Folie Wittgenstein, 1991),* I have been "playing hooky" with "Forward Psychiatry," as the psychotherapy practiced on the Front was named. Coming directly out of the trenches of 1917, its principles were formulated by the American psychiatrist, Thomas Salmon. A physician on Ellis Island in 1904, he had the job of examining the immigrants who were filing through. Between America's entry into the First World War in April 1917, and the arrival of its Forces to the Front in October of that year, Salmon was sent on reconnaissance to England to study the effects of "shell shock." His report included comprehensive recommendations for addressing future psychic casualties among those involved in the war. Through the clinical experience of analysts engaged in the war—Sandor Ferenczi in Hungary, William Rivers in England, Frieda Fromm Reichmann, first a neurologist working with head injured soldiers in a military hospital in Königsberg, Germany, and then an analyst at Chestnut Lodge in the United States—this war psychotherapy contributed to the invention of a psychoanalysis of the psychoses and of traumas. This clinical tradition was thus born on the Front, of war, but also of immigration.

Beginning at Hull House, co-founded by Jane Hull in 1889, a psychotherapy of traumas related to immigration began to emerge. Hull House, which took in immigrant children and their mothers for whom it sometimes "spelled the difference

between life and death" (Perry, p. 235), had a significant impact on the development of American psychiatry, especially through the work of Adolf Meyer. Harry
Stack Sullivan, in 1915, while still in medical school, served as an "industrial surgeon" at a steel mill in Gary, Indiana (Perry, pp. 165–166). Steel mills employed
large numbers of immigrants. Since the last decade of the previous century, there
was the phenomenon of the Chicago School of the social sciences (so named by
William James). This evolved from the work of researchers at the University of
Chicago, who looked on the city of Chicago as their laboratory and who were
responsible not only for the emergence of a new social science that included as
foundational the principles of American pragmatism but also for the creation of
a new American psychiatry, beginning with Meyer and continuing through Sullivan who came to think of himself as a "social psychologist." The Chicago School
coined the phrase "marginal man," which Sullivan considered himself to be. During the war, he became a liaison officer with Saint Elizabeth military hospital.
These experiences of working with immigrants and with soldiers in a military hospital oriented his practice toward a psychoanalysis of schizophrenia considered as
a response to the traumas and catastrophes of History. He continued developing
his intensive dynamic psychotherapy of psychosis with Frieda Fromm Reichmann
after her exile to the United States in 1935. This tradition was largely ignored in
France where electric shock treatments flourished during the war and continued
once peace returned, along with a medical discourse on psychosis that objectified
patients.

Yet, during "the long weekend" between the two wars, to quote Bion's title, the
new paradigm of quantum mechanics had appeared, which privileged the interferences between the observer/researcher and the objects observed. The physicist
Erwin Schrödinger, a contemporary of Wittgenstein, warned psychologists "against
yielding to the illusion of objectivity by enclosing their patients in definitive struc-
tures." In Ireland, where he had gone into exile during the Nazi period, giving up
the Max Planck chair in Berlin, he got to know Drury in Dublin, as his wife was
hospitalized in his ward.

After its release in 1992, this book pointed me toward the warpath of those who
can possibly overcome the consequences of traumas, on condition of their finding
someone to talk to about "what they cannot speak and therefore only show" as
Wittgenstein would say. "*Therapon,*" *the* ancient name for this "someone," was
attested to by Homer in the Iliad, showing that war psychotherapy had developed
already so that Achilles could find his soul in the last song and begin to breathe
again (Psyche). Our current psychoanalysis of madness and traumas is as old as the
world. The Harvard Hellenist, Gregory Nagy, emphasized the role of "*therapon*"
in the *Iliad,* of Patroclus for Achilles, meaning the second in combat, and the ritual
double, responsible for the funerary honors.

This word "*therapon*" identifies the place of the analyst working with patients
who defy the limits of classical psychoanalysis. Wittgenstein installed himself in
this book right away and pushed the analyst to find her friend Paul for "supervision" of a situation as strange and as old as war. Cervantes immortalized it in

the person of Sancho Panza. And after him, inspired by Don Quixote, Laurence Sterne, in *The Life and Opinions of Tristram Shandy, Gentleman,* created Corporal Trim, Captain Toby's aide-de-camp. "A book I like greatly," Wittgenstein said to Drury, "is Sterne's *Tristram Shandy.* That is one of my favorite books . . . . I am particularly fond of the character of Corporal Trim in *Tristram Shandy"* (Drury, pp. 133–134). Trim is the *"therapon"* of "my uncle Toby," who was injured in the battle of Namur in 1695, during the Nine Years' War between England and France. Thanks to Trim, he goes through a war psychotherapy which he will transfer to his young nephew already traumatized in the womb, if we trust the first chapter. Captain Toby is a paradigmatic figure for the psychoanalysis of traumas, as Captain Rivers and Captain Bion—who must have been familiar with Sterne's novel—would also become.

Such is probably the role that I had Wittgenstein play with the analyst in this book. But he also has another function, that of "a surviving image" coming back like a ghost. This expression was coined by Aby Warburg, an art historian of the Renaissance who became mad during the First World War and was confined in the clinic of Freud's disciple, Ludwig Binswanger, during the early twenties. He overcame this madness thanks to his own disciple Fritz Saxl who acted as his *therapon.* Such images, which he calls *"nachleben,* after life," arise at the border of the unnamable and unrepresentable that Lacan calls the Real.

In this book, Wittgenstein comes up with this definition since he enters it as a spooky character to disturb the analyst and to teach her how to give up the posture dictated by neutrality. Twenty years after, I continue to think that he is a major analyst on the question of the Real, believed to be "impossible to be written," whereas it may be first approached through a specific transference, in the oral tradition, before being inscribed in books or otherwise. Wittgenstein himself privileged the oral form, publishing only two books during his lifetime.

Continuing playing hooky, I finally learned that in the Middle Ages, madness was, as today, the object of shock treatments and of purely organicist theories. In a parallel way, "it took refuge in literature," to transmit to us what she has learned. Indeed, Folly claims that her speech is that of a woman in Erasmus' *In Praise of Folly.* The Medieval dictum: *"La folie est plus* engin *que destin"*—madness is more intelligence than destiny"—indicates that, yes, it is possible to come out of madness, on condition of having encounters, in the dialogical space of wonder; *"l'espace de la merveille."* In medieval novels, the fool inhabits the wild space of the mountain and the forest, where time stops, where coincidences happen, where monsters show themselves (to show, *"montrer"* in French, is akin to the word "monster"), and where fairies speak, which can make you crazy.

And so, to quote the first verse of Jacques Prévert's poetry, *"En sortant de l'école, nous avons rencontré,* going out of school, we came across . . . ." In my case, after leaving my schools in social sciences and psychoanalysis, I came across, thanks to Wittgenstein, medieval fools, those traumatized by war, inventors of new scientific paradigms and other co-researchers in the knowledge of madness, who led me then to write *History Beyond Trauma; Fighting Melancholia: Don Quixote's Teaching;*

A Word to the Wise: Don Quixote Returns to Fight Perversion; and *Mother Folly: A Tale.*

I also encountered precious translators for this book: Tununa Mercado in Argentina, Alberto Montoya in Mexico, Roberto Aceituno in Chile, Johannes Myrrä in Finland, Angelos Voutsas in Athens, Ariel Omert in Tel Aviv and William Hurst in New York. Ariel Olmert and William Hurst's introductions to their translations are published at the end of this book. I extend my thanks to all, in fond friendship.

Most especially I want to recognize Helene Thomas and Marc Bernardot who have made this new edition possible at Editions du Croquant, in Bellecombe-en-Bauges, near the birthplace of my paternal grandmother, *la Dame Jeanne,* whom the reader will encounter in the next to last chapter of the book. She was a native of Doucy-en-Bouges.

Notes

1 Ludwig Wittgenstein, *PI,* Preface, p. VIII.
2 Cf. Harry Stack Sullivan, *Schizophrenia as a Human Process* (New York: Norton, 1975). Introduction and Commentaries by Helen Swick Perry.
3 This book is a collection of Sullivan's principal articles published during his career as a psychiatrist and collected by Perry for his biography.

Chapter Introductions

Chapter 1

Wittgenstein intrudes on a meeting of psychoanalysts where the author FD is giving a talk about transference with psychosis, occurring at the limits of mainstream psychoanalysis. FD confides to Paul, FD's colleague and friend, that his name is Wittgenstein.

Chapter 2

Paul invites them into his Parisian apartment to discuss about dreams of fear which were raised by Wittgenstein, in contrast to dreams of desire. To the question: what unconscious knowledge is at stake in this case, Wittgenstein answers with the question: how do we get to know? For instance, how a diviner gets to know the message sent by his god? Paul invites FD to his log house in the woods to recount her uncanny encounter with Wittgenstein.

Chapter 3

FD tells Paul how, at first, she was introduced to Wittgenstein by a former catatonic patient whom she calls the Philosopher. Then, Wittgenstein's voice interfered between them, speaking of language games. Wishing to discover what language game took place in the positive outcome of the Philosopher's analysis, FD decides to visit a psychoanalyst of psychosis in the United States.

Chapter 4

FD tells Paul the story of her geographic transferences: first in England where she visited an anti-psychiatrist, and also to the north of France, where she became an analyst with confined patients in public psychiatric hospitals. Looking beyond theories, she discovers a tradition in the United States devoted to the practice of transference with psychosis since the First World War, still at work at Chestnut Lodge and Austen Riggs Center. She then takes the plane to visit Otto Will, its former medical director, where she meets Wittgenstein, who was concerned by the limits of speech between pain and its expression.

Chapter 5

Otto Will puzzles her more than he enlightens her problem, as he displays his unorthodox practice at the limits of language and fragments of his analysis with Harry Stack Sullivan who broke the rule of neutrality so that he could reach a cut-out episode of his infancy. Her own training did not prepare her to grasp Frieda Fromm Reichmann's statements, who became his analyst at Chestnut Lodge after Sullivan's death. Wittgenstein's voice supports Otto Will against FD's prejudice.

Chapter 6

The debriefing of her disillusion unfolds in the plane back to Paris, as Wittgenstein is sitting next to her. As he contends that in three stories disclosed by Otto Will, "an ostensive definition" takes place, showing what cannot be said, which interferes with the analyst's so-called private life. Then he discloses that resonance instead of staying silent. His criticism of psychoanalytic theories makes her unable to grasp that the philosopher's analysis followed Otto Will's path, which Wittgenstein supports, insisting on the creation of new language games from ostensive definitions.

Chapter 8

As Wittgenstein states that Casimir's problem was linked to a broken tool of a name, he exposes to FD his method to deal with broken names, which he describes in § 41 of his Philosophical Investigations. Although she sticks at first to Lacanian signifiers, she follows Wittgenstein's process and has to acknowledge that she "nodded" in response to the broken tool, creating a language game by performing unwittingly a kind of "strip tease" that linked Casimir to the erasure of a village in his linage, where women were stripped off to be tortured. The analyst's nod comes from analogous experience in her linage too. This is the story she will carry over the ocean.

Chapter 9

After the visit of Paul's neighbor, an authentic diviner, FD recounts her presentation at Austen Riggs Center which she started by quoting Lacan's Seminar on the Ethics of Psychoanalysis. Martin Cooperman stresses the part she plays in "the folie à deux" with Casimir. An ancient flight surgeon at Guadalcanal, he tells her that after years of "defeating process," a session may happen when they meet, getting out of hiding behind their respective symptoms and theories. Wittgenstein appears to quote his own Conference on Ethics where he spoke in the first person and introduced the topic of ghosts.

Chapter 10

At the Red Lion Inn garden, in Stockbridge, FD wonders why the process of naming, in the transference, triggers so much violence. Wittgenstein exposes that a
name survives the absence of its bearer, such as the name of Arthur's sword, which
is known even after it has been broken into pieces. Could it be, she argues, that rage
is necessary to destroy the things into which people are reduced by ruthless agen-
cies so that their name can prevail? As she asks Wittgenstein about his own ghosts,
he quits the scene after drawing a scribble on the paper cloth that Jerry Fromm,
who attended her presentation, calls a Winnicott's "squiggle."

Chapter 11

Another psychotherapist, Jerry Mohatt, who came to Riggs from the Rosebud Reservation where he lives in Sud Dakita, attended FD's presentation. Finding reso-
nances with Sioux ceremonies, he invites her to share her experience with medicine
men. There she participates in a giveaway set up by a family to honor its members killed in a car accident and in ceremonies performed by Joe Eagle Elk. When
Wittgenstein appears, he calls "association of practices" her exchanges of clinical
stories with Joe and his helper Stanley Red Bird, on the same footing as with her
colleagues at Riggs. However, she fears that her colleagues back home would call
that witchcraft.

Chapter 12

On her way back to Paris, she discovers a lump in her stomach, which necessitates
a surgery. At the same time, she receives an alarming letter, announcing her patient
Theodore's hospitalization. In her office, Wittgenstein and Harry Stack Sullivan
watch her panic. They try to help her concentrate on what happened between her
patient and herself during their last session, and to consider his madness not as an
illness, but as a social relationship that he observed intensely. Her fear increases
to be condemned by psychiatrists, when a delusional Theodore enters the room.
Plagued by witchcraft, he is assailed by demons and leaves the room, for half an
hour, he says. Suspense!

Chapter 13

Paul, to whom that story is counted, wonders if Theodore was aware of the presence of Sullivan and Wittgenstein. Indeed, when he comes back half an hour
later, he agrees with their comments of situations which suddenly lose all meaning, and their many examples that he heard when he came back. Joining their
conversation, he enters their language game, discarding totally her presence.
When they decide to go for a walk and continue to examine the collapse of language that only the fools may witness, FD is relieved that she can at last take care
of her health.

Chapter 14

After the surgery, she apprehends to resume her work a month later, especially with Theodore. Wittgenstein appears to help as usual, with the image of a fly-bottle that caught her patient at first while she was observing him from outside, and in which she is now trapped, not knowing how to escape. A good start for their future encounter, says Wittgenstein, is to find a point of agreement for a new language game between them.

Chapter 15

Having been diagnosed "borderline" for cancer, FD goes back to the psychiatric hospital and interacts with a borderline girl. Asked for supervision, Wittgenstein advises her to let go the research of causes for mental processes inside the psyche. She should turn toward what happened between them and find an agreement in the weird language game they shared. Back to her office, she waits for Theodore while talking with Wittgenstein about his notion "paradigm." A new paradigm emerges indeed, when Theodore discloses his perception of something going wrong for FD, before her summer vacations. As she had no clue about it, he looked for the cause of his impression in the attacks by demons.

Chapter 16

Wittgenstein's insistence about the use of language between pain and its expression takes place in a dialogue with Constance, as he now dares to speak directly with FD's patients. Fighting the notion of private experience, he replays with her the dialogue starting his "Notes on Private Experience," between the philosopher and a person with a faraway look. The story goes back to Constance's first arrival in FD's office and the strange dream she made afterward, which triggered a first agreement between them. Such interference with her "private life" contradicting the rule of neutrality, she decides to go to Vienna for sound supervision.

Chapter 17

While FD visits Freud's house in Vienna, she starts a conversation with him on the limits of classical psychoanalysis, when another unconscious is at work, unrelated to the language game with wordplay, but related to the analyst's life. Freud patiently replies that he spoke about an unrepressed unconscious in his comment on Wilhem Jensen's *Gradiva*, a story about the healing of a delusion. In this text, he considers creative writers as our more precious allies. As she confesses her relationship with Wittgenstein, he appears in a hurry to quit his native city. In the train, she perceives his pain, while he contends that somebody can feel a pain in another's body.

Chapter 18

This question is enacted in the ward where she works and takes Wittgenstein the following day. A delusional patient linked to a "telepathic machine" asks for her diploma in psychiatry, after having helped, with her case, many interns to write their theses. Wittgenstein starts a discussion, from his own experience of madness related to the First World War, with her who, as a child, helped to care about the wounded, in a hospital near the D-Day beaches, where her mother was dying. An intern compares such chance of meeting to the encounter with "ready-mades" considered by Marcel Duchamp as a start of language. Hence, Wittgenstein claims that abnormal language games need to be validated on the ruptures of speech.

Chapter 19

At the clinic in the afternoon, where she sees patients discharge from the hospital, everybody tells animated stories about ready-made pipes talking to patients and also to Marcel Proust. FD leaves the place in a state of indifference which will be interpreted by the philosopher who comes back to elucidate a haunting number. Happy to meet Wittgenstein again who had advised her to read, they both enjoy discussing on the topic of unfelt pain and leave her office together. She is quite relieved to get rid of them.

Chapter 20

In Paul's log house, she confesses to him that she is the one who called Wittgenstein for help when she saw a huge beetle crawl on her office floor. Hence the lecture he bores her with on the beetle that each of us may have enclosed it in a box, whose name has no place in a language game as long as we do not open our box. In French, "*ouvrir sa boîte*," meaning to disclose oneself, is the favorite expression of a young man whose appointment she is expecting later that day. She recalls the day of her presentation (Chapter 1) when Wittgenstein argued that the subject of pain might be located in another person's body.

Chapter 21

This issue is debated in a seminar organized by FD's colleague Bernard Mottez on sign language at the Institute of Social Sciences where she also works. Wittgenstein contradicts a psychologist stating that deaf-mutes have an inner vocal language. FD, whose computer has swallowed the text of her future presentation, wonders if some evil spirit is talking to himself inside that box, and, in her confusion, she forgets to quote Sullivan's statement who supports Wittgenstein's argument in a book she had brought on purpose, and without opening her box, she heads off to the hospital.

Chapter 22

After meeting the medical doctor's dog who waits for his master outside, she attends the interview of a man brought by the police, who refuses to say anything. The same question is asked again of what he tells to himself Sullivan answers in a passage of the book that she reads to a nurse concerning the private life of dogs. In the same vein as Wittgenstein, he contends that we will never reach their private life, except in a language game that we create with them. Such invention takes place with the lady connected to a machine, who comes back claiming that her organs have disappeared, replaced by the telepathic device. Her requests to be "authenticated" eventually happens through a language game with FD, related to her traumatic experience.

Chapter 23

Back in her office, she discovers Wittgenstein reading Diderot's invention of a feeling harpsichord. Commenting on the lady's disappearance of organs, he quotes the same experience described by Descartes, probably related to his war experience during the Thirty Years' War. While he speaks, she gets the fleeting impression that something is wrong with him, which increases when Wittgenstein looks down from her balcony, watching people behave like automata, in a mechanical way. Coming back into the room, he stares at her window in a peculiar way.

Chapter 24

To suppress her impression, she pretexts a medical appointment and takes him down to the boulevard, where they go pass a lady who stands there for years, warning mothers with a Yiddish accent to take care of their kids. The catastrophes of History enter the scene without Wittgenstein bulging in spite of FD's inquiry about what he saw at her window. In total contradiction with his claim against private experience, he keeps for himself what happened. Perhaps she feels his pain at his place while he withdraws to the last sentence of his "Tractatus": "Whereof one cannot speak, thereof one must stay silent", denying that after ten years spent in Vienna in a terrible PTSD condition, he changed his formula when he returned to Cambridge, which became so to speak . . .; thereof one cannot help showing what is silenced.

Chapter 25

In total contradiction with what is happening between them, he continues to hammer his aphorism: "One does not choose the mouth which says I have toothache." To take his mind off this idée fixe, she takes him to the Luxembourg garden. While he takes a stroll around, she sits by the playground and opens Descartes' book that she took with her, intending to find the quotation which, disturbed him, at least to her opinion. Leafing across the pages, she falls on an echo of Wittgenstein's formula in Descartes' image of a vibrating cord which may connect us to each other. When Wittgenstein comes back, he alludes to a window frame shaped like a Swastika giving her the clue of nausea that she felt at his place. At that point, Paul asks her what part was put into motion on her side of the vibrating cord.

Chapter 26

When she started an analysis, long ago, she fell from a rock called "La Dame Jeanne," showing her analyst the rupture of a cord linking her to her paternal grandmother called Jeanne. She was forbidden to know her by her mother who, after the war, cut out all relationships reminding the period of the Résistance in Savoy, fighting the rule of the Swastika, which had imprisoned her pregnant of FD. Hence, the project of her presentation, which began with a passage of Kleist's "Theater of Puppets," shows the transformation of a graceful young man into a grotesque puppet by a perverse language game. My point, she says, was to present transference in psychosis as a way to weave a thread of trust, so that a subject may emerge from the erasure of traces.

Chapter 27

After leaving Paul's log house, FD goes back to the hospital from where one of her patients who doggedly refused to be psychoanalyzed has escaped. When she comes back, she asks to talk to FD, out of the blue. Their meeting brings back to life an abused child who had remained ostracized in a timeless time. Now, FD may allow Wittgenstein to go. The book ends on his departure in the company of a little boy who knows how to play with ghosts.

Chapter 1

Who Is He?

A meeting of analysts.
FD, PAUL, DEEP VOICE, SWEET VOICE, MAN WITH AN OPEN
SHIRT COLLAR, A GERMAN-SPEAKING ANALYST, PAUL

I like making presentations only when I've finished. The one I had just brought to a close was addressed to psychoanalysts and entitled, "Transference and Psychosis."

I had already forgotten what I came to say, fascinated by the people looking at me, all perfectly silent except one, who was fidgeting in the back of the room. His shirt collar was open, and he seemed to be talking to himself. I was trying to catch his eye. He seemed to be somewhere else. Yet for two years, he'd never failed to rush to my rescue. This time I feared he would disappear, leaving me all alone in this absurd space. Finally, someone spoke up. A deep voice from somewhere in the front rows said, with a sigh of boredom: "What about your desire to analyze psychotics?"

I didn't know. I no longer knew. I didn't want to know, and I had no urge to answer. There was a void. So many competent ears gave me vertigo. Was I the analyst here or the patient? I seemed to hear the man with the open shirt collar muttering: "This is as if one said: 'wherever you are, you must have got there from somewhere else, and to that previous place from another place, and so on ad infinitum.'"[1]

No one budged. Too bad that I made things worse:

FD: What happens to this desire when there's madness in the air? That's exactly the question I'm raising in talking about "psychotic transference." Maybe you'll understand this better with the help of some particular cases. For example, one of my patients claims he's a voyeur. He seems especially attached to this characteristic. He came to see me after having used and misused another couch. And besides, he doesn't believe in psycho analysis. One day . . .

DEEP VOICE: Why speak of psychosis? It's a case of perversion.

DOI: 10.4324/9781003437451-1

FD:	I never told you he was mad. "Psychotic transference" refers to a link with the analyst, not to a diagnosis.

Deep Voice rolled his eyes. This type exasperated me, and forgetting that I hadn't finished my story, I got even more entangled.

FD:	I could recount a lot of cases like that. Another patient pro claims in front of everyone that something is being concealed from him—a plot. Yet I had to admit to him that, just before what he himself calls his "delusion" started, I had in fact "concealed" a tumor [*tumeur*] from him—a tumor that I had also concealed from myself and ignored until I got to the operating room.
ANOTHER VOICE—SWEETER:	"You're dying" [*tu meurs*]*: you had an operation on a signifier that was not benign.
FD:	All the less benign in that I really believed I might find that I was at the end of my journey. But if you'd made this brilliant interpretation at that time, it would have been a wasted effort. In the moments of psychotic transference, we're outside ordinary language games, including those in which the unconscious is understood as the repressed: the analysis is about the unspeakable and the unimaginable, which are impossible to repress. The tools of classical psychoanalysis no longer work.
SWEET VOICE:	So what works then?

To answer, I repeated what the man in the back of the room so often said to me: "What cannot be said can only be shown."[2]

SWEET VOICE:	Then one can at least imagine it.
FD:	Not necessarily. One can very well show something that one has registered but cannot imagine. The patient I just told you about showed a catastrophe that was at once imminent and already past: the deaths of babies, with himself as the sole survivor. He took from this the certainty "that his body is now the seat of that which truly lives."[3]

---

* *tumeur* (tumor) and *tu meurs* (you are dying) sound the same.

Sweet Voice took on a sullen look. The man in the last row gave signs of impatience. He was going to leave without warning, which was what he usually did. I continued:

FD: One doesn't have to be a confirmed madman to be familiar with madness, according to Harry Stack Sullivan, an American analyst who had lost all his siblings—dead at very young ages—before his birth.[4] From such an experience, some children become convinced that they are true survivors of a catastrophe that has engulfed every living thing—in their family, and therefore on the earth. In this particular context, in which nothing can be said, the philosopher Ludwig Wittgenstein claimed: "the tool with the name "N" is broken."[5] One can, therefore, give expression to this ever-present death only by showing it, with the hope of becoming free from it.

SWEET VOICE: So, you're pretending to free your patients?

FD: Yes, from a thing outside discourse, which materializes through interferences with the analyst, and which, in a second time, can be expressed, forgotten and finally repressed.

SWEET VOICE: Then the goal of treatment would be repression? But this is psychoanalysis upside down!

FD: You don't know how right you are! Everything unfolds in effect as if the analyst were a piece of soft wax for recording words removed from language and not an echo reflecting the language of the unconscious.

The audience seemed also to be removed from language. As in the goat's beard game, their faces were almost totally without expression.* There was a noise from a chair. It was Paul, arriving very late, and smiling sheepishly at me, as if to excuse himself. I tried to draw him in by telling a story he had told me:

FD: In the register of the psychopathology of everyday psycho analysis, an analyst caught himself responding to someone who phoned for a first interview by saying: "I am laying you out."(*Je vous* étends) instead of "I am expecting you." (*Je vous attends*).** With such a lapse, the analysis, as he said, was launched.

---

* A reference to a children's game in which the players attempt to grab each other by the chin, as if it were a goat's beard. Once caught, the child must try to keep his face free of expression, while the others attempt to make him laugh. If he laughs, he loses.

** This is an easy mistake to make, since there is only a slight difference in sound between the two expressions.

No one laughed. Paul smiled at me again, without lending a hand. He turned to the right, to the left, and then gave me a questioning look, as if to ask me what hornet's nest I was trying to goad him into.

DEEP VOICE: You're confusing the place of the analyst with that of the patient. What about the desire of the analyst? I'm asking you that question again.

From the back of the room, the man with the open shirt collar stood up to speak. Finally!

MAN WITH THE OPEN SHIRT COLLAR: A man who cries out in pain, or says he has pain, doesn't choose the mouth which says it. The place of the pain may be in another person's body.[6]

Everyone turned toward him. Who was that crank with the German accent? Whose patient was he? He went on in a strong voice:

MAN WITH THE OPEN SHIRT COLLAR:	An innumerable variety of cases can be thought of in which we should say that someone has pains in another person's body; or, say, in a piece of furniture, or even in an empty spot.[7]
DEEP VOICE:	Particular cases, again!
MAN WITH THE OPEN SHIRT COLLAR:	Why do you despise particular cases? If I am going to analyze the word "desire," I shall not be dissatisfied if I describe various cases of desiring.[8]
DEEP VOICE (ANNOYED):	Why are you answering for the speaker? I asked her the question.

My old demons again took hold of me—always the same feeling of uneasiness. I felt that words were going to fail me, that the French language would abandon me— first the vocabulary, followed by the syntax, and then an emptiness in my mouth, and a slight nausea. I looked at the door. It appeared to be miles away. The more I looked at it, the farther away it seemed to be.

MAN WITH THE OPEN SHIRT COLLAR: What a queer mechanism, one might say, the mechanism of desiring must be if I can desire that which will never happen.[9]

SWEET VOICE:	So, what is desire for you?
MAN WITH THE OPEN SHIRT COLLAR:	Your question makes it appear that what we want is a definition. We mistakenly believe that a definition is what could remove our trouble (as in certain states of indigestion we feel a kind of hunger which cannot be re moved by eating). The question is then answered by a wrong definition. However, we are tempted to think that we must replace a wrong definition by a different one, the correct one.[10]
SWEET VOICE:	I didn't ask you for a definition, but rather for what desire is for you.
MAN WITH THE OPEN SHIRT COLLAR:	On this point of desire, I don't agree with my friend Russell. For him it's a kind of hunger. We don't know what we expect until our expectation has been fulfilled. Thus, in Russell's way of using the word "de siring," it makes no sense to say: I desired an apple, but a pear has satisfied me. Therefore the pear and not the apple was the object of my desire, since it sufficed to satisfy my hunger. Yet, it could very well be that the pear had satisfied my hunger without my desire being fulfilled.[11]
SWEET VOICE:	Lacan spoke of this long before your Russian friend,* in distinguishing the object cause of desire from the object of need, which suffices to satisfy the hunger.
MAN WITH THE OPEN SHIRT COLLAR:	I too use the word "desire" in a different sense than Russell's, to indicate that the tension of desiring was relieved without the desire being fulfilled; and also that a desire was fulfilled without the tension beiing relieved. That is, I may, in this sense,

* Sweet Voice apparently misunderstood the reference to Russell.

become satisfied with out my desire having been satisfied. A real apple is not enough to satisfy my desire.[12] Saying "I should like an apple" does not mean: "I believe an apple will quell my *Wunsch*."[13]

A GERMAN SPEAKING ANALYST: *Wunsch!* There we are! What is the object of this desire?

MAN WITH THE OPEN SHIRT COLLAR: The answer to this question of course is "I desire that so-and-so should happen." Now what would the answer be if we went on asking: "And what is the object of this desire?" It seems as though, as I said, I could nev er entirely explain what I desired until it had actually happened. But of course this is a delusion. The truth is that I needn't be able to give a better explanation of what I desired after the desire was fulfilled than before.[14] Now suppose you asked me: "Do I know what I desire before I get it?" If I have learned to talk, of course I do know.[15] And in your opinion, whence this determining of what is not yet there? This despotic demand? The imperious character of the *Wunsch* and "the hardness of the logical must"?[16]

In response to these remarks, although they had a rare, ortho dox Lacanian meaning, almost everyone left the room, probably to demonstrate that they knew all that already. Indifferent to the hustle and bustle, the man continued to address a small number who remained intrigued by I don't know what—his assurance, perhaps, or his tone of voice:

MAN WITH THE OPEN SHIRT COLLAR: Do you know why a man thinks? Is it only because he has found that thinking pays? Does he bring up his children because he has found that it pays?[17]

Strange question! I suspected it referred to the tragedy that bore the imperious Wunsch *of his own father. They say he had brought up his sons so that they would succeed as heads of his firm, and that the first three had paid with their lives. He gave me a look that stopped me in the tracks of my suppositions. It was not the first time he seemed to read my thoughts. He insisted on hammering away with these words:*

MAN WITH THE OPEN SHIRT COLLAR: To bring up children because it pays—that seems impossible . . . even though there are cases in which one could say that. But I still have a question for you, psychoanalysts. It seems to me that my dreams are always an expression of my fears—not, as Freud thought, of my desires. I could build up an interpretation of dreams just as cogent as Freud's in terms of repressed fears.[18]

Paul took him at his word and proposed that we continue this conversation the next evening, at his apartment on the Boulevard Saint-Michel. We all went our separate ways. "By the way," Paul asked me in a low voice, when we were shaking hands, "Who is he? Do you know his name?"

FD: Wittgenstein, Ludwig Wittgenstein. I will explain. See you tomorrow.

Chapter 2

The Uncanny

In Paul's apartment, in Paris.

FD, PAUL, WITTGENSTEIN

I had gotten to know Paul some months earlier during a meeting of psychoanalysts, when, in order to relax, we talked about mountains—his passion. But this was the first time I visited his home. Wittgenstein came with me. He walked beside me, taking large strides, perhaps thinking about the question of dreams of fear, which he had thrown out as a challenge to psychoanalysis. Probably wanting to meddle in it, I said:

FD: You should read the *Essays on Psychoanalysis*, composed in the 1920s. In that work, right from the beginning, Freud considers dreams of fear. Deeply moved by the traumatic dreams of soldiers from the Great War, he had to change the direction of his theory, which until then interpreted dreams in terms of repressed desires. He admitted then, alongside sexuality, another instinct, which he called the death instinct, the repetition compulsion or aggressivity. Could it be that your concern about dreams of fear dates from that same war? They say you were decorated for your heroic conduct on the first line of the Russian front. Then, there was Monte Cassino and your captivity. Were you, like the soldiers Freud wrote about, attacked every night, over and over, by the same bombs?

WITTGENSTEIN: At any moment the sky can always fall on your head I thought I understood, however, that Freud had not attempted to interpret this kind of dream.

FD: Don't you believe it! To address this question, he begins—curiously enough—by analyzing a child's game.

WITTGENSTEIN: Good. I myself have said that if I wanted to define it at a single showing, I should play-act fear.[1]

DOI: 10.4324/9781003437451-2

FD: Freud's solution resides in the game of *fort-da*, invented by his grandson at the age of 18 months. This child's fear was connected to the prolonged absences of his mother. He play acted it by throwing a spool of thread over the side of his crib, and then pulling it back, all the while punctuating his gestures with the sounds "o-o-o-o" and "a-a-a-a." His psychoanalyst grandfather immediately recognized the rough shape of the pair of words, which in your language mean: "gone" ("*fort*") and "there" ("*da*"). The important point is that paradoxically, the child's enjoyment reaches its peak in the act of throwing, in the "o-o-o-o," which reproduces the disagreeable event. Thus, in repetitively playing out the traumatic event, the child succeeds in mastering through language a disappearance he is not in a position to understand. So, this was the source of his jubilation.[2]

WITTGENSTEIN: But what if the mother does not come back? And what if the child discovers in the talk of those around him, neither *fort* nor *da*?

FD: There, you're hitting the limits of this solution. It may be, in fact, that the traumatic event repeats itself as a curse. And indeed in Freud's case, the nightmare didn't stop. In a note at the bottom of the page, at the very beginning of his *Essays*, he informs the reader that his grandson lost his mother, when he was five years old.[3] Freud's daughter Sophie died from the Spanish flu, toward the end of the war. He writes that this time the mother had really left her son ("o-o-o-o"), but the child, busy with jealousy toward his little brother Heinele (born not long before their mother's death) showed nothing—no sadness . . .

WITTGENSTEIN: Then how did the child manage? How did he imagine this absence? Was it through nightmares? And what if he did not dream? Imagine a family in which fear and sadness reach such intensity that it becomes impossible to show whatever it might be. . . .

FD: Imagination is often inferior to reality. Heinele died, in his own turn, a little later, at the age of four. Freud was all the more traumatized in that he learned (after several months of those around him keeping secrets) that he had cancer of the jaw. He took refuge in an apparent total indifference. We know this from a letter he wrote in response to a letter from Binswanger, who had informed him of the loss of the youngest of his children, born around the same time as Heinele.[4]

WITTGENSTEIN: Sometimes there is no language to say something to oneself, and one finds the words through someone else, by way of a response.[5] It may be that another dreams your fear in your place . . .

FD: We'll see what Paul will answer. We've arrived.

When Paul showed us in, I stopped for a brief instant, perceiving on the wall over his head a picture representing a rock suspended in mid-air above a peaceful valley.

PAUL: It's a reproduction of a work by Magritte, *le Sens des réalités* (*The Sense of Reality*). It's what I picture to myself of the Real, the unnamable, the unimaginable.[*]

FD: And are you waiting for it to fall on your head?

PAUL: You don't know how right you are! I actually saw this rock one day, over my head. One summer, when I was climbing, I heard a rumble of thunder. Rocks were shooting out into the air—you could say that the whole mountain was crumbling, creating a kind of fireworks. One of the rocks seemed to be hesitating in the air, suspended above my head. Since then, I'm always looking for it, even if it doesn't exist. It's not that I imagine it, but it's always there. At this moment, it's even there a little more than usual.

Something struck me in the way he spoke these words. It wasn't the tone—which was, as always, cheerful—so I brushed aside this touch of uneasiness.

FD: You're making this up.

WITTGENSTEIN: But the danger must be somewhere, since you are looking for it, even if you don't find it, even if it does not exist.[6] Such an experience leads us to revise what counts as the domain of the imaginable. Yet, it is what happens when one looks for something in mathematics; you have to leave the sphere of what can be imagined.[7]

The mention of mathematics brought us to attention, through a kind of reflex acquired in some psychoanalytic seminars.[**]

WITTGENSTEIN: That's right. One can look for somebody when he is not there, but not hang him when he is not there.[8]

---

[*] Links: http://www.iutc3.unicaen.fr/~moranb/accueilperso41.html;http://www.tendreams.org/magritte2/SR.htm

[**] Mathematics (specifically topology and the theory of knots) had become an important focus in Lacan's seminars at that time.

Once again, death was there, and I couldn't prevent myself from associating these words with other gloomy notes, which resound here and there in the Philosophical Investigations. Here a shot is fired;[9] there a person gets ready to take two powders, and declares coldly that in a half hour he is going to be sick.[10] But no, the conversation remains calm; it is I who must be out of it. I gave my discomfort an intellectual turn:

FD:	I don't understand very well. Are you talking about making something exist which exists only too much? That's absurd.
PAUL:	Not necessarily. If someone has hanged himself, and his ghost haunts you, you would do well, in a dream, for example, to make this dead person exist, in order to let this ghost die at last. One can call this a desire for death, but a death wish on a dead person—that's weird, isn't it?
WITTGENSTEIN:	It is not, for all that, less real.

I found it odd that Paul had answered so quickly in place of Wittgenstein, as if he had not stopped thinking about the question. After saying all this, Wittgenstein got up, and went straight to the library. Seeming to have noticed something, he took down a yellow book from a shelf, and read a passage aloud to Paul:

SOCRATES—And if someone thinks, mustn't he think something?
THEAETETUS—Yes, he must.
SOCRATES—And if he thinks something, mustn't it be something real?
THEAETETUS—Apparently.[11]

WITTGENSTEIN:	We have yet to know what meaning should be attached to the word "real."

No longer following very well, I extended my hand to take this book. Mechanically, I put it in my bag as I asked:

FD:	But these thoughts Socrates is talking about—are they conscious or unconscious?
WITTGENSTEIN:	You psychoanalysts, you imagine you have done much more than discover new psychological reactions; you believe you have discovered conscious thoughts which were unconscious.[12]
FD:	For example?
WITTGENSTEIN:	It might be found practical to call a certain state of decay in a tooth, not accompanied by what we commonly call toothache, "unconscious toothache," and to use in such a case the expression that we have a toothache, but don't know it.[13] It is in that sense, I think, that psychoanalysis talks of unconscious thoughts.[14]

PAUL:	Not quite. We have moved somewhat beyond that. Lacan asserted that the Freudian unconscious is structured like a language, and not by unconscious thoughts. For example, I dreamed one night that I was in a gondola on the canals of Venice. On awakening, I had a terrible toothache. I hurried to the dentist to hear him tell me that he had to do a root canal immediately. His friendly tone and engaging smile inspired me to open my mouth to tell him about my dream. He then took the pins (nicknamed "Venetian instruments"), which were to be used on me, clamped my jaw, and got to work. So, I never did find out what the objects of desire were, towards which my signifier "gondola" might be navigating . . .
WITTGENSTEIN:	The verbs "fearing" and "desiring," when they describe sensations not referring to objects, are intransitive. I can say, "I feel a fear, but I don't know what I'm afraid of."[15] In your dream the tension was discharged, but you still don't know what you desire. But, on other occasions, you can also say: "I am afraid of something, but I don't know of what." In the two cases, how do you use the verb "to know"? Would it be the same in each case?[16]
PAUL:	We use it in the sense of unconscious knowledge looking for the object causing the desire. For you, then, what is the object cause of the fear?
WITTGENSTEIN:	You seem to confuse the object of fear and the cause of fear. Thus a face, which inspires fear, is not on that account its cause, but—one might say—its target.[17] The grammar of the word "to know" is connected precisely with that of "getting to know."[18] For example, someone can say to you in a smiling tone of voice: "I must tell you, I am frightened." "I must tell you: it makes me shiver."[19] Or even: "How strange it is that I feel no fear at all." Ask yourself how you get to know that he is afraid.
PAUL:	I know it's often difficult to know if it's fear that one feels. Thus, while under this rock, I didn't feel it and, what's more, I still don't feel it.
FD:	Well, so much the better.
PAUL:	A propos of this, do you know the Grimm tale "The Story of a Youth Who Went Forth to Learn What Fear Was"?[20]
FD:	Do I know it! I have even lived it. It was while on a trip to China. At the very beginning of the trip I discovered a lump in my stomach. Overcoming my uneasiness, I said nothing about it to anyone, and I continued my trip without concerning myself too much with it. Some days later I visited a zoo with my children. I became curious about an area enclosed by

a tarpaulin inscribed with some Chinese characters. I rushed right in. It was too late to pull back. There was an exhibition of human monstrosities: fetuses preserved in jars, and photos of anatomical anomalies. The children took it all in. I assumed an objective and disengaged manner, explaining that these things happen—"they are mistakes of nature, and why make a fuss about them?" The follow ing night, my eldest son, then ten years old, started screaming. Sitting up in bed, half asleep, he saw monsters all over his room. "Why be afraid," I asked him, reassuringly, "Why?"

WITTGENSTEIN: It often happens that we only become aware of the most important facts if we suppress the question "why?"[21]

FD: Exactly. The most important fact was not within the tarpaulin enclosure, but I was still ignoring it. I sang songs, told stories, just as in the good old days when he was little. "There are all sorts of monsters in stories," I said,—"it's not so strange."

WITTGENSTEIN: Not everything which is unfamiliar to us makes an impression of unfamiliarity upon us. At the same time, a feeling of strangeness does not give us a reason for saying that every object which we know well and which does not seem strange to us gives us a feeling of familiarity. We think that the place once occupied by the feeling of strangeness must surely be occupied somehow. The place for this kind of atmosphere is there, and if one of them is not occupying it, then another is.[22]

FD: At the point where I was, I had not yet localized the place you're talking about. I started to get nervous. He had passed, I told him, the age of childish caprice: "Be brave. Cheer up." Had I not proved this myself? . . . Just then that unfeeling lump came back to my mind. Having run out of resources, I finally confessed: "You're afraid, but it's I who should be afraid." I told him about the stomach lump, and I promised him I would have it taken care of when we got home. 'Ok," he said, "I was looking for something to be afraid of." With these words, once the true target of his fear was named, he fell asleep, after promising me, inspired no doubt by our visit to the tombs of the Chinese emperors filled with offerings, that on mine he would pour water of life (eau-de-vie).*

PAUL: He was expressing, in your place, your fear of this stomach lump, and he was looking for monsters in an attempt to speak to you about it.

---

* "eau-de-vie," or "water of life" is the name given to certain brandies which, due to the amount of alcoholic content, are thought to be strong enough to wake even the dead.

FD:	He wasn't the only one. On my return I learned that one of my patients had unwittingly sensed this same thing before I became conscious of it. So, as I said yesterday after my presentation, he became delusional in order to be able to speak to me about it. One day, when you have some time, I'll tell you the story, if you want.
WITTGENSTEIN:	I wonder whether we really talk about what we see. Wouldn't it be more accurate to say that we don't really speak about what we see, but to it, for instance, to our impressions?[23]
PAUL:	What you're saying is quite complicated.
WITTGENSTEIN:	Still, it is the only way to get in touch with what we are thinking. Although we are unable to know what we are thinking, yet we may know what someone else is think ing. A whole cloud of philosophy condensed into a drop of grammar.[24]
PAUL:	I wish you could get us out of this cloud . . . I am still in a fog.
WITTGENSTEIN:	An impression received from another, on condition he communicates it to us, can teach us what we are thinking, and even what we are feeling.
PAUL:	Are you making an allusion to telepathy?
WITTGENSTEIN:	No, to logic. When a diviner tells us that when he holds the rod, he *feels* water is five feet underground or that a mixture of copper and gold is five feet underground, what objection can be made to him?[25]
PAUL:	None. I knew a diviner many years ago, when I was building a log house in the woods. He found the location for a well, by using his divining rod.
FD:	Do you really believe all these stories?
WITTGENSTEIN:	If we express our doubts, the diviner could always answer us: "You can estimate a length when you see it. Why shouldn't I have a different way of estimating it?"[26]
FD:	But I need these things explained to me.
WITTGENSTEIN:	We could then ask the following question: "How did you come to know that water is three feet underground—was it by a feeling in your hands?"[27]
PAUL:	Still the question: How do you come to know?
WITTGENSTEIN:	And the diviner's response: "I have never learned to correlate depth of water under the ground with feelings in my hand, but when I have a certain feeling of tension in my hands, the words 'three feet' spring up in my mind." We should answer, "That is a perfectly good explanation of what you mean by 'feeling the depth to be three feet', and the statement that you feel this will have neither more, nor less, meaning than your explanation has given it." But you see that the meaning of the

words, "I feel the depth of the water to be feet" had to be explained; it was not known when the meaning of the words "n feet" in the ordinary sense was known. We had to take it out of its ordinary context.[28]

PAUL: Forgive me for following you badly but we know each other only a short time. While you were speaking I had a daydream. Sometimes, during a session, the analyst's unconscious reacts, tenses up, like that divining rod, in relation to something uncanny in the session, unstuck in space and time. I imagine analysts as diviners of time. The uncanny would be our divining rod. A simple pressure from the uncanny and we become vectors indicating with certainty the presence of a time taken out of the course of history.

FD: Your daydream will definitely give us dreams. . . . It's late . . . I must be going.

While Wittgenstein was also taking his leave, and going downstairs, Paul held me back.

PAUL: You're not going to tell me this man is Ludwig Wittgenstein. He died in 1951. I did some checking.

FD: Why didn't you ask him?

PAUL: I didn't dare. It's strange that he stirs up in me an old passion for psychoanalysis, which I believed had been long dead. I would have loved to pursue this discussion about fears that are difficult to feel.

FD: What stopped you?

PAUL: Tomorrow I have to go to the hospital. There's some urgency since I have cancer. They've scheduled some hospital stays. Like you, I'm going to do everything I can to take care of myself. But tell me, how did you meet this man you call Wittgenstein?

FD: It was around two years ago, through a patient. In the beginning I was speaking to him in my head. He was whispering in my ears; I didn't see him. Then he appeared to me. I was the only one to see him, and then some patients saw him. No wonder—I was feeling isolated in the barrenness of my work. So I had taken up the habit of consulting him. And he was not stingy with his advice.

PAUL: But how can it be that we see him today?

FD: It took time. Still, little by little, he became more and more imperious. It's almost as if he took my place with my patients. One fine day, I decided to put an end to it—to terminate the transference. He pretended to disappear. And can you believe it? He came back, like a ghost.

PAUL: A true ghost, always coming back.*

FD: Who had a true experience of madness. He could have been an analyst.

PAUL: Is that your own opinion?

FD: No, it seems that he confided in Drury, an Irish psychiatrist, who was one of his former students. He had already given him the same advice he offered me: "Always take a chair, and install yourself at the side of the patient. Do not remain at the foot of the bed like the statue of the Commander. Patients should have the feeling that they have time to speak with you."[29] And he, in fact, took the time to speak with me. But for some time now, he's been very hardheaded, and he insists on appearing in public. I wonder what people think of him—they must take him for a German researcher. To some extent it's my fault. To be honest, I find him more and more disturbing; all the more because I have the impression that he takes me for an idiot . . .

PAUL: What if you told me this whole story from the beginning?

FD: It's a long story.

PAUL: Well, now I have a lot of time. I'll call you when I return from the hospital.

I knew Paul would keep his word. As I left him I was feeling sad and reassured— sad about his illness (which he seemed, though, not to take tragically), and reassured at having found someone to talk to. I no longer found the uncanny charming, and the company of this ghost was beginning to weigh on me.

---

* This is a play on the French word "*revenant,*" which means "ghost," but is derived from the verb "*revenir,*" which means "to come back."

Chapter 3

Language on Holiday

At Paul's house in the woods.

PAUL, FD

In the analyst's office.

THE PHILOSOPHER, FD, THE VOICE OF
WITTGENSTEIN (then WITTGENSTEIN)

One month later, Paul phoned to invite me to spend a weekend with him at his log cabin in the woods, where he was recuperating. "Here, there's nothing to do but tell stories," he said, as he welcomed me. It was raining that day. I looked around, not knowing where to begin. On my right, beyond the trees, I saw a hill where some cows were grazing.

PAUL: Do you feel a little out of place?

Paul's words launched me into my story.

FD: There are days when whatever I do, whatever I say or don't say, wherever I am, I am not "with it." "Once again, you are not 'with it' . . ." The one who summoned me to order with these words, session after session—with patience certain patients seem to have—I nicknamed for myself, "the Philosopher." One day, he added: "You should read Ludwig Wittgenstein."

The next time he brought me some books. I read "The Notes for the Lectures on Private Experience and Sense Data,"[1] and then the "Remarks on Frazer's Golden

DOI: 10.4324/9781003437451-3

Bough."[2] These texts spoke to me. When I began the Philosophical Investigations, *they drew me into a secret conversation with their author.*

PAUL:	About what?
FD:	I have a hard time answering you directly, since at the beginning I ignored what was going on. It was my Philosopher who, once again, put me on track, by announcing at the start of a session:
THE PHILOSOPHER:	It is when one is the most delusional that one is the least delusional; one is only playing the game of language.

He had guessed it exactly. For some time, I was somehow using Wittgenstein's language-game for my own fantasy, but I kept this little delusion for myself. I remained silent; he went on:

THE PHILOSOPHER:	Does it mean nothing at all to you? "Philosophical problems arise when language goes on holiday."[3]

I did indeed recognize this sentence drawn from a paragraph of the Investigations, but I had been trying to keep Wittgenstein for my private use. And so I hid myself behind a cloud of psychoanalytic silence, which he took advantage of by announcing his departure.

THE PHILOSOPHER:	With respect to holidays, you're certainly close to taking a holiday yourself. Me too, for once. I've finally obtained my medical card identifying me as an "invalid." Don't make that face. Listen to what the "metro mouths" were whispering in my ear while I was on my way here. First there was "invalid" (*Invalides*), then "pleasure" (*Plaisance*) followed by "cheerfulness" (*Gaîté*), where I got off and went down the stairs to get another train. These were all auspicious. Farther along the line there was *Balard*, which is an exquisite combination of "*balaise*" and "*malabar*" (slang for "strong" and "huge").* I will therefore cheerfully accept this card that invalidates nothing at all. As you see, my energy has returned. I have started to write again. I'm swarming with ideas. I don't want to

---

* All these references are to subway stations along the Paris metro. Thus, *Invalides, Plaisance,* and *Gaîté* are place names corresponding to those stops, as well as words that have a particular significance for the Philosopher. The "metro mouth" refers to the opening or entry from the street, which leads to the staircase that goes underground. Many of these openings, beautifully adorned in the grand modern style of Guimard, display the name of the station.

	return to my work. You may object, but it's decided. All these stupid tasks are no longer for me. I have no more time. I accept the name "invalid" because I have never in fact been in such great shape. Logical, isn't it?
PAUL:	It is logical. I understand this paradox perfectly, especially right now.
FD:	Meanwhile, I was feeling as if I had made an interminable solo crossing while in his company. He was leaving the boat and I was left in a lurch. You would have thought that this energy had come back to him without any help.

Still, I have never forgotten our first meeting, preceded as it was by his not asking for analysis. He had not deigned even to make a move. I was just then starting out as an analyst. His aunt came to see me; she was quite worried. For some months and weeks her favorite nephew had remained in bed, not moving at all, just like a stone. She wondered what was going on in his mind, and if he was at all open to some feeling. All I could think of saying was: "Let him come see me." He didn't come. At that time, I blamed my inexperience, regretting that I hadn't taken advantage of speaking with this relative of his. Then I thought no more of it. Two years later, he rang my doorbell. I wanted to refresh his memory of our first meeting:

FD:	You remember when you came to my office, some years ago, shuffling your feet, with little steps, like an invalid? As you were saying already."
THE PHILOSOPHER:	You have certainly changed too; you're much better. You say what you have to say more simply. I had difficulty understanding you then. You must have just finished your psychoanalytic training. You were fresh out of school, not knowing how you would deal with my madness, imagining I don't know what drama. . . .
FD:	What concerned me were your months of immobility. As your Wittgenstein puts it: "Did you have frightful pains turning you into a stone for as long as they lasted?"[4]

At that precise moment I heard a clear and distinct voice whispering in my ear:

| THE VOICE: | So, you would like to treat this question right away, without preparation, when I had to take 283 paragraphs before asking it. |

I looked around.

| FD: | Why are you saying that? |

THE PHILOSOPHER: I didn't say anything.

THE VOICE: Since you seem to be referring to my *Investigations*, why not follow the order that is written there?

FD: The order is not at all evident.

I had said this sentence quite loudly. For sure, the Philosopher was going to think I was talking to myself. He looked at me mockingly. The Voice continued:

THE VOICE: I know. I should have liked to produce a good book. This has not come about, but the time is past in which I could improve it.[5] On top of everything, I am dead. . . .

I didn't know what I should say, in this situation. But The Voice went on without waiting for a response.

THE VOICE: I should not like my writing to spare you the trouble of thinking, but, if possible, to stimulate you to thoughts of your own.[6] Even if I jump from one thing to another, I try to follow the thread of my associations.[7]

FD: Admit that you don't make your reader's task easy.

The Philosopher drew me out of my daydreaming.

THE PHILOSOPHER: To return to my problems, what do you think of this new name of "invalid"?

The voice answered in my place.

THE VOICE: So you think that naming is something like attaching a label to a thing?[8]

THE PHILOSOPHER: You're strange today. This label of "invalid" amounts to the very same one that is kept in my file in the hospital: "schizophrenia, with catatonic episodes, unsuited for psychoanalysis or for military service." Don't blush like that; admit that you have made this same diagnosis yourself. Don't worry; there's no shame in playing the naming game.[9]

THE VOICE: Certainly, what we in ordinary life call using language mostly presupposes this game.[10]

THE PHILOSOPHER: In my case, this little game led to a series of electroshock treatments at the clinic where I went of my own free will, because I thought they would be interested in my delusion. The clinic advertised itself as a psychoanalytic and anti-psychiatric institution. My delusion, I thought, was helping me escape from years of Ice Age glaciation. I attempted to share with those so-called analysts, discoveries that were bursting forth as numerous as Alpine snowbells* in the spring. But an electroshock device was waiting for me, and the label of "mental illness" was applied automatically, stopping me in my tracks for many years. Do you know what it means to be "mentally ill"?

THE VOICE: It all depends on how the expression is used.[11]

FD: Well, the most current use supposes that you have a psychotic structure, which, according to the principles of classical psychoanalysis, makes psychoanalysis impossible.

THE VOICE: Is it a material or a logical impossibility?[12]

FD: It's both a material impossibility, in that you are in general unable to pay for your analysis, and a logical impossibility, in that if your psychosis is healed, it's proof that your structure wasn't truly psychotic.

THE PHILOSOPHER: I don't give a damn about my structure. What I'm asking you is if you know the meaning of these two words, "mental illness," for the person concerned? Do you understand?

FD: Rather say, I shouldn't have tried to understand you (as I had been advised in my training). But I couldn't help wondering what on earth had put you in such a state— you, an invalid of 20 years—without apparent wounds, walking in small steps, with a falling voice, your movements scarcely defined. I would have liked to have been more attuned to your signifiers. What does "invalid" evoke for you? Or I might have attempted a nice Lacanian interpretation such as: "what? valid" (*hein? valide*)†— what validity are you talking about?

THE PHILOSOPHER: Shut up! You're no good at this game. Without flattering myself, I surpass you in puns.

---

* These are Alpine flowers that are the first to bloom in the spring, evenwhile the snow remains on the ground.

† This is simply mocking the Lacanian technique of the "echoing signifier," which consisted in repeating a word with a different emphasis, thereby giving it a different meaning—a technique that was used indiscriminately at that time.

I plunged again into a sullen silence. The Voice drew me out of it:

THE VOICE: Think of the tools in a toolbox. Words are like these tools.
                        Their functions are diverse. There are not only word
                        games; there are also language games . . .[13]

But the Philosopher persisted:

THE PHILOSOPHER: What, then, do you include under these words: "mental
                    illness"?
THE VOICE: When one says a word, one means this word. One does not
                    mean something *under* this word, *hidden in* the thought.[14]
THE PHILOSOPHER: I don't agree with you; the words "mental illness" cover
                    some ulterior motives.

To my surprise, the Philosopher had indeed answered the Voice in a perfectly natu-
ral way. I wasn't therefore the only one to hear it. What a relief! Certainly, it would
have been more professional to ask myself about this delire-à-deux, *but I preferred*
to play the fool.

FD: Who is speaking through this voice? You must indeed
                    have an idea, since you answer him.
THE PHILOSOPHER: Don't make yourself more foolish than you are. Why
                    make me say it since you know it already?
FD: No kidding—what's the game we're playing?
WITTGENSTEIN: Imagining a language.[15]
FD: That's all?
WITTGENSTEIN: That is to say imagining a form of life.[16]
FD: How's that?
WITTGENSTEIN: Think what happens when you speak—the tone of voice
                    and the look with which the words are uttered . . .[17]
THE PHILOSOPHER: If you had known me at the time I came to see her, with
                    my toneless voice and my look of exhaustion, you would
                    have seen immediately the form my life had taken when
                    it was caught up in therapeutic discourse . . . you know,
                    the discourse that confines mental illness to the interior of
                    thought where it is hidden like a secret disease, leading to
                    an inexorable deterioration, until the day it breaks out in
                    an acute crisis, or worse, and so undermines you that you
                    are totally wiped out.
                        Do you understand now what "mental illness" means
                    for the person concerned? It condemns him to madness,
                    pure and simple. It's easy then to imagine what form his
                    life will take. Relegated to solitude and humiliated, he

will have to utter his words softly and very close to himself, as if he is both asking and answering the questions.
He will be forced to be himself and another at the same
time. He'll fear that sometime he'll be taken for someone else. And the day he believes himself to be another,
they'll say he's demented.

WITTGENSTEIN: That's what I call a language-game: a language and the
actions into which it is woven.[18]

FD: But, right here, who are the players in the game?

THE PHILOSOPHER: Decidedly, you're not "with it." It's a game with someone
else. With whom do you wish it to be? The most inco-
herent delirium addresses itself to someone, preferring
the other who's looking at you, and imagining that you
no longer know what you're saying, nor to whom you're
speaking, and that you're no longer in contact with reality. Well, the delirium is reality. But there is never anyone to attest to it. It's the doubt and not the delirium that
makes you "lose it." You others always doubt what we
say. You believe that we believe every bit of it. But the
madman doesn't care. A single thing is important to him:
to say and to bear witness. Do you remember the time
when I couldn't open my mouth without saying: "I want
to say."?

WITTGENSTEIN: The French expression "*vouloir dire*" ("mean" or "want
to say") carries simultaneously the connotations of
explaining what one is saying and of expressing a desire
to speak.[19]

THE PHILOSOPHER: As you say. By dint of saying over and over things that
meant nothing to anyone, I had nothing more to say. I
even had no more strength left to "want to say," and I suf-
fered unknowingly from no longer desiring to speak.

And reciprocally: By dint of finding no one to speak to,
all that I said no more meant anything, leading to debility.
I was confined to bed, captivated by an interior show of
astounding beauty. But at the same time, I was forbidden
speech, sequestered. You're right; what followed confirmed it. I couldn't say anything but this simple and clear
conviction: "I want to say." If I don't express myself, I am
going to drop dead. But right now, I'm speaking; it's as
easy as that.

FD: You find that easy! Yet for an awfully long time we had to
follow the rhythm of your little steps. You said you were
a dissident from the western world, escaped from a gulag,
in possession of a samizdat, an underground writing on

the crisscrossing of your little history with the big History I couldn't help looking over your shoulder to try to decipher it, but I never succeeded.

WITTGENSTEIN: Your mistake is to look for an explanation where you ought to look at what happened as a proto-phenomenon. Wishing to ascend again into the great chain of causes when you ought to say: this language-game is being played.[20]

FD: But what language-game? You know I'm not really gifted at driving out a delirium. I envy those who know so well how to describe, at great length, the world of the schizophrenic, as if they were "with it."

THE PHILOSOPHER: You're still not "with it."

FD: And where do you wish that I should be?

THE PHILOSOPHER: It's for you to discover. You have all your vacations to think about it. I'm not sure about returning in the month of September, but I leave you with Wittgenstein. He'll tell you what language-game is involved here between us, threading through these years.

When the Philosopher left, I believed myself free of the voice he had evoked. It nevertheless stole its way into my thoughts: "There are countless language-games— new ones come into existence, and others become obsolete and get forgotten."[21]

PAUL: It's left for you to discover where you have to be, to be "with it."

FD: Wittgenstein and the Philosopher had left me no indications, and by myself I was sure to arrive at nothing at all. I do wish I had known you at that time.

"You have nothing to regret," said Paul, while getting up to wash some potatoes at the pump, placing them then in a piece of pottery called a devil, which he set on the embers at a corner of the hearth. Then he added: "I have never had the impression so much of being 'with it' as now."

Chapter 4

Transference

The house in the woods.

PAUL, FD, LACAN

In the days that followed, just before summer vacation, I tried to focus seriously on getting to work describing what had happened—what had worked—between the Philosopher and me. Since there was a language-game, what had we exchanged so that instead of the label of "mental illness," he was able to bring his philosophy on the world's folly out into the open, and say what he wanted to say? But instead of concentrating, I was daydreaming.

This criticism of labeling brought me back to the 1970s. I saw myself arriving at Heathrow airport, on my way every month to London near Hampstead Heath. Every month I used to visit the home of Morton Schatzman, an anti-psychiatrist, who generously offered me his hospitality, without ever asking anything of me.

In London I had very quickly become acquainted with all sorts of therapies, which a little time later were going to cross the Channel for the conquest of Paris. I had tried out the craziest methods on myself, verified that they worked, discovered that there are no limits to therapeutic tinkering, and tried all sorts of tricks for laughing, crying, shouting, gesticulating, and running through a marathon of emotions. But I was not letting go of psychoanalysis, which still seemed to me to be the surest method for accounting for what worked, and for why it worked.

There were a great many people there. I didn't know very well whether they were therapists or patients, or indeed which was which. And frankly, I didn't care; I loved being there. Laing was then in India; Cooper was between two books, and Kingsley Hall was on the point of closing. Under the initiative of Joe Burke, some other therapeutic communities opened in nice English houses with English gardens, in the London suburbs. One could encounter there, mixed among those rescued from madness, young American psychiatrists, and conscientious objectors to the Vietnam War ("drop-outs" as they called themselves), and talk for hours day and night. Mary Barnes was a leading figure. She had escaped from a spectacular

DOI: 10.4324/9781003437451-4

madness—in which she would cover her room with her excrement—to become a painter.[1]

PAUL: Madness and war In France, in the period after the war, the focus was mainly on institutional reform, called institutional psychotherapy. I worked with Tosquelles at St. Alban's Hospital, where the movement started. At that time, madness was still our central concern. Then I left the hospital to become an analyst. What about you?

FD: Not being a physician, I wished, on the contrary, to get to know the psychiatric hospital. After having pondered and tried various "alternative" solutions, I decided to work as an analyst in an asylum. Since I had no power over either a good or a bad use of the keys, I had to renounce the effort to open the doors of the mental hospital. Indeed I preferred and I always prefer to see them open. But opened or closed, I work the same, even in the isolation room. All the more so because one day or another, those whom I see at the hospital come through the exit door themselves, without my opening it for them, never when I hope for it, nor when I'm trying hard, but always when I'm not expecting it. In your opinion, what is it that works in that case?

PAUL: As a physician who worked for a long time in a psychiatric hospital, I can at least tell you what doesn't work—to sit behind or opposite someone, asking him to free associate; to wait, like sister Ann,[2] for the patients to make the first move, and, meanwhile, teach the nurses about Lacan's theory. On the other hand, I tell myself today that it isn't enough to flee the institutions in order to practice a purer psychoanalysis. More lucrative, certainly. Sometimes, one hears it said that an analyst such as Lacan himself healed a psychotic patient, without knowing why. The pirouette is easy; I have said it too. If I understand your Philosopher well, he pushed you to come to know what happens in these moments when the analyst doesn't know what's happening.

FD: But how do we come to know it? Lacan wrote something that has always puzzled me. It's the conclusion of a text in the *Écrits* entitled "On a question prior to any possible treatment of psychosis." I have read it and reread it; I know it by heart: "I will leave the question prior to any possible treatment of the psychosis at that for the time being. It is a question that introduces, as we see, the conception to be formed of the handling of the transference in such treatment."[3]

"To say what we can do in this area would be premature, because it would be to go now 'beyond Freud,' and it is out of the question to go beyond Freud when psychoanalysis after Freud has, as I have said, returned to a pre-Freudian stage . . . For to use the technique he instituted outside the experience to which it applies is as stupid as to toil at the oars when one's ship is stuck in the sand."[4]

As you know, this chapter developed the formula for the "foreclosure of the Name-of-the-father" which, in the Lacanian lexicon, is the mark of psychosis. When the "Name-of-the-father" tool is broken, nothing responds from where it is called. Then a delusion or other psychotic symptoms rush in instead.

PAUL: You've learned your lesson well.

FD: But it tells me nothing about how to proceed with the analysis of psychosis, and nothing about the conception to be formed of the handling of the transference in this situation. Conversely, it seems to prohibit any advance beyond Freud who, by the way, didn't refrain from inviting the reader to move ahead. Yet by sticking to preliminary considerations, the concept of "foreclosure" is finally reduced to a kind of label.

PAUL: You're exaggerating.

FD: Probably, but this is what I've thought for a long time. When I went to the United States at the end of the seventies, I was expecting to encounter representatives of a sort of psychoanalysis, which Lacan had judged to have returned to a pre-Freudian stage. To my great surprise, I discovered that American psychoanalysis was not reduced to the movement baptized "ego psychology." I was welcomed by analysts belonging to a tradition contemporary with Freud, analysts who had never ceased handling the transference in psychosis, without having the impression of toiling stupidly at the oars in the sand. Obviously, they had no problem situating themselves either "before" or "beyond" Freud. Rather, they were oriented by the challenges thrown at Freud's theory by madness itself.

PAUL: Freud had, however, claimed to be bringing the plague when he came to the United States.

FD: The plague was already there, since the end of the previous century. In that period, in Chicago, a whole group of social workers, psychologists, sociologists and physicians were gravitating around Hull House, founded by Jane Addams[5] for welcoming immigrants set adrift, whose symptoms were different from those of Freud's clients in Vienna.[6] There, the Chicago school of urban sociology originated, to which we are indebted for a psychiatric current inspired by Freud and by George Herbert Mead. From Mead came the concept of the self as a node of social relations; from Freud's fundamental psychoanalytic concepts, they created an original approach to psychosis in the context of public service.

PAUL: And who were they?

FD: Their names will probably say nothing at all to you, since they are not yet translated into French.[*] They are scarcely mentioned by Jones in

---

[*] Since this was written, some of the works of Harry Stack Sullivan and Frieda Fromm-Reichmann have been translated into French, specifically, *Schizophrenia as a Human Process* by Sullivan, and *Principles of Psychotherapy* by Fromm-Reichmann.

his account of Freud's trip, and they were certainly eclipsed by the academic and medical notables who scrambled around the great man. Among these pioneers at the beginning of the century were: William Alanson White, a psychiatrist at Saint Elizabeth's, a military hospital where many were trained during the two wars, and also Clifford Beers, who had been through madness and confinement himself, before taking part in the reform of American psychiatry. Then came Harry Stack Sullivan, after the First World War, to Sheppard Pratt Hospital near Baltimore,[7] Frieda Fromm-Reichmann to Chestnut Lodge around the time of the Second World War, and more recently, Otto Will to Austen Riggs Center. These last two institutions being committed to the intensive psychoanalytic therapy of psychosis.* Each analyst works, on a daily basis, with three or four patients, who elsewhere would be subjected to heavy medications. At Austen Riggs, the unlocked doors and front lawns extending out to Main Street give no indication of any sort of enclosure.

PAUL: Don't you think you're idealizing?

FD: Perhaps, but I'm under no illusion. Since my first visit, there have been some changes. Private insurance companies don't like treatments to take too long, and cost them too much money. Besides, they're very fond of disputes. Each analyst has to have a lawyer behind his armchair ready to jump up to the bar at the least complaint. If somebody threatens suicide, it's better to hospitalize him or her in a closed ward. If not, there's a professional liability case. In other words, the passion for research transmitted by the elders whom I have mentioned to you diminishes in inverse proportion to the caution demonstrated by young analysts today in the exercise of their craft.

PAUL: Now you're exaggerating in the other direction.

FD: I prefer to talk to you about a very recent time, when I encountered analysts over there capable not only of taking risks with patients diagnosed as psychotic, but also of giving an account of their work. They came from an analytic tradition confronted originally with patients coming out of poverty and from immigration, knocking their heads against the American dream—at quite a distance from the tradition of East Coast "ego psychology" and from West Coast systemic analyses. I wonder what indeed had prevented Freud from discovering, during his trip to the United States in 1909, this endemic theoretical virus, which has been sufficiently hardy to survive all the way to the present. Was it his proselytizing concern or his difficulty speaking English? Whatever it might have been, the arsenals of the pharmaceutical companies will have soon eradicated this plague.

---

* Chestnut Lodge closed in 2001.

PAUL: Rather than prophesy, I would rather have you recount what made you return to the United States, for apparently you have gone there more than once.

FD: Yes. That time, the date for my vacation was approaching and I was still wondering how to account for what had happened in the analysis of the Philosopher—"this language-game with madness," as Wittgenstein put it. I regretted having practically committed myself to describing it, and I felt I was trapped in a stupid bet. In rereading Lacan's text, it seemed to me so stupid to remain toiling at the oars in the sand. Then suddenly I felt like changing to another mode of transference.

PAUL: Theoretical?

FD: No, geographical. I had the idea of taking a trip to the United States, to meet Otto Will, the former director of Austen Riggs Center. He had been close to Sullivan's way of thinking, and at the same time he had encouraged the creation of a Lacanian reading group at Austen Riggs. I had missed him on my first visit, because he had just left for his retirement on the California coast. I wrote to him to introduce myself. A short time later, he welcomed me to his home.

Chapter 5

Do *You* Believe in Psychoanalysis?

Otto Will's house, near San Francisco

BEULAH PARKER, OTTO WILL, FD, THE VOICE OF
WITTGENSTEIN, HARRY STACK SULLIVAN,
FRIEDA FROMM-REICHMANN

*That summer I happened to be near San Francisco in the company of Otto Will and his wife Beulah. We were sitting in a garden on a hill that sloped down toward the bay. Beulah was also a psychoanalyst and the author of several books on schizophrenia. I had read one of her novels on the airplane—*The Mingled Yarn*—and we were talking about it. It's written as a tragedy about a family that dies out, without any descendants, three generations after the Civil War, with members on both sides. At the end of the book a brother kills himself and his sister remains childless.[1] I was impressed by the forceful tone of the novel, but a silent musing came into my mind. Beulah read my thoughts.*

BEULAH: In fact, the story is akin to mine. I'm old enough now to tell it without hurting anyone.
OTTO WILL: What about you? What made you become a psychoanalyst?

This question took me by surprise. We knew each other for scarcely an hour. I answered without thinking.

FD: The war, probably. When my mother was just pregnant with me, she secretly crossed the demarcation line while carrying some compromising letters. After some months we got out of prison, barely escaping assassination or deportation. I was born sometime later.
OTTO WILL: I had no intention at all of becoming an analyst. I spent the war in the Pacific, as a physician on a destroyer. I was at Guadalcanal, and then back home. After my return I was in charge of a ward at the

DOI: 10.4324/9781003437451-5

military hospital of St. Elizabeth, until a serious operation cut short my activities. I then undertook an analysis with Sullivan. During my convalescence I resumed my duties on the ward, where I was really just dragging myself along. In the meanwhile a soldier had been admitted. No one knew what to do with him. He was traumatized by violent combat, and he was letting himself die, without any physiological causes. He was vomiting, refusing to eat, and lying in his bed in his own excrement, like some kind of shapeless and foul-smelling thing. He had cut off all contact. Being useless for anything, I visited him. One day I sat down beside his bed, with no particular purpose in mind. I became accustomed to passing the time daydreaming, and talking to myself, as if he were not there. By the way, was he truly there in that state of living death?

The telephone rang. Otto got up and called Beulah. In their absence I distinctly heard a voice in my ear: "He was speaking to himself since no one else seemed to be present. But does that mean that he was speaking to himself?"²
This time I had indeed recognized Wittgenstein. I wasn't surprised.

FD: So there you are! I'm told that you were very popular in the universities around here.

I stopped myself as Otto was coming to sit down again.

OTTO WILL: If someone is talking even when no one else is present, it doesn't necessarily mean that he's talking to himself. I learned this little by little as I discovered that a subliminal conversation was unfolding between this inert being and myself. More exactly, my reveries were not unconnected to what this man was expressing without saying a word. I ended by telling him whatever came to mind. Speaking loudly to myself, I must have seemed nuts. But one thing intrigued me: I had no feelings for this man. The situation struck me as particularly absurd, and I spoke to Sullivan about it:

OTTO—I couldn't work in your field; I have no empathy at all for this kind of patient.
SULLIVAN—Then perhaps there's a chance they'll teach you something.

FD: Yet American psychoanalysts have the reputation of being great lovers of empathy.
OTTO WILL: Not Sullivan. It was not his cup of tea. Not mine either. I remember the hard time I gave him session after session:

OTTO—This analysis is not moving forward; it doesn't help; you don't listen to me; how long will it go on like that? You never say anything; you are hateful.

SULLIVAN—You too are a terrible bore. Naturally I could tell you that you have aggression toward your father, your mother, or God knows who, but today I find you especially disagreeable.

Otto burst out with a roar of laughter. I didn't exactly see what was so funny. He seemed to be speaking for his own amusement, not mine. And not Beulah's either. There was nothing to laugh about—an analyst, intervening shamelessly in reality, giving up his neutrality and showing that he was affected! What's more, Otto, totally caught up in his memories, paid no attention to our private indignation.

OTTO WILL: That was a long time ago! No doubt I'm rambling. A little later, I became an analyst and worked at Chestnut Lodge. Compared to Austen Riggs, Chestnut Lodge had more closed wards, in order to accept more disturbed patients. I hadn't changed very much, and I always succeeded in exasperating Sullivan. Again one day, he exploded: "If you're not happy with me, then go and consult the dear little lady who lives at the top of the hill."

The dear little lady was Frieda Fromm-Reichmann, who was the director of psychotherapy at Chestnut Lodge. She lived in a cottage located on the grounds of the Lodge. In fact, she became my analyst upon the death of Sullivan. As you know, he died in Paris in 1949.

I prudently acknowledged this, but I didn't know it at the time.

OTTO WILL: Frieda Fromm-Reichmann had come to Chestnut Lodge while fleeing Nazism. Before that she had worked in Heidelberg and in Frankfurt—with sociologists, I believe. She was very close to Groddeck in his last years. Do you know her?

FD: The official doctrine has it that American psychoanalysis is an adaptation to the "American way of life," and that the work of Sullivan has nothing in it that would stir a movement of interest in France.

OTTO WILL: Whatever it might be, those two truly led people out of madness. They were very close and understood each other well. Still today, in this country, there are analysts who ask if what they did was truly psychoanalysis! You will judge for yourself. . . .

He went to look for a book by Frieda Fromm-Reichmann, from which he read me the following passage: "Other analysts may feel that treatment as we have outlined it is not psychoanalysis. The patient is not instructed to lie on the couch, he is not asked to give free associations (although he frequently does), and his productions are seldom interpreted other than by understanding acceptance."[3]

I agreed. Whether the patient is seated, standing, or lying down, the important thing is to trust his nonsensical productions. Why obsess on this question of position? As if the true psychoanalysis must be done on the couch, while the seated position, face to face, would come under the name of psycho- therapy, reserved condescendingly for a category of patients decreed incapable of being analyzed. Didn't Freud say that he asked patients to lie on the couch so he wouldn't have to tolerate being looked at for the whole day?

Otto Will invited me to continue reading: "Freud says that every science and therapy that accepts his teachings about the unconscious, about transference and resistance, and about infantile sexuality may be called psychoanalysis. According to this definition, we believe that we are practicing psychoanalysis with our schizophrenic patients.

Whether we call it analysis or not, it is clear that successful treatment does not depend on technical rules of any special psychiatric school but rather on the basic attitude of the individual therapist toward psychotic persons."[4]

I said to Otto that this book addressed precisely the question I had come to ask him, about the use of psychoanalysis in the case of patients said to be schizophrenic. Well, Frieda Fromm-Reichmann spoke a lot about transference, but under the form of a "basic attitude," with disdain for rules and for schools . . .

Otto signaled to me to read more. "If he meets them as strange creatures of another world whose productions are not understandable to 'normal' beings, he cannot treat them. If he realizes, however, that the difference between himself and the psychotic is only one of degree and not of kind, he will know better how to meet him."[5]

This text began to arouse my suspicion. I hadn't thought that between the Philosopher and myself such a meeting had ever occurred. This word "meeting" exuded too much feeling for my taste and training, and I couldn't help showing my reluctance.

FD: Does that mean the analyst must be mad in order to function as an analyst under these conditions?

What followed was scarcely more reassuring: "He will be able to identify himself sufficiently with the patient to understand and accept his emotional reactions without becoming involved in them."[6]

I was not grasping this, but the reference to "identification" ended my confusion. Everything in me, and above all the way in which psychoanalysis had been transmitted to me, rebelled against such participation by the analyst. On the contrary, she must absolutely remain at a distance. There again, Otto ignored my silent disapproval.

OTTO WILL: I forgot to tell you that the soldier on my ward left the hospital some months later, rehabilitated. I understood that our uncanny conversations had mattered for something. Thus I began to become an analyst, and I came to Chestnut Lodge. Today psychoanalysis is done with people who don't really need it, but it's not done with those whom it could really help.

The light-hearted tone had become dull in spite of the sky that was ever so blue, and of the fragrant eucalyptus over our heads. We were looking at a boat crossing the bay.

FD: And you? What you did with that soldier—do you call that psychoanalysis?

Otto didn't answer me. The Voice whispered in my ear: "One has already to know something in order to be capable of asking a thing's name. Ask yourself what you may already know."[7]
    I knew nothing, since I had come to learn Wittgenstein was getting on my nerves with his comments. He was choosing this moment when I was assailed with doubts to confuse me even more. Beulah saw my embarrassment.

BEULAH: You should ask Otto to write a book on the subject.
OTTO WILL: I'm not a writer.

The silence weighed heavily once again and became even thicker. The boat had disappeared. I was no longer so sure that I would find here what I had come looking for. I was afraid of losing my theoretical moorings, and I was trying to hold onto them. I thought again of Sullivan. What familiarity with a patient! Otto too seemed preoccupied.

OTTO WILL: And you—do you believe in psychoanalysis?

I attempted to evade the question:

FD: When patients ask me this question, I answer them that I wouldn't do this work if I didn't "believe" in it, as they say. What about you? Do you believe in it?
OTTO WILL: Not especially. I believe in only one thing. Men suffer and are injured by the links that join them to one another. The way out of this suffering is found in the same links. Very simple: you have only to talk about what's impossible to say. Psychoanalysis starts with that. Nothing but a tool, an instrument—more or less reliable, more or less precise, depending upon the moment, depending upon the people.
FD: Then it would be enough to talk. Everyone's doing that today. Isn't everyone trying to "say the unsayable"?

THE VOICE: I would like to add the following point: you regard it much too much as a matter of course that one can say anything to anyone.[8]

The Voice had spoken so loudly that I looked at my hosts. Otto continued as if he had heard nothing:

OTTO WILL: It's so rare that something is said by somebody that truly tells something to someone. It happened to me with Sullivan. That day, it wasn't that I believed him; I always had a hard time believing. But, I trusted what he had to say to me; I gave him my trust. Moreover, if I remember well, I believe he said . . . nothing.

BEULAH: You could be clearer.

OTTO WILL: Sullivan was not always the cold and sarcastic man he is often said to have been. A long time after my operation, I happened to be overcome by periods of violent nausea. Right in the middle of a session one day, I had to rush to the bathroom to throw up my guts. I felt miserable and ashamed. Sullivan went with me, and helped me get up. He took me upstairs, gave me a bed to lie down on, and phoned my wife so that she might come to spend the night. And all of that without the least comment, without the least "it's no accident that precisely during this session, etc." The next morning, I came downstairs to leave. He was in his office. I mumbled something about thanks. He raised his head from his book and said tersely: "There's no need for thanks."

BEULAH: What harm would there be to accept thanks?

I was even more skeptical than she. I was finally grasping it—this famous American psychoanalysis, obsessed with the well-being of the patient, responding to the demand to cure the symptom instead of listening to what it might tell us. Sullivan had certainly missed an opportunity to articulate a signifier. Besides, I didn't see why on earth Otto was recounting all this, and I looked for a polite way to take my leave. But he went on:

OTTO WILL: And yet what took place that day was decisive. It's incredible all that can happen to babies. One wears oneself out as an analyst, finessing this muddle of concepts of frustration, separation, privation, anxiety, and who knows what else . . . and Beulah could tell you the anxious and impossible type I can be at certain moments. But after this crazy episode in which I found myself confined to bed in Sullivan's home, an idea came to me.

FD: Sullivan made you see something?

Maintaining the suspense, Otto got up to go look for some ice cubes. Beulah asked me if I would enjoy taking with me one of the abalone found in the bay. She left for a while to go to the beach. Wittgenstein took advantage of it: "Your question is stupid. You see very well that he is going to tell you about an ostensive definition."

FD:	About what?
THE VOICE:	When one cannot say, one points . . . But an ostensive definition can be interpreted in very various ways in every case.[9]
FD:	What does it depend on?
THE VOICE:	On the circumstances under which it is given, and on the person I give it to. And how he takes the definition is seen in the use that he makes of the word defined.[10]

I heard nothing of all that. Otto returned with his ice cubes. I asked him by the way:

FD:	What use did Sullivan make of what you had shown him?
OTTO WILL:	He made me see what I had shown him by being sick in bed. Listen to this. I had the idea of asking my mother a question. I knew that my father had been stricken with tuberculosis just before my birth. He believed he was doomed and he had chosen to finish his days in New Mexico, where the climate and the altitude would be less harsh. He was cured. So Santa Fe was also the city where I grew up. I spent my youth without problems in that wonderful place. But I was coming to realize what my mother had had to endure, and I went to ask the old lady:
OTTO:	It mustn't have been pleasant for you, life in Santa Fe, with a husband confined to bed and a newborn in your arms.
HIS MOTHER:	But you couldn't know about it; you didn't know how to talk. What's more, you weren't with us. You spent all the early years very far away from there, raised by a black nurse, at your grandmother's . . .
OTTO (TO FD):	Looking at my face, she seemed surprised by my surprise. But the strangest part of this story was a memory that clarified itself retrospectively. It had left an impression on me of the "uncanny," a word Sullivan loved. As an adolescent I had to attend a cousin's funeral in the area where my grandmother had lived. Someone, they tell me, wanted to see me. I was taken to a black woman whom I didn't know from Eve, or from Adam. Seeing me, she melted into tears and took me in her arms. "My baby, my baby boy," she said, sobbing. I was the same size then as I am now. Very embarrassed, I did my best to calm her, thinking that Southern people are really emotional. How would I have been able to recognize in this woman my nanny whom they had never

mentioned to me? When I left again, two days later, I had understood nothing at all, and I had not even thought to ask her name.

I didn't know what to say after such a story. Evening fell, and I had to go. Taking my leave of my hosts, I returned to San Francisco with Frieda's book and my abalone, still more puzzled than when I arrived.

PAUL: And yet Otto Will had at least shown you that the analyst's transference to the death zone of his patient, the deteriorating soldier, had been the only possible way out. Your geographical transference had brought you to the discovery of an atypical form of analytic transference.

FD: It took me quite a while to understand it—all the time I needed to go through some analogous experiences. By then I was still very far from figuring out that the fragment of autobiography delivered with a tone of confidence by Otto Will contained the elements of the language-game, which Wittgenstein and the Philosopher were urging me to describe.

PAUL: And how have you "come to know"?

FD: As we go along, I'll present to you those patients who led me, little by little—as if they had given the password to each other—into the language-game with madness that I call "psychotic transference."

Chapter 6

An Ostensive Definition

The house in the woods.

FD, PAUL

On a flight from New York to Paris

WITTGENSTEIN, FD

Paul went to take down various sausages and hams, some of which he was slicing into several piles on a board, defying, I suggested, the dietary plan that applied to his case. Since he was turning a deaf ear to my suggestion, I resumed my narrative.

FD:	The next evening, at Kennedy Airport in New York, I had scarcely placed my foot on the escalator when I began reciting the usual litany of "should haves" to myself. I felt I was returning empty-handed, very disappointed that, by offering me anecdotes, Otto had eluded my question about the transference in psychosis.
PAUL:	And what then was the "spirit of the stairs,"* in an after- thought, whispering to you?
FD:	I should have told Otto Will about some moments in the Philosopher's analysis. I should have asked him how, in spite of his experience of madness, the tool of psychoanalysis had been able to function. What did the transference consist of in his case? What was being transferred when transference was considered to be impossible? and so on. I was blaming myself for letting myself be swept along by the flow of the

---

* A French expression that refers to the afterthoughts that occur to one while on the stairs and on the way out, and hence too late for the conversation just ended.

DOI: 10.4324/9781003437451-6

conversation, and for not having had the presence of mind to make use of my own theoretical references, which, to tell you the truth, had also abandoned me. But then, what was the point of this trip!

In order to think about something else I bought some comic books, and as soon as I took my seat in the airplane, I plunged into the adventures of Calvin and Hobbes. The one named Calvin, a scamp of about six years of age, fiercely resists every form of education—at school, at meals, from baby-sitters, from parents. His principal ally in rebellion is Hobbes, a plush tiger. He's the only one who truly responds to Calvin and the only one who truly plays with him. He comes to life only through Calvin's and the readers' eyes, whereas in the eyes of other characters who intrude on their play, he appears in his plush form as banal, silent and inert.[1]

While turning the pages I was thinking again of my visit. Why had I gone on to tell my life story to this analyst whom I didn't know? Why had I talked to him about the war? And what about him, laying out his private life as though it were theory for him. In what way were these confessions my concern?

THE VOICE:	That's it. You have to manage everything for yourself.[2]
FD (TO PAUL):	This time, the Voice came from my right, from a passenger seated beside me. I recognized Wittgenstein in the flesh. Paul, this time you must definitely take me for a fool.
PAUL:	Right now, as matters stand. . . .
FD:	I'm positive it was really him. Just like the photographs—serious, stiff, and unwelcoming. How can I put it? In my confusion I stammered: "I should manage it all by myself? Naturally, how could I do otherwise? Have you understood something about this story with Sullivan? Americans truly do implicate themselves too much. They have no theoretical distance."
WITTGENSTEIN:	Otto Will put you on the path; he showed you something—an ostensive definition. Think about it. What did he show you, and above all, how did he manage to show it to you?
FD:	All right. He recalled three scenes, each one containing a person confined to bed. Each time he showed me someone sick and very close to dying. Is that what you call an ostensive definition?
WITTGENSTEIN:	Go on. Describe these scenes for me.
FD:	First there was the meeting with the soldier, in the ward Otto was in charge of after his return from the

war; then his own illness at his analyst's, and finally, his father's illness, in Santa Fe, with his mother, when he was a baby, and far away He had to be far away for fear of contagion. What more can I tell you?

WITTGENSTEIN: Don't forget the circumstances. An ostensive definition depends on the circumstances under which it is given.[3]

PAUL: What exactly is meant by "ostensive definition"?

He asked this while pouring me some peach wine to give me some courage.

FD: It's a way of pointing to what one can't name. Thus, with the gesture of sitting down beside him, Otto Will gave form to what the soldier was showing— dying from being unable to get out of his stupor. At the time, I myself would also very much have wanted Wittgenstein to provide me with some details, but his peremptory tone permitted me no way out at all, just as in the old days when he was teaching in his room at Cambridge. So, I did my best to describe the circumstances he asked me about.

FD (TO WITTGENSTEIN):   In the first two scenes, the circumstances are simple: psychoanalysis isn't working. For example, with that soldier—how can one ask him to free associate if he has renounced all communication? What's more, you yourself are no stranger to such circumstances. When you were at the front, during the First World War, you must have known men like this soldier. . . .

Wittgenstein frowned, and made me regret at once that I had said too much. During that war, David Pinsent, his best friend and an aviator during the war, had been killed, and his own brother Kurt killed himself with his own officer's pistol. This was the third suicide to hit his older brothers, after Hans, who had drowned himself in Chesapeake Bay, and Rudi, who had poisoned himself. He had only one brother left, Paul, the pianist who lost an arm in the war, for whom Ravel composed his Concerto for the Left Hand. *I didn't dare say anything more. But he came out of his muted silence:*

WITTGENSTEIN: In the end, if you want to interpret an ostensive definition, I repeat that everything depends not only on the circumstances, but on the person to whom it is given.[4]

FD: Let's suppose then that this soldier is what you call an ostensive definition—a near corpse covered with a sheet. It was given to Otto Will. Besides, no one else wanted to look at it. Otto had his reasons, having himself experienced one of those states between life and death, a state in which time has come to a standstill.

PAUL: I see what you mean—Lacan's concept of "a space between two deaths", in *The Ethics of Psychoanalysis*,[5] looks like that: you are progressively erased from the circle of the living, but not yet inscribed in the Great Beyond.

FD: Wittgenstein confessed to me that during the war he also had experienced this kind of state. But he didn't want to tell me more about it, and he insisted that I pick up the thread of my description.

FD (TO WITTGENSTEIN):   Picture Otto feeling empty, unable to do anything. He sits down at the soldier's bedside, daydreaming, a little like Alice, feeling sleepy on a hot summer afternoon, unwittingly registering a rabbit hurrying by. This is how I imagine his state of mind—a state of being somewhat dazed, capturing what vigilance excludes from the rational mind. And at that point this absurd, bed-ridden presence speaks to him, without evoking anything in Otto—no reminiscence, no resonance at all. Nevertheless, he can't prevent himself from responding to some slight movements of this body in the crumpled sheets, to this soldier who can do nothing but show for all to see the thing he has become. Would you say he's a living definition of what it is impossible for him to say?

WITTGENSTEIN: . . . and which is waiting to enter a language- game. Go on.

FD: You want me to describe the second scene? Otto Will occupies in his turn the place of the patient surrounded by his own vomit. Now he presents himself as one about to give up the ghost. The "bedridden man" was transferred onto him. The circumstances always concern the limits of psychoanalysis. His analysis with Sullivan wasn't moving ahead. It was going nowhere. It was a failure. Otto Will was at his wit's end, and so was Sullivan.

WITTGENSTEIN: And who was the person to whom the definition in question was addressed?

FD:	What to say about Sullivan, except that he doesn't accept thanks? Was that to indicate that the language-game being played between them was not one between patient and physician, and not even one between friends?
WITTGENSTEIN:	What was the language-game then?
FD:	Probably one played in the catastrophic zone into which the soldier, unable either to live or die, had fallen. But there's still that third scene that Otto Will went through. When Sullivan pointed to the bed on which he could lie down, Otto discovered there the place occupied by his father; he then questioned his mother for what she might say about this bed-ridden man. The game is up. Do you truly want to push me to say that Otto has shown us the primal scene, a drama of his childhood played out around his parents' bed? Now can I return to my comic books?
WITTGENSTEIN:	He said that his childhood had passed without drama.
FD:	He'd repressed it.

Wittgenstein exploded. I feared he was stirring up the other passengers. But everyone was sleeping while waiting for the film.

WITTGENSTEIN:	Typical psychoanalyst! Fascinated by the *Urzene!* Always the primal scene! It seduces you into giving our lives this dramatic pattern, as if we were all tragic heroes, repeating fate's decrees since the day we were born.[6]
PAUL:	He wasn't completely wrong; you had overdone it.
FD:	I could no longer stop him. Now he was out of his wits.
WITTGENSTEIN:	You need only to transform the banality of your patient's life into a "thriller" in order to give these patients the impression that they're interesting, and to push them to show off on the couch. Psychoanalysis is a powerful mythology—which makes it all the more harmful.[7]
FD:	I wasn't expecting this outburst. Noting my crestfallen look, he conceded:
WITTGENSTEIN:	Sometimes it's useful . . . but its utility proves something only if it can assume a critical distance on itself.

FD:

I recognized I had bungled the end of the story with this standard primal scene. Otto's childhood had passed without drama. His father had been cured, and although drama had been narrowly missed, things were arranged to make it all commonplace. In Santa Fe, the atmosphere of the house, with his father bedridden and critically ill, had not been able to impress him because it had been "cut out."

PAUL:

What's that again?

FD:

A word in my private language . . . to refer to circumstances "in which one acts as if nothing has happened."

PAUL:

Do you want to say "denial"?

FD:

I call it a "cut-out impression." Otto saw his father sick and lost, before he himself was able to speak. Then they sent him away in order not to traumatize him, implicitly requiring him to act as if nothing has ever happened. What could be more banal! There's an upheaval in the family, and the baby will be the last to be informed, although he's the first affected because his life is just beginning, and he offers little resistance to the impressions he's receiving. "He can't understand," as they say. On the pretext of helping him start a new life, not overshadowed with our troubles, we deprive him of the language that could authenticate what he's registering. I made this point to Wittgenstein.

WITTGENSTEIN:

Babies are treated as if they came from a strange country, without knowing our language—as if they could think, if need be, but not yet speak.[8]

FD:

This image of a strange country comes up often. Many bear witness to a childhood passed in exile, and to a loneliness lived in good surroundings with their dear ones—surrounded by affection, but excluded from the language that would have permitted them to name their sensations. Some people have the memory of having been stowaways in a territory in which language eludes them, and with it bits of life, lived through without having been lived. That's how it was with this nameless black nanny. One day, coming from nowhere, she startles Otto in an uncanny way, calls him "my baby,"—disturbing the course of his "official" history—and he doesn't bother at all to ask her name.

WITTGENSTEIN:	Right now you do understand that in order to ask this simple question "What is her name?" he had to have access to a language about her.
FD:	But why was this access refused to him? What misfortune were they trying to avoid by that?
WITTGENSTEIN:	Be careful, you're again falling into tragedy.

This was the moment for me to strike back:

FD:	And how not to bring up tragedy! You who make so much of the "circumstances"—how can you conjure away, in a Southern state, the Civil War and the slavery from which Otto Will's nurse had barely escaped with an identity? And what about the other war from which more recently his soldier emerged in his rotting state? What about this historic scene, primal or not, where chaos prevails, where social relationships disintegrate? If you'd like to know, that's what psychoanalysis runs up against when it ceases to be a mythology and loses its power— when it no longer works.
PAUL:	What happens when it no longer works?
FD:	What happens is the Grand Entry of madness . . . this was one of the leitmotifs of the Philosopher. He said that madness arises when the upheavals of the big History, objective and public, encounter our little history, subjective and private, pulverizing all social relationships, including families. Such were the "circumstances" of the language-games he encouraged me to explore. The succession of stories that Otto Will had disclosed to me presented exactly this kind of interference, which on my return to France, I myself would have to face. Meanwhile, I continued to lecture Wittgenstein on this theme:
FD (TO WITTGENSTEIN):	Let me tell you: the use of psychoanalysis, when one assumes a critical distance toward it, is to inscribe in someone's history "bits" of time uprooted from History. No matter that we are heroes of our own history. What's important are those roaming, surviving images, like this nameless woman, or this dying man without any past. Wouldn't you say, then, that when all masks fall away (including the psychoanalyst's), an ostensive definition appears, waiting to be spoken?

PAUL:	Finally, you caught hold of your psychotic transference.
FD:	I didn't quite realize what I was talking about, especially since my talk ended up putting Wittgenstein to sleep. He woke up only when they turned off the lights in the plane, at the start of the film—one of those disaster movies beloved by airlines, which seemed to fascinate him. I was upset; my enthusiasm had fallen.

From Otto Will's story I had gathered that he himself had been able to understand his patient only from unspoken pieces of his own history. But that point was quite cumbersome, actually. Ruminating on my disillusion over and over in my mind, as if it were a piece of old chewing gum, I finally fell asleep without waiting for the end of the film. I was eager to be in France, back in my own theoretical home. Otto's confidence seemed to fade further and further away from me. As I stepped on the moving walkway at Roissy, I concluded that this whole story came down to a veteran's memories unrelated to the sessions that were waiting for me almost at the door of the airport.

Chapter 7

Host and Visitor

Back to Paris, FD is confronted to a heated session with Casimir who threatens to kill himself. Diagnosed as a voyeur, he already spent years with another analyst. To Wittgenstein who witnesses the scene, she complains about the logical impasses in which he traps her, analogous to riddles staged by T'chan master Lin Tsi in rough dialogues between "host and visitor." As Wittgenstein asks her what his voyeurism is showing her. The answer is given later on by revealing "a crossroad" between his story the analyst's story and History, opening a cutout scene of events, and a therapeutic outcome. Her intention is to tell that story, next summer, at Austen Riggs Center.

The house in the woods.

PAUL, FD

The analyst's office.

FD, CASIMIR, WITTGENSTEIN, LIN-TSI

Noticing that the pile of hors d'oeuvres had almost disappeared, I felt the moment had come for me to attack the "main course" in my narrative—the "interferences"* between my little history, the big History, and the history of my patients. I was hesitating before approaching this kind of confession—preferring, like any self-respecting psychoanalyst, to stick to happy endings. Paul saw me hesitate.

PAUL: So, on your return you had barely moved beyond where
                    you were when you left.

---

* An "interference" is a technical term, taken from the vocabulary of physics, and understood here by the author as a coincidence and a feature of her own life that comes up through the transference. It constitutes a kind of common ground of experience for her and the patient.

DOI: 10.4324/9781003437451-7

FD:	I had, however, gained a companion—this Wittgenstein—who at that time was appearing only to me, in a private way, like Calvin's tiger, Hobbes. . . .
PAUL:	And appearing to the Philosopher as well, if I remember correctly.
FD:	Exactly. From both Otto's Will's story and the Philosopher's analysis, I got the idea that one's never totally alone when talking to oneself. But the comparison ends there. I had always more or less known this, for my grandmother never stopped talking aloud to herself.
PAUL:	Mine also talked to herself, when she was alone. She was a widow of the First World War. I was a little ashamed of her, and I used to explain to my pals when we were outside her door: "No, no, she's really with someone."
FD:	On my return, I tried, without success, to convey to a patient, Casimir, that he was with someone. But he claimed that in my presence he was really and definitively all alone, with no other person to talk to.

One day, while waiting for him, in Wittgenstein's company, I was recalling my summer trip—in particular, a little scene that had struck me:

FD (TO WITTGENSTEIN):	In the middle of a square on the Berkeley campus, I saw a man wearing a coat spotted with multicolored stars. He was making large gestures aimed at the four directions, looking like either a wizard or like a fool. You know, like the Epinal riddle: "Look for the peasant in the old Alsatian"*—or like that duck-rabbit image at the end of the *Investigations*.[1] I stayed there staring at him, lost in conjectures, trying to sort out the confused impressions inside me. Then I went on my way.

---

* Epinal is a town in the East of France, known for the colorful images, riddles, and stories which have been very popular since the eighteenth century.

WITTGENSTEIN:	You should really lose this habit of analyzing your internal experiences. Once again, this man was pointing to something.
FD:	His gestures made no sense to me, and yet it's true that they hinted at something. I thought at first of the circular movements the old people make at dawn, in Beijing's parks—martial arts figures, in spite of their very slow movements. I occasionally encounter someone practicing Tai-chi in the Luxembourg Garden. Through his eyes one can trace the outline of an invisible adversary he never loses sight of.
WITTGENSTEIN:	Suppose then that this guy, by making his circular movements, is simply giving you an ostensive definition: "This is called a circle." Wouldn't you, however, still be able to interpret his definition differently, even if you see his eyes following this outline, and even though you feel what he feels? In fact, your interpretation will consist in the use you will make of the word he points to, for example, a circle.[2]
FD:	But to grasp the point of all these circles—what use do you want me to make of them? I know nothing of martial arts.

Meanwhile, Casimir had arrived. Seeing the door half open, he came in, greeting me in his usual way: "I'm late, I know, but in any case, it's the last time I'm coming to see you. It's a vicious circle. We go nowhere, just around and around. You're even dumber than my previous analyst. He at least wrote books."

As you can imagine, I didn't respond. Then he stood up.

CASIMIR:	I knew it; it's not worth coming here. Always the same story: you keep quiet. You think you have the upper hand. Since that's the way it is, I'm going to kill myself—and this time for real. Yesterday, one of my friends did it the moment he left his analyst. There's no dumber place than this!
FD:	Even so, tell me what you had to say to me.
CASIMIR (SITTING DOWN AGAIN):	I want you to listen to me and to answer me. Is it clear? Either you believe in psychoanalysis, and admit mine was a failure, and then the only option left is to

shoot myself. Or you don't give a damn about it, and you're a crook—all the more reason for me to get rid of myself. Answer right away! What've you got to say?

I immediately pulled together what was left of my presence of mind:

FD: There's at least one thing you're succeeding at perfectly, and that's at making your analysis fail. That should be acknowledged here, as dumb as this place might be.

He got up as if moved by a spring, and left without saying a word, slamming the door behind him. I immediately regretted what I had said. If we had been in the United States, I would have had to hospitalize him in anticipation of the artillery of lawyers, and all the chicanery of malpractice suits that would certainly have followed. Perhaps, in that case, I would have been less worried. . . . Wittgenstein, who was watching the scene without a word, didn't seem flustered.

WITTGENSTEIN: And before that, what had happened?
FD: I don't know what to say. He gets me so muddled. He's confused about "before" and "after." He has a strange notion of time: it doesn't flow, since no event takes place to make it flow. Time is dead for him. As he says, he's on death row, with a half-rotten body. His life is not a life; for him death is life. Nothing can get time moving again. He has no future, no past to talk about. As far as anamnesis is concerned, he says he's already given enough of it to his previous analyst, to whom he'd said everything—so it's my job to ask that guy about it.
WITTGENSTEIN: I was simply asking about what had happened the session before. Today, he showed you that there was something to kill.
FD: "Kill"! This last word slapped me like an ominous call to order. What if he was really going to kill himself?
PAUL: Don't you think that we all have, one day or another, a monster to exterminate?
FD: Suddenly too upset, I couldn't think anymore. I bore a grudge against Wittgenstein, who had done nothing to stop this catastrophe I reproached him for it: "Would you still be able today to maintain that psychoanalysis invents tragedies?" He didn't deign to respond. I was fed up and eager to let everything drop. Already, the preceding week, a young woman had stormed into my office in the clinic

	for her appointment, screaming: "Let me die like a human being or I'm going to die like a dog. When I'm healed, I'm sick; and when I'm sick, I'm healed. Quick: Answer me right away!"
FD (TO PAUL):	I was petrified. She rushed out to the secretary's office and publicly called me all sorts of names, and then she left with a big commotion. Disheartened, I assumed that psychoanalysis was impossible in her case, and also that, because of me, she was going to return to the asylum (which was bound to happen). I asked Wittgenstein if he knew a trick for escaping from these logical impasses. He joked:
WITTGENSTEIN:	Well, train yourself in martial arts.
FD:	You're not funny, but not far off either. These patients really are fighters. Sometimes, you think you've been transported to the Tch'an* monasteries of ninth-century China, where logical impasses often gave way to violent assaults between master and disciple.[3]
PAUL:	Watch out! Beware! Psychoanalysis—"a relation between master and disciple"?
FD:	Let go of the stereotype. These turbulent Tch'an sessions have a family resemblance to psychoanalysis, when it reaches its limits. During those sessions the places of master and disciple, still called "host" and "visitor," are not stable, but are occupied alternatively by the antagonists in an extremely rapid dynamic.[4]

. . . as happens between patient and analyst in the moments of a psychotic transference. What's more, the sinologist Demiéville himself, translator of the *Sayings* of Lin-tsi, one of the great figures of Tch'an, suggests that analysts could learn something from these Tch'an sessions. They should take a page from this collection of *Sayings*[5]. . . .

I knew Wittgenstein was a lover of cross-cultural relations; besides, at that point, anything was better than thinking about Casimir's future. I then described for him these "battles" about enigmas to which one had to respond immediately, without thinking. This is what Lin-tsi called "acting with one's whole body"[6]: words, cries, belches, hits with the stick, departures from the room in a gust of wind. They said of

* In this section, where the author refers to Lin-tsi (d. 867 CE), to Tch'an Buddhism, and to the T'ang Dynasty (618–907 CE), I have followed her spellings, which are also in accord with Demiéville's translation of Lin-tsi's *Sayings* into French. The current pinyin for these words are "Lin-ji," "Chan" Buddhism, and the "Tang" Dynasty. It should also be noted that Tch'an Buddhism developed in China around the sixth century, and moved sometime in the twelfth century to Japan, where it is known as Zen Buddhism, and "Lin-tsi" is known as "Rinzai."

him that instead of being a monk, he could have been a general in one of the armies that ravaged China in endless civil wars.[7] In this dooms-day climate, Demiéville assumed that the monasteries served as refuges, and were more similar to bedlams than to the Cistercian Order.[8]

PAUL:	Well, at the time of its foundation, our big History was hardly more peaceful.
FD:	Perhaps Lin-tsi, says Demiéville, had a great clinical experience of madness, which, by the way, has always been part of the tradition of Chinese wisdom.[9] Thus, in spite of all my efforts to distract myself from worrying about Casimir, this tradition took me back to him. Beneath the pitiful demeanor he cultivated, he too was deploying a fierce energy. After our sessions, I always felt as though I had received a sound thrashing.

Suddenly the telephone rang. Casimir was calling me from a telephone booth to let me know I should be happy he hadn't killed himself. He had something to give to me. I told him to come up.

PAUL:	Was he going to lay down arms?
FD:	I don't know whether he would have made a great general. On the contrary, he was complaining about leading a life too quiet for his taste, and of being under the influence of some images that prevented him from acting. Instead of doing what he had to do, he could spend whole hours behind the shutters of his windows, looking at women undressing in the apartment building across from his. A nice case of voyeurism, he often told me, a most classical one. He knew what the literature said about this, and above all he knew his previous analyst's theory. At least that analysis had been "didactic," whereas not only was he learning nothing with me, but he often left me gaping, as a result of his sticky questions.

One day he spent the whole session persuading me that he wished to be pregnant, and he demanded his share of interpretations. As you might imagine, I didn't react. My silence seemed suspect to him. At that time, coincidentally, I was the one wanting a child, but I certainly wasn't going to let him know about it. The next week, I learned that I was pregnant and I forgot Casimir's fantasies about it. Filled with joy, I phoned a friend with the good news, at a moment when I thought I was alone. But that day Casimir was waiting in the room next door, having arrived a good hour early. Through my office door, which was slightly ajar, without my suspecting his presence, he heard everything, including some very free speech I was exchanging with my friend about the changes my body would be going through. In short, a true telephonic "strip-tease" offered up to those voyeuristic ears, which didn't miss a bit of it. Finally, he coughed. I was mortified by having let myself go on in this way . . .

PAUL: By undressing, in a way. What did you say to him?
FD: Nothing. Once again, I was stunned, unable to utter any-
               thing whatever. Once again, he wanted to leave immedi-
               ately, furious at my amateurism. "And you call yourself
               an analyst!" he roared, as he walked through the doorway,
               with a burst of anger just like the one he had later on, on
               my return from California, when he wanted to die.
PAUL: In that session, on your return, what precisely happened
               when he had something to give you? What was it?
FD: A piece of paper.
CASIMIR: During the period I used to call and wake you up at night,
               you told me, no doubt urgently wanting to go back to bed,
               to draw something and to bring it to you. I am beyond the
               age of children's drawing, but at least, in case it might
               amuse you I found this scrap of paper in the bottom of my
               pocket that I have always forgotten to show you.

He unfolded a piece of paper for me. I turned it around in every direction.

FD: It looks like a chessboard.
CASIMIR: You're definitely not gifted. It's the apartment building
               across from mine—the one I look at.
FD: And those scribbles in the squares?
CASIMIR: You're kidding. Do you want another drawing to explain
               this one? What do you want them to be? Women undress-
               ing themselves?

I regretted not being Françoise Dolto—and for want of anything better, I came out with what was going through my head.*

FD: Those silhouettes seem quite distorted. What indeed can
               that mean?
CASIMIR: And you're asking me? You're too much! I'll no longer
               presume upon your interpretations. *Ciao!* And don't forget
               to throw that in the garbage, where it belongs.

---

* A well-known child analyst, a contemporary of Lacan. She lived from 1908 to 1988.

He left. Wittgenstein looked at me in total dismay.

WITTGENSTEIN:	Never ask what it means. The description alone must take its place.[10]
FD:	The description of what? There's nothing more to describe. Do these scribbles inspire you?
WITTGENSTEIN:	When pointing out the chessboard, you had identified pieces in a game, which you must describe now as pieces in this game.[11]

At that point, he also got up to leave. Nevertheless, I took his counsel to heart. The next week, when Casimir, as fresh as a daisy, again took up the charge, I was ready with a comment for him. Nevertheless, I let him open the hostilities.

CASIMIR:	You're not in very good shape. You should close up shop and call it a day.
FD:	Instead of throwing away your piece of paper, I counted the squares on this chessboard, which were filled with silhouettes supposedly undressing themselves. There are nine of them.
CASIMIR:	Nine squares. Wait! In German one would say "*Neunfeld.*" That's the name of a village, just on the other side of the border, which one day my grandmother left.
FD:	You never mentioned it to me.
CASIMIR:	It wouldn't have gotten us much further. She never went back. Why recall the past? Anyhow, I was not born.
FD:	But your grandmother—had she ever mentioned it?
CASIMIR:	Never. The village was destroyed during the war. Her family perished—her first daughter, her first husband. I don't know what it was, bullets or some epidemic. Now she herself is dead too, so it's too late to find out.
FD:	Wait a minute! Might those women who are undressing be tortured women?
CASIMIR:	You're romanticizing. What does it matter? My mother was born in France, where my grandmother had remarried. I'm not concerned.
FD:	You think so . . .
CASIMIR:	Well, there was this dialect, which my mother and my grandmother spoke to each other, when they didn't want us to understand them.
FD:	A forbidden language and a country erased from the map.
CASIMIR:	I see you coming with your theories; you're going to sing the refrain for me: "What is foreclosed from the symbolic order makes a return in the real," Amen. But I can make

it stronger. As a Lacanian analyst you might be interested in the name of the village, in the East of France, where I already wanted to die last year, you remember, from love trouble. It's called "*Wiegen*"; "cradle," in this language. Well, my dear Watson, the cradle of her older daughter, who died before her exile, was the only object my grandmother carried with her when she crossed the border. At least the only object I have known from there. Think about it. If I were you, I would end the session on the scansion of this signifier. Don't you find it compelling? You could at least dazzle your colleagues with it.

PAUL: And did you see him again?

FD: For several months, he had left his window to resume the activities he had given up for many years and he was able to pay me. Until that time, he had objected to paying, thinking that the time past in my office was, according to his own estimation, enough of a fee. So we called it quits and I had the idea to taking him at his word by going on to recount this story the following summer at Austen Riggs where I had been invited for Otto Will's jubilee.

Chapter 8

When the Tool with the Name "N" Is Broken

The house in the woods.

FD, WITTGENSTEIN, LIN-TSI: "It's ready," Paul observed, opening the "devil" halfway to test the steamed potatoes with the point of his knife. Then, rekindling the fire, he threw into a frying pan some black and yellow mushrooms, which had been dried the previous autumn and were soaking since the day before. I easily identified the chanterelles, whose color contrasted with the purplish black flesh of the others. "Trumpets of death," he informed me, with a sarcastic tone of voice, while pouring the fricassee onto my plate and saying: "I prefer these—the woods are full of them. And you—were you going to show the Americans what theories we're cooking up over here?"

FD:	I wanted only to tell them that, with Casimir, unlike Otto Will and his soldier, I had managed, without falling sick and without mixing the ups and downs of my personal life into my analytic work.
PAUL:	Really?
FD:	I certainly believed it. My intention was to make for these Americans this simple demonstration: to put back into circulation the names excluded from a language-game, one simply has to be skilled at the game of signifiers.
PAUL:	You forgot the episode of your confession on the telephone—that intrusion into your private life.
FD:	I had censored it as an enormous blunder, feeling only shame at having let (what I believed to be) my territory be violated.
PAUL:	. . . and apparently it was Casimir's territory too.
FD:	You're right. I had buried the whole story, without suspecting the obvious: my inner experience was also out there.
PAUL:	Did you wonder what this pregnant woman—whom you put right under his nose—was doing there in the series of tortured women?

DOI: 10.4324/9781003437451-8

FD: Your question would have seemed absurd to me at that time. Following the advice of the Philosopher, whenever the transference turned out to be impossible, I looked for the rules of a possible language-game. For the moment, I could only baptize this eventual game "psychotic transference," discovering the rules as I played it. At first what was at stake in this transference seemed to me a kind of naming process. Wittgenstein had been absent from the session when Casimir had handed over his scribbles. When I told him about it, as a true connoisseur, he recognized the story of "a broken tool with the name "N." He's a real handyman, you know. You can tell he studied engineering. If you invite him to your home, he will fix everything that doesn't work. From the flush in the toilet to the sewing machine, but also the apparatus of language. He has a method for that.

Paul wanted me to explain this method to him. I felt hopeless—and preferred to be entranced by the incomparable flavor of the mushrooms. But he insisted, so I had to try to reconstruct Wittgenstein's argument for him:

WITTGENSTEIN: Suppose that the tool with the name "N" is broken. Without knowing this, A gives B the sign "N." What is B going to do?[1]
FD: I've no idea.
WITTGENSTEIN: Well, perhaps he will stand there at a loss, or he could show A the pieces. But, at such an impasse, it's always possible to imagine a convention. For example, B would have to shake his head in reply if A gives him the sign that belongs to the tool that is broken.[2]
FD: That's all?
WITTGENSTEIN: It could even be a sort of joke between them.[3] In this way the command "N" might be said to be given a place in the language-game even when the tool no longer exists, and the sign "N" to have meaning even when its bearer ceases to exist.[4]
FD: Let's try to apply that. Casimir would be B facing the other, A, but not any kind of other. It's the one who unwittingly sends him an incomprehensible sign, "N," such as this name "*Neunfeld*," which cannot be mentioned within his family. If I understand this well, A is not necessarily a person. In the first place, this other for Casimir would be the apartment building facing his, a wall with some windows—a huge chessboard on which his life is being played out. From there signs are being sent to him in the form of women undressing. He takes pleasure in looking at them, until he realizes that he's caught in a

trap, and cannot free himself from them. So he's completely lost behind his window, with these naked women, whose lure little by little becomes horrible, like rotting flesh. Would you say that these images are ostensive definitions? Could they be signaling that there is something there to be named, this "*Neunfeld*," which has been banished from memory and become unmentionable?

WITTGENSTEIN: That's what I told you: pieces of a game must be described as pieces of this game.[5]

FD: OK, but the whole problem is that Casimir at first took this game with the wall facing him for a "peep-show," which led him nowhere. In the second place, he tried to transfer these pieces to another other, another A—this time the analyst—supposed to be more eloquent than his concrete wall. A wasted effort, for the more concrete-walled of the two is not whom you might think. From this new other, interested only in the maneuvers of the neurotic transference, came neither a nod nor a raised eyebrow. Finally, sliding from one Analyst into Another, Casimir ends by falling upon me. Unwittingly, I awaken some sleeping wounds in the language-game between us—that is to say, in the "forms of life," which gave Casimir the idea of killing himself.

He chose this critical moment to bring to my office, this graffiti— a "tag," as taggers say today—a convention analogous to the shaking of the head that B directs at A when the latter gives him the sign for the tool that's broken. Thus, the ostracized name "Neunfeld" came out of banishment and secretly passed the border, toward the minimal social circulation that constitutes a session.

WITTGENSTEIN: You forgot one detail.

FD: Which one?

WITTGENSTEIN: Under what form did you, as A, address B with the sign N, with which he was unable to do anything at all?

FD: Well, I told you, the wall opposite his apartment was transferred to my place.

WITTGENSTEIN: But you, with what sign did you address him?

PAUL: A good question. To begin with, you tell this damn story as if you needed only to decipher a hieroglyph, while denying completely your stake in this story. Remember Otto Will's story. You couldn't play this transferential game unscathed either. Well, what have you yourself shown your patient—in the way that Otto Will showed Sullivan a man confined to his bed? A pregnant woman? Exposed to voyeuristic "looks," shown, so to speak, through the phone? What had she to do with those tortured women?

FD: I didn't know at that time. Unable to answer Wittgenstein, I hadn't even grasped the meaning of his question. But, I questioned him in return about a striking feature of this entire story. Was this violence, in which the analysis had unfolded, avoidable? As a matter of fact, nothing in the directions for use that he proposed for A, B, and N, indicated the necessity for it. He remained evasive—as if this question was perhaps premature.

PAUL: Nevertheless, your question was relevant. A name breaks, and so what? Why make such a fuss of it? After all, that's what life is, for language. Its tools break normally, like some old first names that were once very much in fashion, and have finally been replaced by others, and even eventually used again.

FD: It's not so much the breaking of the name, but rather the process getting blocked. With disastrous effects on familial and social exchanges. You're going to tell me again, as Wittgenstein did, that I'm over-dramatizing. Why not consider the life of language like all lives: it has its misfortunes? Imagine that the tool with the name "N" breaks too soon, by force. Though still usable, it's foreclosed—withdrawn from circulation. What's bound to happen?

PAUL: Casimir was prompting you with the answer: it comes back in the Real, actualized in these bodies that turn into rotting flesh.

FD: Precisely—it does make a return, but it comes back as a ghost. Such as names of countries once erased from the map, or of houses that have fallen, or of commitments that have been broken, or of catastrophes that lurk in the silences registered by children . . .

PAUL: Your "cut out impressions" again . . .

FD: . . . which occur where the tool with names breaks, and then breaks again, always in the same place, on these inexpressible impressions. Wittgenstein must have known quite a lot about this violence, and about these silences. Think of the disavowal of Judaism by his family three generations earlier, and the successive suicides of his three older brothers.

PAUL: You're haunted by this idea. Why haven't you talked to him about it?

FD: I don't dare. He has a visible horror at intrusions into his private life . . . However, I understood well the violence that always accompanies the circumstances of the destruction of names. Still, I was asking him about Casimir, if violence was

	necessary in order to fix a makeshift link. Such was the topic of my presentation before you arrived.* In fact, I was referring to those rough dialogues called mondôs in Zen. What's more, Lin-tsi compares these clashes to actual stripteases.
PAUL:	If you said that to Parisian analysts, then don't be surprised . . .
FD:	. . . I know. Still, as a matter of fact, Lin-tsi doesn't shrink from any "striptease." He even describes his own transference technique in this way. After removing, little by little, all sorts of clothes, before his disciples, he notes: "There they are—suddenly lost and stupefied; they start running around, saying I am naked! Then I say to them: Do you finally recognize the man in me who puts on these clothes? And suddenly they look at me, and they recognize me on the spot."⁶
PAUL:	And who is this man who removes his clothes? Is it the ego, the self, the subject of desire?
FD:	Lin-tsi calls him "the man without a situation," a close kin of Wittgenstein's compatriot Musil's "Man without qualities," but also of Otto Will's bed-ridden man, and of the naked women in Casimir's drawing. In sum, they are the pending subject of a language-game at the limits of the speakable. Lin-tsi compares him also to "some kind of shit-wiping stick."⁷

As far as Casimir was concerned, my problem at that moment was to survive this iconoclastic rage. When I had got stripped of my theoretical as well as practical rags, when Casimir, at his wit's end, had his brush with death, we were reaching the shores of a zone, where nameless images waited for us, surviving in order to be named . . . These images served as targets for murderous actions. Analysts usually label them as "neurotic failure," "negativism," or "negative therapeutic reaction"—probably in order to cover their own failure. But Casimir's problem was that these image-targets moved constantly. Had they been confined to that wall opposite, he would have been able to stay ensconced behind his window. Now they popped up at any moment, from all directions, like that pregnancy I was tricking him with, against all the rules of the game. We had not agreed at the start, that his analyst should be authorized to do a strip-tease. Trust me—that was strictly reserved for the ladies in the windows.

Nothing describes this situation of analytic violence better than Lin-tsi's celebrated blasphemies: "Whomever you encounter inside or out, kill him! If you encounter a Buddha, kill the Buddha! If you encounter a patriarch, kill the patriarch! If you encounter your father and mother, kill your father and mother! If you

---

* This refers to Paul's arrival, described in Chapter 1.

encounter your neighbors, kill your neighbors! It's the way to free yourself and to escape being enslaved by things."[8]

PAUL: The moral, then, is: if you encounter your analyst, kill your analyst. Your Lin-tsi was commenting in his own way on Lacan's definition of the symbol. "The symbol is the murder of the thing."[9] If I understand correctly, you're proposing, for this type of transference, to take this formula literally.

FD: You're anticipating the presentation I was preparing for some American analysts. I would soon be flying to Austen Riggs Center, for the celebration of Otto Will's seventy-fifth birthday.

Chapter 9

Folee-ah-deeoo

The house in the woods.

PAUL, FD, THE DIVINER

Austen Riggs Center, Stockbridge, Massachusetts.

A NAKED MAN, FD, MARTIN COOPERMAN
(THE OLD MAN), ESS WHITE (THE MAN SITTING
NEXT TO FD), THE MAN WEARING
COWBOY BOOTS, WITTGENSTEIN

After this attempt to hand over to Paul this little sample of Wittgenstein's teaching, I persuaded him to take a nap, while I took charge of washing the dishes at the pump. I wanted to go out, so I could recall some long forgotten gestures at the big black wheel that brings the water up with the sound of its chain. This pump happened to have a handle, but the expectation was the same, and as the chain sound got louder, the water, held back in its throat, suddenly gushed out. I was wondering whether these confessions I was unraveling to Paul, like Ariadne's thread, would lead me toward I don't know what Minotaur.

Still busy with soaping and rinsing, keeping time with the sound of the pump, I suddenly heard a harsh voice asking me if Paul was there. Turning around, I saw next to me a big fellow, about 60 years old, with piercing eyes and a goatee like that of Mephistopheles. Before I answered him, Paul was standing on the doorstep, and already inviting him inside. When I joined them, Paul introduced his neighbor, the diviner who had located for him the site for his well. They inquired about each other's health. The diviner had brought a bottle of sloe gin. We had to have a nip. I put on airs: "No thanks—just a little, a 'canard*'," etc. But Paul brought out some other bottles of Alpine brandies, all more or less medicinal: wormwood or

---

* Although this word is used in English, its usual meanings are un- related to the present one, which is from a French usage, and means "lump of sugar" to be dipped in brandy. The literal French meaning is "duck." In another semantic field, it may mean a false note: in music, a "quack."

DOI: 10.4324/9781003437451-9

vulnerary, chamomile, white bouillon . . . I tasted everything, and from canard to canard sank into a sweet torpor, half-listening to the endless discussions which had lulled me to sleep when I was a child. As if there were the same harvests, the same droughts, the same cows, the same politics. I wondered where my grandfather's still could be—not the officially approved one, but the other secret one for moonshining mirabelles, plums, grapes, pears, and the peaches whose pits were poisonous because of Prussian acid. That undeclared still had so poisoned my grandmother's life that when her husband died she had nothing more pressing to do than to pierce it and make it useless. It was probably relegated to the attic of the farmhouse. Since my grandmother's death, I had never wanted to return. Were there demijohns, filled with golden alcohol, still waiting in that cellar where the bottling took place?

The two men went on talking. A cow had been found choked— caught in the barbed wire of an enclosure she had tried to jump over. They said she'd been terrified by a she-wolf that had been roaming around the countryside; Large footprints had been spotted, and the wolf seemed even more awesome as a "she." Paul wanted to see the place of the crime, and so we set out through the meadows. Emboldened by the "nip" of spirits, I asked our guide how he managed to find springs. Without saying a word, he took two forked twigs from a nearby hedge, cleared away the buds, and placed one of them in my hands. I had to hold the stick between my pinkie and my third finger, with my palms facing up, spreading the branches apart with a light tension, and follow him, walking along slowly, while he held his in the same way. Obediently, I followed his instructions, and after a moment of great concentration, during which nothing happened, I began to laugh at our gait, as we marched along as if in a Rogation Day procession.

At that moment my stick chose to straighten itself up, under some irresistible force, and completely apart from my will. The diviner had stopped; "It's done it for you," he noted. Paul was laughing. I thought he was making fun of me.

PAUL: No, really—I don't doubt you've found water, even if for me it doesn't work. I was just thinking about the phallic comments our analytic colleagues would make about this erection.

Vaguely upset, I let them go ahead, and I went back without a guide, divided between disbelief and secret pleasure when I felt the stick rise by itself again. Later, when we parted, I thanked our neighbor for this mysterious gift.

When we came back to the log cabin, it was already late in the afternoon, for we had stopped several times at molehills to gather the dandelion salad for the

---

* These were processions made around the fields in the spring to bless the crops.

evening. Paul seemed more interested in hearing the rest of my narrative, than in evaluating my future as a diviner.

PAUL: Who, then, was this Austen Riggs, whom I've never heard tell of?

FD: Riggs was a physician and the founder of that clinic in Stockbridge, which is devoted to the analysis of psychosis.[1] On my first visit, in 1977, Stockbridge was covered in snow. This time it was summer, and the town had a vacation look to it. In the evening, some would go for picnics on the nearby lush lawns of Tanglewood, where they listened to the Boston Symphony Orchestra.

At the end of the meeting devoted to Otto Will, young fellows of the Center, enthralled by their recent reading of Lacan, questioned me, especially about the place of the death instinct in his theory. The director of research during Otto Will's time, William Richardson, a philosopher and a specialist in Heidegger, had, along with two colleagues, John Muller and Jim Gorney, introduced them to Lacan. They had dared to bring within the walls of this venerable institution this "typically French"—translate: "incomprehensible"—theoretician, at a time when Lacan was not yet in fashion in the United States.

To answer their question, I took up Lacan's commentary on Sophocles' *Antigone*, from his Seminar, *The Ethics of Psychoanalysis*, which is described there as a tragic ethics.[2] This idea displeased Wittgenstein. Still, I took advantage of his absence to talk about Casimir's analysis as a journey of a tragic hero, who in life prefers death. He had renounced his own good in order to reach, beyond the pleasure principle, a paradoxical space, for the conquest of a new signifier . . .

PAUL: And were your hosts managing to follow you?

FD: My presentation, seeded with Greek references in Greek, was also perhaps a little too "typically French." Still, I hoped that the obscurity of my abstruse remarks would be attributed to my clumsy English.

Curiously, no one fled. Politeness, I thought, or snobbism. Little by little, older people came into the room, and took their places around the large table, without saying anything. In particular, there was a grumpy looking old man, who, after he had sat down, seemed to doze off immediately. I was just beginning not to find my words, as usual, when a hubbub broke out just outside the room. A totally nude man appeared in the doorway, howling to the assembly: "Is there an analyst in the room?" Then, without waiting for an answer, he turned around and left, wrapped solely in the pleats of his dignity.

A lively exchange then took place among those present, which I had difficulty understanding. His therapist seemed to be the ill-at-ease young man trying to justify himself and asking for help, while the others bombarded him with questions. The old man, awakened from his nap, ended all the excitement: "When will you stop grilling him on what he hasn't analyzed?

If Donald creates a disturbance in front of visitors, and in an instant ruins years of progress, his therapist is the last one who should be asked about it. What his therapist hasn't been able to hear, he knows nothing about, for goodness sake, or else Donald would not have gone through all this trouble to show it to him!"

As the excitement settled down, I had, regretfully, to continue with my talk. In the meantime, the old man had gone back to sleep. When I finished, the silence that broke into the background noise of my words woke him up again. He began by letting the others ask me questions, and then he said: "That's all well and good, but just tell us now how you yourself make use of what you're speaking about." This was the ideal time to tell them about the memorable session with Casimir. So, I expounded on the death instinct, which was at work in our confrontations, until the production of the signifier "Neunfeld," which gratified me very much. "Yes," said the old man, "we all perform miracles. But what was actually going on, for you, before you reached that point?" My gosh, Wittgenstein had spawned disciples in that place. Yet I didn't find it very gallant of the old man to question me so directly in front of people I didn't know. However, I told the story of the telephone blunder, without knowing very well why.

THE OLD MAN:	It's a 'folee-ah-deeoo.'
FD:	A what?
THE OLD MAN:	'Folee-ah-deeoo'

Damned Americanisms!

FD:	I don't understand.
THE OLD MAN:	Then you haven't got a clue, and you don't even speak your own language.

With that, he got up and made his way toward the door, walking kind of sleepily. When he had disappeared, the idea came to me like a flash of lightning: 'folee-ah-deeoo,'—folie-à-deux? I wanted to know that old man's name.

THE PERSON NEXT TO ME:	He's Martin Cooperman, our medical director. My name is Ess White.* Your stories of lost names, of Civil War, of tragedies, and of ghosts introduce a change for us in the never-ending parade of mothers of psychotics we are so tired of hearing about. I myself was born in the South. Read Faulkner's *Absalom, Absalom!*[3] The hero is haunted by ghosts

---

* Ess A. White, MD was a preeminent figure at Austin Riggs Center from 1951 until 2005, when he died.

of the Civil War. It's very close to what you've
been telling us about.

A MAN IN COWBOY BOOTS: Very close also to what Sioux medicine men talk
about, in South Dakota, where I live. I'm going
back there tomorrow. Come and pay me a visit.

*After the discussion and the customary "How terrific!" and "How spectacular!" I
met Martin Cooperman in the hallway, and he showed me into his office.*

MARTIN COOPERMAN: Good effort—your talk. You know, the analysis of
psychosis is extremely simple. This idea came to
me during the war, when I was a flight-surgeon
in the Navy, in your country, among others. On
returning, I continued to think about it. I was working at Chestnut Lodge, where I remained for several years before coming here. Over there, it was
different; they had closed wards. Here, as you've
been able to see, there are neither walls around the
property, and patients move about freely; they can
even work in the town before their final discharge.
One of them, at this very moment, is a teacher's
aide at Paula Meade's Montessori school, where
we send our children.

FD: What about this simple idea?

MARTIN COOPERMAN: Take Donald, for example, whose behavior
seemed absurd to you. Look out the window.

I was looking desperately for what there was to see.

FD: "I see only the grass, which is green,"* and some
hundred-year-old trees.

MARTIN COOPERMAN: Yes, you see only that, because the window frame
is concealing a part of the scene from you. Now
imagine that you're seeing Donald, through the
window, in the middle of a fight. But, since you
don't see anyone toward whom his attacking or
defending movements are being directed, along
with his kicks, his punches, his dodging and evad-
ing, you judge his behavior absurd. For you, he's a
naked man, gesticulating in a void. He makes you

---

* This was part of sister Anne's reply to Blue Beard's wife, who repeatedly asked her if she saw her
brothers coming.

laugh, or he frightens you. Psychosis is exactly that: a paradoxical social relation. The other is all the more present, to the extent that he has been cut off. One tends to forget about that.

FD: And you—what do you see from your own personal window?

MARTIN COOPERMAN: Well, shift and change your point of view; you will then see that his real adversary was hidden by the window frame. Of course, what happens when you're least expecting it is you find yourself being at the place of that formidable antagonist.

FD: Right, and then what do you do?

MARTIN COOPERMAN: I tell the patient that he's fighting with me, since obviously we're the only people in the room.

FD: And does that produce the miracle?

MARTIN COOPERMAN: Not necessarily. It may happen that things get worse, in an escalating process—which you experienced with your patient, and which I have baptized, a "defeating process."[4] A true sabotage of the analysis can take place. All collaboration ceases, with the return of flamboyant symptoms. If the patient comes to his sessions, he has lost all his talents except that of directing insults, full of hatred, toward his analyst, who is too cold, or an idiot; who talks too much; who is too young, too old, a man, a woman, and so on. The power conflict is overt. Sensing he's losing hold of the situation, the analyst blames the nurses, and says of himself that he's not cut out to be an analyst, that he's not the analyst this patient needs, unless it is that analysis is not indicated for this diagnosis, and then, in any case, that analysis is not possible in an institution. In short, the fighting spreads, and the search for causal explanations becomes hellish. It's because of his father, or his mother, or his analyst, his psychiatrist, the devil and his hell. The patient's family is called in; there are interdisciplinary discussions to improve communication . . . What the patient gains at the end of it all is an increase in medications, and a "transfer" to another institution.

FD: And then?

MARTIN COOPERMAN: If however the wish to chemically bludgeon the patient is resisted, it becomes obvious that another "transference" is at stake—engaged in a struggle without mercy. The patient will not stop until he puts his analyst out of play, no matter what the price, even the price of his own life.

Then I tell him he's welcome to take the big jump, if he's decided to have my hide, but he should reconsider the price he's ready to pay, since I don't give a damn, whether he jumps or not. The only thing that counts for me is whatever has brought him to see me. His craziest behavior is a statement addressed to someone, and it's the most sensible reaction to the degrading manipulations he's been subjected to. That's what we, together, have to analyze. Thus, to come back to your patient, what have you challenged him about, and what battle have you engaged him in?

At that moment, in my ear, I recognized the usual voice starting to speak to me, very distinctly: "There we are! The battle is against the bewitchment of our intelligence by means of language."[5] Surprised, I answered him in a very loud voice:

FD:	Did you come in through the window?
MARTIN COOPERMAN:	Who came in through the window?
FD:	No one . . . I was wondering whether the invisible adversary who's not seen through the window, could be a ghost and enter through that window.

"Who knows?" Martin Cooperman answered, as he got up to lead me out. He had an appointment with a patient. On the doorstep, I could not help saying to him:

FD:	I don't believe in ghosts, you know.
MARTIN COOPERMAN:	After listening to so many patients, I have come to think that even the most bizarre behavior is always addressed to someone.[6] Come back and see me when you want to.
PAUL:	And did you see him again?
FD:	Of course. But after this first exchange, I thought of not seeing him again. I was furious with Wittgenstein, whose intrusion had interrupted our conversation. Once outside, while walking about Main Street and pretending to be interested in the local artifacts, I was bawling him out in a low voice. He had done it on purpose, wanting probably to make a fool of me as someone "seeing

	things." What was he doing here? I thought he was in France.
WITTGENSTEIN:	Ethics—the subject of your talk—that interests me. Your presentation was so-so.
FD:	You should've told me you were there; I would've gratefully let you present in my place.
WITTGENSTEIN:	The question he asked you was relevant: "What then was happening for you?" I myself, at the end of my lecture on ethics, in Cambridge, around 1930, spoke in the first person.[7] I believe it was essential to do so.
FD:	I didn't want to talk about myself; I wanted to talk about ethics at the limits of language.
WITTGENSTEIN:	Language isn't a cage . . . No, when there's an ethical question, it's essential not to provide sociological, or even psychoanalytic, descriptions, but to speak from one's own proper ground.[8]
FD:	Well, for me the essential thing was to try to develop some theoretical connections.
WITTGENSTEIN:	But at this level, you agree, nothing can be an object of observation; you can only enter the stage and say "I." Here, theory has no value. A theory gives us nothing.[9]
FD:	Ordinarily, your "I" enters the stage rather concealed, doesn't it?* Okay. The day I forgot to close the door on my private life by letting Casimir know some details about me, which were not his business, I had indeed entered the stage as "I," but with what a result!
WITTGENSTEIN:	I know—you can think that I'm trying to undermine your intelligence. And you wouldn't be wrong, but it's the only way to show you these questions.
FD:	What questions?
WITTGENSTEIN:	Those you're interested in—questions about ethics and about madness. Am I mistaken? What need was there to justify yourself by talking about not believing in ghosts? Were you afraid to appear mad?

---

* Cf. René Descartes, *"Cogitationes Privatae,"* in *Oeuvres de Descartes*, Volume X (Paris: Vrin, 1964–1972), 213. FD's line derives from a famous sentence of Descartes, in which he speaks of entering the world's stage, masked, whereas before he had been simply a spectator.

FD:	Because, really, I don't believe in ghosts. But that doesn't stop me from encountering them.
WITTGENSTEIN:	Me too. Suppose for example that I lost a friend, and that you said to me: "Don't bother; you will see your dead friend again." Would I say that you're a bit superstitious? Not at all. Even if, in saying that to me, you put on a queer smile, I know well that you would never make any search for a deceased person. Believe me, these stories have a dream-like quality.[10]
FD:	I believe you, but let's admit that I've seen the ghost of your deceased friend.
WITTGENSTEN:	Even if you tell me you have visions, I wouldn't say offhand that you mean something different. Another example: Imagine that you've decided to go to China, and [11]
FD:	How could you have guessed that I have the intention of going to China? I very much want to know the country of Lin-tsi.
WITTGENSTEIN:	All the better. Imagine that before leaving, fearing you'll never see me again, you say to me: "We might see one another after death." I'd understand you entirely, and would not necessarily have to say that I don't understand you.[12]
FD:	That would be the last straw! Be reassured, I have no intention of dying in China, for the pleasure of rejoining you in the beyond. I'm in perfect health . . . You're giving me chills up and down my spine.
PAUL:	I'd have another response—I wouldn't be that displeased to see him again in the Elysian Fields. But, let's leave that alone. You were walking around on the streets of Stockbridge . . .

Paul poured out the dandelions onto a newspaper so that we could begin to clean them for the evening salad.

Chapter 10

Excalibur

The house in the woods.

PAUL, FD

The Red Lion Inn (Stockbridge, Massachusetts)
FD, WITTGENSTEIN, SOCRATES, GERARD FROMM

At the sight of the Red Lion Inn on the other side of Main Street, I suddenly felt very hungry. A plaque at the entrance identified it as one of the innumerable places where George Washington had slept. I ordered a salad in the garden. Wittgenstein didn't want anything, preferring to speak of death, and of a brother who had died in America, as if this were a completely abstract example. Probably he was thinking again about Hans, his oldest brother, who had run off to America and disappeared from a boat in the Chesapeake Bay.[1]

PAUL: And, again this time, you didn't dare say anything to him at all.

FD: Yes—I did try a little. When he said to me: "If you think of your brother in America, how do you know that what you think is, that the thought inside you is, of your brother being in America?"[2] I snapped back at him: "You're mistaken; your own brother, not mine, went to America."

PAUL: And what did he answer?

FD: I wouldn't know what to say, for the expression on his face immediately ordered me to keep quiet. An embarrassing silence set in, filled only with the crackling of the salad, which I was conscientiously crunching, while, out of the corner of my eye, I was watching his features, which had so suddenly changed. His face calmed down, little by little. He was absentmindedly following the ballet of the

DOI: 10.4324/9781003437451-10

	waiters and waitresses. Weary of watching this little game, I murmured.
FD:	Cooperman exaggerates. I wear myself out observing the rule of neutrality as if it were sacrosanct, trying to keep cool and working serenely without spoiling everything with my subjectivity . . . and yet he asks me about what was going on "for me" with Casimir! Do I ask you to tell me what's going on, at this moment, for you?
WITTGENSTEIN:	Why not? You could actually ask me the name of what I'm looking at. That would be interesting . . . What's the relation between name and thing named?[3] Do you think it's enough to keep your eyes or your ears open, and stare at what's in front of you, while repeating a name over and over?[4]
FD:	No. Casimir tried that, but it wasn't enough. He correctly named what he saw as "voyeurism." Still, time was passing, dragging on, without his being able to free himself from this psychological stance.
WITTGENSTEIN:	To escape from it, he had to know what naming is.
FD:	Go for it; you're eager to redo my presentation.
WITTGENSTEIN:	First, you would have to wonder how you had such trouble getting at a name your patient already knew.
FD:	True—"*Neunfeld*" was indeed conscious—not at all repressed.
WITTGENSTEIN:	This objection could be formulated in this way: names really signify simples. Then, since you love to show that you read Greek, you should have cited the *Theatetus*, instead of the tragedies so dear to psychoanalysts. Socrates says there that there is no definition of these primary elements (*stoicheia aloga*), which do not involve any reason (*logos*). Every element in its own right can only be named; no other determination is possible. Neither that it *is*, nor that it *is not*. For it, nothing is possible but the bare name; its name is all that it has. "But," he adds, "only by names being woven together does reason (*logos*) come into existence."[5] So, you'd have to conclude that nothing in fact happens when a thing's been named. One could even say that it hasn't yet received any name until it's brought into a language-game.
FD:	It's crystal clear. What has to come about is not simply a name, but a language-game. But again I ask you: Why is the start of this interweaving of names, as Socrates put it, accompanied by such destructive rage?
WITTGENSTEIN:	Here's the reason for it: Take "Excalibur," Arthur's sword, or "*Nothung*," Siegfried's sword. They're proper names, in

the ordinary sense of the term. The sword Excalibur consists of parts combined in a particular way; if they are combined differently, Excalibur doesn't exist. And yet it's clear that the sentence: "Excalibur has a sharp blade" makes sense, whether Excalibur is still whole or is broken in pieces. On the other hand, if "Excalibur" were only the name of an object, then once Excalibur is broken into pieces, the name would no longer have meaning.[6]

FD: Okay, but it's a long way from that to breaking the sword in order to demonstrate that its name keeps, or loses, its meaning . . .

WITTGENSTEIN: Think about it, when X dies, they say the bearer of the name dies, but not that his name dies. It would be completely nonsensical to say that; for if the name ceased to have a meaning, it would make no sense to say that X is dead.[7] And in the same way, the sentence, "Excalibur has a sharp blade" makes sense, even when Excalibur is in pieces, for in our ordinary language-game names are also used in the absence of their bearer.[8]

FD: That—I know by heart. But according to you, does another language game exist in which names would be used only in the presence of their bearers?

WITTGENSTEIN: We could totally imagine it. In that game, the names could always be replaced by demonstrative pronouns, or by gestures of pointing, that is, by ostensive definitions.

FD: And in that case, to suppress a name and to erase it from the map, it would be enough to destroy its support. It's the politics of those who raze towns and villages to the ground, who chisel away stone faces and inscriptions, and even murder others or themselves, so that the names cease to exist. In order to have those names back in circulation, one would have to hallucinate the disappeared and then destroy them. What do you think?

He had a vacant look and didn't answer me. Stupidly, I became upset. I hadn't stomached his small amount of enthusiasm for my presentation, and I let my rancor burst forth:

FD: I wonder if we're not going astray by letting ourselves be dragged along by these ideas of murder and death. Why couldn't you yourself stop speaking of ghosts and of death? Why this obsession with death?

PAUL: You're going too far! You can indeed moan about others' indiscretions . . . but at the very moment when he's about to

answer a critical question, you antagonize him with innuen-
dos about his private life.

FD: The retort wasn't long in coming. Getting up quickly, at
wit's end, he answered me:

WITTGENSTEIN: We all use the word "death," which is a public tool . . .
if you treat it as something private, by what right do
you call it "ideas of death"? It no longer belongs to the
language- game we play with the word "death," which we
all know and understand, and which links every naming to
destruction.[9]

*I retorted very unjustly that Lacan hadn't waited for him to summarize in only a
single formula his whole theory of naming, but he was no longer listening to me.
With an angry pencil, he scribbled something on the tablecloth. "Here," he said,
"if you absolutely want to know the idea I have of death, I can make you this scribble, which could be psychologically interesting."*

PAUL: And what did it look like?

FD: Like that.

*After which, he left the place, and I stared down at my salad bowl, wondering about
who the sporty-looking man at the next table was, with his eyes ogling this shapeless scribble. After a few minutes, he approached, smiling, and told me knowingly:
"It's a squiggle."*

FD: A what?

MAN: A squiggle.

*I felt I was stepping into a film that was already shot. Obviously, I would never
get used to this American accent. But, he didn't lose patience, and sitting down
at my table, he introduced himself: "GERARD FROMM." He had attended my
presentation, and he gave me thousands of compliments, which, true or false, made
me suddenly enthralled by this lovely afternoon, flooded by the fragrances of the
garden. Then, pointing to the scribble with his finger, he added:*

GERARD FROMM: Winnicott, whom I know better than Lacan, found these
squiggles so interesting that he used them in his analytic
practice with children.[10]

At that moment, once again I had an illumination:

FD:	Squiggle . . . you mean . . . the squiggle game? His smile was as engaging as if I had made a slam dunk in a game of basketball, his favorite game, which I later saw him play. I seized the opportunity to ask him what use could be made of the squiggle that was right before our eyes.
GERARD FROMM:	Winnicott said you didn't have to make this technique into a therapeutic formula. For him, it was sim ply a way of entering into communication with the child, while showing how, as an analyst, he plays the game, in so far as it's unconscious. Starting with this kind of drawing, made by the child, and by himself too, he can find a way of bringing the case to life.[11]

So, I thought that it was in such a way that Wittgenstein could have tried to establish this kind of communication with me, as with a child, or even as a child. That was rubbish! This idea upset me so much that I lost the thread of the conversation, which I pretended to follow by nodding my head. I only got hold of it again when Fromm said that, in Winnicott's view, the difficult part of his thesis was that destruction played a role in making reality, and in placing the object outside the self. For him, the object was always being destroyed.[12]

Suspicious, I thought for an instant that he had been eavesdropping on my talk with Wittgenstein. I tried to find out why he was so interested in this question of destruction. He seemed surprised:

GERARD FROMM:	You didn't stop mentioning it throughout your presentation. If I understood correctly, destruction is essential to every process of nomination. While listening to you, I even understood two stories told by a Japanese colleague at Riggs. They were taken, he said, from a Chinese book of the eleventh century, *Wou-men-kouan* (*The Pass With No Gate*), an evocative title for a Lacanian . . . These stories unfold in two sequences, around two transitional objects: a bamboo cane and a carafe. In the first story, a master shows his bamboo cane to his disciples and says to them: "If you call it a bamboo cane, you fix its meaning. If you don't call it a bamboo cane, you're going contrary to fact. So, you can neither say something, nor avoid saying it."[13]
FD:	Then say it. Say it quickly.
GERARD FROMM:	Do you know the story?
FD:	No, but I see what you're getting at with this kind of pass.
GERARD FROMM:	In the second story, with another master, the pass is cleared. This master takes a carafe, puts it on the ground, and asks:

"If you don't call it a carafe, what is it called?" While the learned argue: "One can't say it's a piece of wood, etc.," the master turns toward a young monk, a lowly fellow who washes the dishes at the monastery. Without hesitating, he knocks over the carafe with his foot and breaks it. The story recounts that the master laughed and nodded consent: "In this test," he said, "superiors have been defeated by this simple monk." But when our patients knock over and break our carafes, we neither laugh nor nod consent, and we don't like admitting defeat either.[14]

PAUL: Nice story! All the same, when a patient sets out to destroy everything he meets—not only carafes, but people he takes to be carafes, including his, or eventually your own, noggin—you may very well say he's looking to produce a signifier, or to put an object outside the self, but what do you do? From this point of view, the method of close-combat advocated by Cooperman seems quite efficient . . .

FD: I no longer wanted to fight and I started to feel like I was on my vacation. To the devil with psychoanalysis! Gerard Fromm had invited me to finish the afternoon at Tanglewood, where a concert hall, called "The Shed," opens out onto a wide green. The Boston Symphony Orchestra and the Boston Pops have their summer quarters there. The man in the cowboy boots who was at my presentation would also attend.

Chapter 11

Give Away

The house in the woods.

PAUL, FD

The Lawn at Tanglewood, Massachusetts.
JERRY MOHATT (THE MAN IN COWBOY BOOTS), FD,
GERARD FROMM, WITTGENSTEIN

Rosebud, South Dakota.
JERRY MOHATT, STANLEY RED BIRD, ISIDORE, JOE EAGLE ELK,
THE INDIAN

That summer my children were also on the trip and spent their days in a nearby summer camp. After picking them up, we went on to Tanglewood, joining the flow of cars pouring into the parking lot—a multicolored throng, filled with blankets and picnic bags. Once through the entrance gate, everybody found a place on the lawn facing the shed, which had been built to direct the sound toward the outside. The cowboy was there already, with his family, and he told us to take a place near them, under a tree. While the children were running around, jumping over the paper plates, he repeated the invitation he had extended to me right after my presentation. I was very willing to accept, and I wasn't surprised to hear that Wittgenstein would be joining us in this project, for I knew of his taste for Westerns.

PAUL: They knew each other?
FD: These Americans seemed not to be surprised by anything. They treated us already like old acquaintances. The cowboy maintained that Indian ceremonies resembled psychoanalysis. Without having the least idea of these practices familiar to him, I took the contrary view. I criticized the tiresome tendency of people in Western societies to measure the

DOI: 10.4324/9781003437451-11

culture of others with a yardstick of their own. I doubted, on my part, that an American cowboy understood something of these strange practices. Gerard Fromm was just smiling, while serving a round of wine and cheese. Wittgenstein was reading the program, which announced Brahms, Schubert, and then, after an intermission, Strauss—all under the direction of Seiji Osawa. The arrival of the conductor silenced the noise, and against the background of the tuning up of the instruments, I heard Wittgenstein talking with the man from the Plains: "In the way you speak about those strange practices, there's something similar to the association of ideas, which is related to it. Could one speak of an association of practices?"[1]

I very much would have wanted him to answer his own question, but Brahms's Academic Festival Overture resounded. Some people were stretching out on the lawn, while the night was gradually falling. During the applause that preceded the intermission, Wittgenstein leapt to his feet and announced to us that he was leaving, because he couldn't stand Strauss's music. I came upon him again some days later at the airport, ready to board the plane for South Dakota.

PAUL: Does the "Far West" still exist?
FD: All I can tell you is that while landing at Pierre, the State Capital, I remembered having read recently in a French newspaper filled with commiseration for indigenous people: "Everywhere on the roads one comes across solitary Indians walking along with their eyes forward, without looking at you, as if seeing visions, when there's no one around for tens of miles." That was about the extent of my anthropological knowledge about them at that time.

Jerry Mohatt, the man in the cowboy boots, was there, in his big hat, waiting for us as we got off the plane. While driving toward his ranch, situated on the Rosebud Reservation, he informed me that we were in Sioux country—a name the French trappers gave to Amerindians who called themselves "Lakota." In their language it means simply "the human beings." The rolling plains, green and mauve in the twilight, under a horizon unbroken by any tree, were indeed quite a vision. But the people, to whom my host was going to introduce me, chose to show an image of themselves other than that of "dropouts," forged by European media in condescending sympathy with their cause.

The next day we set off again for some hundred miles, to the homeland of the Sioux Brûlés, who were coming together for a powwow, on the banks of the Missouri River. While approaching the festival, the rhythm of the drums, the Missouri shining below, the circle where men and women in paraphernalia were dancing, the feathers, the beads, a few teepees, made me wonder if this was not all in a film. I believed I could smell another tourist trap; I'd soon have to come up with a dollar for the customary photograph. But there wasn't a single "pale face" in the circle.

The dances went on, lasted for ages—and although it was superb, for me the time was beginning to seem long.

Then the music stopped; the circle of dancers broke up, and they all returned to their tents. We went to have something to eat with a friendly family. There were introductions. These typically Indians had family names typically French, which they bore, Jerry pointed out, from their ancestors, who were trappers. They were named Toulouse, Beauvais, Bordeaux, Roubidou. Then they brought out the food without talking to us, without looking at us, signaling us to help ourselves again, without asking us any questions. I would have liked very much to say something, but the absence of eye contact dissuaded me. My children were playing with the other children. While making an uproar, they knocked over some pans, and I told them to behave themselves. The head of the family, impassible to that point, under his plumed headpiece, broke out laughing. The drums and the singing started up again. Everyone re-joined the circle.

PAUL: It feels like "Lucky Luke."*
FD: I had just experienced a form of courtesy in which silence comes first,
           and in which an angel has to pass by before we begin to speak to one
           another.** I was a Huron among the Sioux.*** Perhaps the French journal-
           ist had diagnosed, as suffering from hallucinations, the Indians who
           were politely avoiding looking at him.

To my tenderfoot's ears, the style and rhythm of the songs had changed. The dances also were slower, more solemn. At the center of the circle, objects were being placed in miscellaneous piles: cushions, sheets, pillows, patchwork-quilts embroidered with stars, saucepans, Tupperware, and other things I couldn't distinguish. I wondered what it all was doing there, when my attention was drawn inside the circle, to a folding chair—one of those nylon ones with an aluminum frame carried in supermarkets from one end of the country to the other. Folded into this chair was a very old, little woman, with what was probably her family standing besides her. They seemed to preside at this festival, which was imperceptibly turning into a ritual.

A funeral ritual—Jerry explained to me. This family had lost several of its members in a car accident three years before, and it was honoring their memory by taking care of the living. He greeted, in passing, several men seated around an enormous drum. While modulating high-pitched notes from their throats, they were

---

*   *Lucky Luke* is a popular French comic strip about a "lonesome cowboy far away from home" and
      his horse, "Jolly Jumper". It features some well-known episodes of the Frontier.
**   "*Un ange passe*," a French expression translated literally as "An angel passes," refers to the act of
      breaking a protracted silence in a social situation, by this first utterance
***   An allusion to Voltaire's "*Le Huron*," or "*L'Ingenu*," an eighteenth-century tale of a "good sav-
      age," who comes to France in the middle of the seventeenth century.

beating out the rhythm forcefully, each with a stick. We sat down on the terraces next to them. After a moment, the dancers formed a procession and marched past the grandmother, in a rhythmic, solemn motion, punctuated by speeches and songs. Her relatives carried objects to her, which she distributed, one after the other. Little by little, the pile got smaller. I was given a comb. When there was nothing more, the last ones were given dollar bills. In that place, Jerry told me, were all the family's possessions. After having lost their own in the prime of life, they had waited for enough time to pass, so that they could lose again, but this time willingly.

PAUL: Was it a potlatch?
FD: Here they call it a "give away"—a gift, the contrary of saving or invest-
          ing. That paradoxical practice, in which one deals with a loss with
          another loss, reminded me of the preoccupations I thought I had forgot-
          ten upon my arrival.
              The festival was over. A tall Indian, quite old, slim, with the gait of
          a horseman, wearing a black cowboy hat with a pony-tail of his gray
          hair sticking out, stopped drumming and came to sit near us, accom-
          panied by another plump one next to him, looking like Sancho Panza.
          With no respect for local courtesy, the tall one eyed me up and down
          from behind his dark glasses. In a strong accent I didn't recognize, he
          declared: "You whites, you put everything into accumulating. We sav-
          age have known for a long time that desire is based on loss, and desire
          is what we have that's most precious. That's why we prefer to give
          away, rather than to amass."
PAUL: Your Indian seems to me quite Lacanian.
FD: Lacan had read the anthropologist Marcel Mauss's *Gift: The Form and
          Reason for Exchange in Archaic Societies*,[2] in which Mauss worked on
          data collected from among American Indians from the West Coast. In
          sum, I was standing right at the source of the Lacanian theory. And that
          source was continuing to give me a lecture, as if I alone represented the
          enemy of the entire Sioux people: "We, the Lakota, have known for a
          long time that we are the owners of nothing. Our treasure was in sworn
          faith, in the given word; you Whites have debased it; you've given us
          lies to swallow."

The mustard started coming up into my nose.* Ignoring the code, I didn't know if I should laugh or give it back. Pitiless, he went on: "The Indian way goes through dreams and visions. Look!" he warned us, while pointing his arm toward the sky. Everyone was looking up, in the direction of a circling bald eagle.

"Don't listen to Stanley Red Bird," interrupted the short fat one; "he just has hallucinations."

---

* A French expression that indicates one is beginning to become irritated.

Stanley Red Bird burst out laughing: "Don't believe a word of what I say. Isidore's right; I'm just an old alcoholic. But you've come here; what do you want to know?" Jerry made the first move, and on the way back to our cars, he informed him about where we had met.

PAUL: Like Otto Will, Red Bird was playing on the two English words for the French verb "*croire*"—"to believe" and "to trust." Did you see him again afterwards?

FD: Very often—he was from Rosebud. A former rodeo champion, he had later worked for his people on the reservation, and had notably spent a lot of time with Jerry Mohatt, raising money across the country to create the Indian College of *Sinte Gleska*, or Spotted Tail, the name of a Lakota Chief. Both of them introduced me to their friend Joe Eagle Elk,* a medicine man. They invited me to a ceremony of thanksgiving for the success of a research project at the College. I wasn't understanding much, apart from the fact that Robby, Jerry's wife, and myself, had to spend the whole day cooking some boiled beef tongue, some *wajapi*, a kind of wild cherry (called chalk cherry) marmalade, and some fried bread—all in preparation for the ceremony.

At the end of the afternoon, Jerry took a red stone pipe from his home, some tobacco, some bright colored pieces of cloth—symbolizing the four directions: yellow for East, white for South, black for West, and red for North—and we set off in the car, women and children, with pots and pans, in the direction of the medicine man's house. As we bumped along on the gravel road, a thunderstorm came up. Bolts of thunder and lightning detonated from all directions on the horizon; gusts of wind slammed against us—such as I had never seen— but it wasn't raining. Although hardened by the triumphs of rationalism, I was beginning to fear the gods' anger—Wakan Tanka, Zeus, or Whoever you want—asking myself what I had unleashed there. I remembered Stanley's question: What was my purpose in coming here, as a tourist? The Great Spirit perhaps didn't like that. I very much wanted to consult Wittgenstein on the point, but he didn't appear.

Once we arrived at the medicine man's, the men headed off for the sweat-lodge, for the purification rite of a steam bath. We women settled down to "visit," as they say there, all the while making a chain of small bundles of tobacco wrapped in little pieces of red cloth. I got the knack, finally. Outside, the children were playing and catching frogs. With the darkness of night, still streaked with lightening, the men came back inside, and we went down to the basement of the house sitting on the floor in a circle. Joe Eagle Elk knelt down in the center and unpacked the contents of a little suitcase for the ceremony.

---

* Cf. Gerald Vincent Mohatt and Joseph Eagle Elk, *The Price of a Gift: A Lakota Healer's Story* (Lincoln, Nebraska: University of Nebraska Press, 2000).

Suddenly the door banged open from a gust of wind. I was uneasy. My concern and my sympathy for our hosts didn't stop me from fearing the worst, as if centuries of bitter struggle against our indigenous demons had not succeeded in erasing the fear we have of seeing them come back again. My younger son, who was then two years old, was sitting on my lap, and he started to cry, and I wanted to leave. The medicine man, concentrated on

the preparation of different objects—a small mound of earth in the shape of a pyramid, surrounded by yellow, white, black, and red pieces of cloth—was going on with his work. His wife Vicky remained quiet, a little out of the circle, with a pipe on her lap. I heard Stanley heckle the chap next to him: "You Indian! Couldn't you try to be less ugly! Don't you see you're frightening that child?" I laughed. My son stopped crying. The medicine man burned some sage and gave twigs of it to us to pass around. Each of us placed one behind our own, and our children's, ears. The drum started its powerful beat. The helper started to sing with the medicine man, and my son fell asleep rocked by this formidable lullaby, as did most of the other children. My devils had fled. It was the medicine man's spirits' turn to come on stage. He was calling his friends and allies with the strength of his song.

All the lights had been switched off, and all the windows covered with opaque blankets. Rattles were rattling. Stanley explained that the darkness dated from a past not so long ago, when these rites, in order to survive, had to stay secret. Joe was singing in an ancient tongue, telling of his vision, which had started him on the path of becoming a medicine man. At some point we had to speak, each in turn, in a clockwise direction. I could say what came to mind, or pass the speech to my neighbor by saying, "All my relatives," "*Mi takuye oyasin*" (the only words I know in Lakota, for having heard them so often). Some spoke for a very long time.

When my turn arrived, it came to my mind that my mother was sick; I said it, followed by "All my relatives," and then it was the next person's turn. When everyone had spoken, which took a good while, the medicine man, or more exactly, the spirits through his mouth, uttered their messages and interpretation. Throughout this process, my neighbor was whispering the translation to me, which I had trouble understanding. Then there were drums and new songs. My neighbor passed me a pipe from which he had taken a puff. I did the same, and passed it along to the next person. Then a large bowl of water was passed around, from which, each in turn, we drank a mouthful. Finally, the lights were turned back on. The pots were carried to the center of the circle, and paper plates were given to everybody. Then food was served all around and everyone ate, while joyously heckling each other. "That medicine man must have had too much to drink last night. He has a hangover. He talked without rhyme or reason." Jokes burst out. It was a way of bringing everyone back to earth, as in the medieval traditional comic inversion rites.

On the following days, we exchanged stories with the medicine man. Sometimes I told of some moments in my analytic work, as I would have done at Austen Riggs, and he made some connections with cases in his therapeutic experience. Or he started with bits of myths and commented on them with examples from the present, to which I associated with other examples taken from my practice or from my mythology. I ended by believing there was a veritable kinship between our clinical approaches.

One day, I asked him in what state he had to be to receive a message from the spirits. Stanley answered in his place: "In a completely normal state; he's completely crazy, like you and me."

And after a silence, he added: "Look at him; you see, he is an Other."

PAUL: Superb definition of the analyst . . .
FD: I again asked Joe Eagle Elk my question. How did he know whether or not he could accept the pipe they handed him as a way of asking him for a ceremony? "I accept it when my mind is completely blank," was his response.

I left this country with the impression of having almost understood, but without comprehending. These rites spoke to me, but I remained puzzled, ignorant of the mythology that inspired them. Sometimes I compared this encounter to that of two potters, where each one, without being able to interpret the symbols engraved on the vases of the other, would have recognized the same gestures of forming clay around a central void. Sometimes I regretted the gaps in my knowledge of anthropology.

As usual, that is, at the moment when I least expected it, I discovered Wittgenstein on the airplane. Avoiding the question which was burning on my lips—Where was he all this time?—I disclosed my dilemma to him: What about this kinship that I so strongly felt existed between two practices nevertheless so different? Was it based on a supermarket of syncretic ideas or on the effect of an illusory transference? In short, what did he think of these free associations of stories that we had shared without respect for any rules of the anthropological language-game? For example, after having mentioned to Joe Eagle Elk, Casimir and the ghosts of his grandmother's village, the conversation had revolved around the numerous suicides on the reservation.

The medicine man had then told me the following story: "In the past, we would take our children down to the river. They would go off to hide and we would erase their traces, while calling them by their own names. Today, we don't know how to call our children with the spirits of our people, and they leave their tracks everywhere, traces of their suicides, traces of their corpses." Do they suffer from the destruction of the tool of their names? From ghosts? What do you think?

WITTGENSTEIN: Nothing shows better your kinship with these wild thoughts than the fact that you use this word, "ghost," or indeed, "spirit," to describe both their practices and yours, their calamities and ours.[3]
FD: And what would be the structure of this kinship?
WITTGENSTEIN: It seems to me that the principle according to which these practices are ordered is a very general one, and we find it in ourselves. One could oneself very easily imagine primitive

practices, as you do, without any inhibition, with your patients. Think how, after Schubert's death, his brother cut certain of Schubert's scores into small pieces and gave to his favorite pupils these pieces of a few bars each, as a sign of piety.[4] I myself, who don't believe that somewhere or other there are superhuman beings which we might call gods—if I can say, "I fear the wrath of the gods," then this shows that with these words I can mean something or express a feeling that need not be connected with that belief.[5]

Then, with a sigh, he added without transition: "To cast out death or to slay death . . ."[6]

PAUL: A child analyst told me that one of his young patients threw some things against the mirrors in the room. Asked about that gesture, the little boy answered that he wanted to kill the dead. Perhaps it was to erase the tracks of their ghosts, which can come back through the mirrors, and to send them back to the country of their ancestors. I have this detail from an Irish patient, who was very surprised I didn't cover the mirrors at night before going to sleep.

FD: Wittgenstein, like that little boy, had perhaps good reasons to want to kill the dead. Perhaps he had invented for himself some primitive use in order to confront the death of his brothers. So, I naively asked him the question: "Why do you want to slay death?" He evaded.

WITTGENSTEIN: This situation is comparable to one in which we have lost a paradigm.

PAUL: A paradigm? The word's been in fashion since Thomas Kuhn's book, *The Structure of Scientific Revolutions*,* where it is used, moreover, to refer to Wittgenstein. Who today doesn't brag about having discovered a new paradigm? But by the way, what is a paradigm?

FD: I had the same question. I'll give you his definition.

WITTGENSTEIN: A paradigm is not something represented, but is a means of representation; it's something with which comparison is made and, without it, names can have no meaning. Think of the metric standard, without which the word "meter" would have no meaning. The standard itself remains indestructible.[7] For what names in a language signify must be

* Cf. Thomas Kuhn, *The Structure of Scientific Revolutions* (Chicago: University of Chicago Press, 1962).

	indestructible; for it must be possible to describe a state of affairs in which everything destructible is destroyed.[8]
FD:	Like Indian people threatened with their disappearance?
WITTGENSTEIN:	The symbolism of language, whether scientific or magical, is meant to protect us against this kind of danger. However, you have this experience in your work every day.
FD:	Psychoanalysis isn't witchcraft.
WITTGENSTEIN:	Isn't the magical treatment of an illness also a language-game in which the symptom is addressed and made to speak? Sometimes I wonder—if the symptom doesn't understand that, then I don't know how I ought to say it.[9]
FD:	Repeat publicly that I indulge in magic in my analytic practice and you'll have me burned at the stake right away!
FD (to Paul):	My fright had the effect of delighting him. "Then your goose is cooked," he said laughing. And he tried to explain to me that this magic functioned like that of Alice in Wonderland, Chapter 3, in which a mouse tries without success to "dry."

Alice, who was wet from the sea of her own tears, by telling her the "driest" story there is.*

I was no more disposed than Alice to let myself be hoodwinked. However, I said to him, to reassure myself, "The difference between that Indian medicine and psychoanalysis comes down to the narrative about his vision that the medicine man disclosed at the beginning of the ceremony. For an analyst to have visions was unthinkable, and for him to tell his patient about them was even more unimaginable! Besides, an analysis takes place in a two-some encounter." Wittgenstein kept smiling. Stanley's good-bye was still sounding in my ears: "See you next year, maybe in Hell!"

Paul also smiled at these words, his eyes half closed. Evening had fallen, and looking at the embers, little by little we gave in to our drowsiness.

---

* Cf. Lewis Carroll, *The Annotated Alice: Alice's Adventures in Wonder-land and Through the Looking Glass.* Introduction and Notes by Martin Gardner (New York: The World Publishing Company, 1963), 46.

Chapter 12

Witchcraft

A walk in the woods.

PAUL, FD

The analyst's office.

FD, WITTGENSTEIN, SULLIVAN, THEODORE

The next day, the trees were glistening in the sun. It had rained all night. A squadron of titmice accompanied our breakfast— all species of them together, diving one after the other at a bird feeder I hadn't noticed the day before. Quickly filling his backpack, Paul suggested that I continue with my narrative along the way to our planned picnic, in an area of young ash and wild cherry trees, which Paul was lovingly caring for.

PAUL:

On waking up this morning, I was thinking that there aren't just two of us in an analysis; there's also a third that speaks through the unconscious, and there's also all those to whom we're related—"all my relatives," as Sioux people say. How many times have I been faced—beyond the person who has come to see me— with parents or friends in touch with madness . . . ? You must have had a thought like this when you got back to France.

FD:

I didn't come back immediately. Wittgenstein took off for the East, probably to stop at Cornell University where he had some friends. As for me, I had decided to continue my search for ways of working with madness and to fly off to China, the country of Lin Tsi. There I discovered that stomach lump I spoke to you about, the last time we met in Paris.

On my return to France, I was exhausted. I had visited cities and towns, palaces and tombs, without finding a trace of Lin Tsi. I came to understand while I was

DOI: 10.4324/9781003437451-12

there that madness is no longer a tradition in Chinese wisdom. Now they go their separate ways. My stomach lump ached since I became aware of its existence. On coming back to France, I had nothing more pressing on my mind than to entrust my health to Western medicine, which decided on an operation. The Lakota and their spirits seemed far away. I was waiting then for the day of the surgery, which was supposed to take place in a nearby hospital, when I received a letter so disturbing that I forgot all about my health problems.

PAUL: It's always the same story: you can never go peacefully on a trip without coming back to a catastrophe . . .

FD: This letter came from an Italian psychiatric hospital and said in substance: "We are writing to inform you that Mr. Theodore is hospitalized here. He says he is in an analysis with you. We have been in contact with the psychiatrist in his case, and we have discharged him with the following course of treatment."

PAUL: One of your patients?

FD: Yes. Yet in June, when I left, he seemed much better.

PAUL: That's what happens when one discards accurate diagnosis! I can imagine the intern on duty, upon the arrival of your patient, saying: Another analyst playing sorcerer's apprentice! Wild, pathogenic psychoanalysis, etc.

FD: I was in my office reproaching myself in exactly that way, when I noticed Wittgenstein sitting on the couch with a man I didn't recognize. He introduced me to Harry Stack Sullivan. They were actually contemporaries, and I had always imagined, while reading Sullivan's book, *Schizophrenia as a Human Process*, that they had a family resemblance. Sullivan was smiling too, as he looked at me with my letter in my hand. I thought he was making fun of me.

SULLIVAN: Hardly any change since the twenties. When one of your patients is hospitalized, I bet you're accused of misdiagnosing him.

FD: But I'm not a physician . . .

WITTGENSTEIN: What does it matter! Will a more accurate knowledge of the nervous system allow us to look into the brain with certitude?[1]

I was not in the mood for their sarcasm, and I wanted to show them that nowadays, since their time, positive science had actually made some progress. So much so that, in England, recently, several serious studies have produced some evidence of some sort of genetic disturbance in schizophrenia. But I became so entangled in my explanations that they weren't even listening to me.

WITTGENSTEIN: Mental mechanisms are not material mechanisms . . . That patient disturbs you by using a language- game you're not

	accustomed to. You have to change your way of looking at things.[2]
FD:	That's too easy! Each time I'm in a mess, you talk about all sorts of language-games, but you have nowhere said what they consist of, what their structure is, what they have in common . . .[3]
WITTGENSTEIN:	You're completely correct; they have no one thing in common, but they are related to one another in many different ways.
FD:	And would you describe these links for me, exactly?
WITTGENSTEIN:	Why would "inexact" always be a reproach, and "exact" praise?[4] Don't think, but look.[5]
FD:	OK—what should I look at?
WITTGENSTEIN:	At what has happened between you and this patient. You have to focus on the details of what goes on, and you must look at them from close-up.[6]
FD:	Well, the more I look, the more I notice we're stuck.
WITTGENSTEIN:	That's not at all alarming; philosophical problems generally have the form: "I don't know my way about."[7]
FD:	You're not serious. Say that to the Italian physicians who wrote that letter and they'll answer you: "Philosophy— that's not what we need here!"
WITTGENSTEIN:	My God! You're wrong to despise philosophy. A philosopher's treatment of a question looks very much like the treatment of an illness.[8] Don't hesitate to compare language-games that seem like strangers to one another. Find the connections; locate the intermediate cases.[9]
FD:	But that's what I do. The sociologist, Alain Touraine,*told me one day that madmen stood for the social link itself. Since then I work to find connections between madness and ruptures in the social link. But look at the result! It hasn't prevented Theodore from being committed.
SULLIVAN:	Your sociologist wasn't wrong; I also came to the view that in dealing with schizophrenics, we discovered manifestations of the subject matter of each of the social sciences.[10] Moreover, to understand social forces, why always think of collective entities? Nothing beats the study of groups of two or three people.[11] Wait to be convinced of it, by having a little more familiarity with schizophrenics. With them, in almost laboratory simplicity, the manifestations of complex

---

* FD entered Touraine's research center at EHESS—École *des hautes etudes en sciences sociales* (The School for Advanced Studies in the Social Sciences)—in 1969. That center is now called "CEMS"— *Centre d'étude des mouvements sociaux* (Center for the Study of Social Movements).

social processes at work in society, which are generally scarcely grasped because of their great complexity, show themselves.[12]

FD: And what are these complex processes?

SULLIVAN: The very ones that attempt to tie social relationships together at the places where they have been ruptured.[13] There must indeed be a link, a knot, a nexus, at the place where our string of words gets tangled or broken. Schizophrenics suffer so much from these chaotic zones that they spend all their time analyzing them.[14]

FD: Not from a scientific point of view. Anyhow, this is not compatible with the very idea of therapy.

SULLIVAN: Scientific research can be, and often is, a thoroughly effective therapeutic tool. And why refuse logic a place in the patients' analyses? Besides, everything depends on what you mean by "scientific."[15]

FD: Well, an ideal of rigor and objectivity to which analytic neutrality is not to be compared. Especially when it comes to mad people!

WITTGENSTEIN: Stop, we cannot breathe.[16] You're sending us in pursuit of chimeras, [17] a super-order, with super-concepts, as if thought were surrounded by a halo . . . You're trying to attach your ideal to reality, like a pair of glasses on your nose through which you see everything in the same way.[18] Let go of this too icy surface . . . To walk you need some friction. Back to rough ground! Start from your experience![19]

SULLIVAN: And how! Here we touch upon one of the most fatuous errors of the humanistic or "un-natural" sciences: to wit, that by some technique—poker face, or other—the "observer" gazes down from a pinnacle of scientific detachment upon subjects from whom he is concealed as if by a *tarnkoph*.[20] As if miraculously, the searcher's contact with his ground, or the psychiatrist's with his patient, had no significance at all for him. Query: why not analyze psychiatrists' dreams[21] and take their observations of their own patients seriously. Trust my word on it, for it doesn't get put in manuals, the schizophrenic most lost in his own autistic world is extremely sensitive to all that goes on around him, and especially to the aberrations in his therapists' theories.

That sentence reminded me immediately of my letter, and threw me into a sudden panic.

FD: Let's end this discussion that by no means helps me in this present situation. Certainly, I must have committed some errors regarding Theodore, for him to have been hospitalized

SULLIVAN:

during my absence. But what to do now? What to say to him? How to speak to him?

It's very simple: use everyday language with him. I don't suppose you're deaf-mutes, so I ask you to realize that in talking about speech, I'm using speech.

WITTGENSTEIN:

I too speak to you using that language. When I talk about language, I must speak the language of everyday. Is this language perhaps too coarse and material for what we want to say?[22] And then, if I were you, I wouldn't obsess over explanations. Don't look for what's hidden.[23] Look at the language-game that's functioned between you. Stop the analysis!

FD:

Stop the analysis?

WITTGENSTEIN:

The analysis of the internal experience of your patient. In order to find the real artichoke, you divested it of all its leaves, and there is no longer any artichoke at all.[24]

SULLIVAN:

Or, analyze your own scotoma, the true source of our theories.[25]

FD:

I have looked very carefully, and I don't see more of a scotoma than an artichoke.

WITTGENSTEIN:

It's what you believe, for you fail to be struck by what is in front of your eyes. The most important details are hidden for you because of their simplicity, or because of too great a familiarity.[26] Trust your impressions . . . .

SULLIVAN:

Especially those that are uncanny, those most often dismissed.

At this word Paul stopped walking: "uncanny," is exactly the Freudian "unheimlich." For a moment he seemed to have shifted into slow motion. I wanted to carry the bag. He flatly refused. So, I went on with my story:

FD:

At that moment, the telephone rang. It was Theodore who was asking for an urgent meeting. I proposed that he come, and I hung up, quite shaken.

(TO WITTGENSTEIN AND SULLIVAN):

Theodore is coming. It's a really bad time. I would prefer to take care of my own health. I don't feel at all like doing this job.

SULLIVAN:

Calm yourself, and trust in my experience. Some schizophrenics impressed me, years ago, as singularly interesting, in part, because of their striking manifestation of some of my own most highly esteemed traits. I refer, of course, to my personal appraisal of my traits. I therefore cultivated them and this gave such complimentary

FD: Speak for yourself. First, who told you that Theodore is schizophrenic? Moreover, today I am doing fine without his company.

WITTGENSTEIN: Don't hesitate to find family resemblances.[28]

FD: Between my symptom and his? Impossible . . .

SULLIVAN: Impossible, really? Not the least coincidence?

FD: No. Well, perhaps a tiny detail. Do you see, on the shelf, those little wooden objects, around which black and white thread is wrapped? I always saw them at my grandmother's, without really knowing their use. I believed they were sewing kits, for the women to take when they went to the fields.

At our first appointment, Theodore was being discharged from the hospital where I had met him a short time before. He only stated: "This time I realized that I was truly nuts." Then he remained silent, staring, as if he saw something behind me. I wondered what he could be hallucinating, and, very illogically, I turned around. "I see those objects in turned wood," he said. "Do you know what they are?" I told him my assumption. He went on: "You're not at all with it. They're "sewing kits" that First World War soldiers used. I kept my father's. Look, there's a perforating tool-punch on the inside." Unscrewing the neck, he showed me a punch, the existence of which I had ignored until then. Without either of us intending it, those objects had managed to meet, and to recognize each other, in order to be named. But today our paths seem to have gone their separate ways.

Theodore rang the bell and entered the room looking as spaced as when I had met him at the hospital.

THEODORE: I had trouble managing to get here. It's the crazy number of police cars and firemen I passed on the boulevard.

FD: On the radio this morning they mentioned a demonstration.

THEODORE: . . . And also that I was a dangerous terrorist. It's normal. You should watch out for me. I don't answer for anything. Dangerous to himself and to others! I have nothing more to lose, I am surrounded by demons, and don't try to convince me of the contrary.

I didn't know how to respond. Then he started obstinately studying the ceiling, acting as if I didn't exist. I took advantage of this to turn toward Wittgenstein, and to murmur very quickly:

FD: "What's he talking about? He's surrounded here only by rational, tolerant, and enlightened minds . . ."

From the corner of his eye, Theodore was watching my ploy. Imagine that! Wittgenstein then had the nerve to answer in a loud voice:

WITTGENSTEIN: Say what you choose, so long as it doesn't stop you from seeing the facts. And when you see them, there's a good deal you will no longer say.[29]

At first I had the impression that Theodore had heard him, that he was going to concur, but he continued to be interested in the ceiling. While I was trying vainly to organize my thoughts, thinking of consulting Jeanne Favret, an anthropologist, a specialist in witchcraft, Wittgenstein asked me:

WITTGENSTEIN: Are you unable to keep your head up, sticking to the subjects of your everyday practice?

He accused me of going astray, in order to sort out subtleties well beyond my power, as if I had to repair a torn spider's web with my own fingers.[30] Sullivan, for his part, agreed with him:

SULLIVAN: The description of schizophrenic experience did not at all require any element different from ordinary, simply human life.[31]

Suddenly unstuck from his ceiling, Theodore responded to Sullivan with a vivacity that took me by surprise:

THEODORE: You missed! You misdiagnosed me. I'm not a schizophrenic. Sorry to deceive you, but I'm just overly sensitive and paranoid. That's what it says in my file. And also in the DSM. This "illness" is not improved by psychoanalysis. They told me that, three years ago, in another hospital. Don't bother about it, either way. I don't care as long as they equilibrate my treatment. I love meds.

Before I had time to ask him what fly had bitten him, he was already up and apologizing:

THEODORE: Make yourselves at home; don't interrupt your conversation. I have to get something and I'll be back in half an hour. He disappeared before I had the presence of mind to hold him back.

Chapter 13

The Cosmos Becomes Uncertain

A walk in the woods.

PAUL, FD

The analyst's office.

SULLIVAN, WITTGENSTEIN, THEODORE

At that point Paul acknowledged he was tired. He sat down on a stump to catch his breath. "Well," he said, noticing me looking at the branches of a hazelnut tree whose golden buds were hanging over our heads, "you're dying to try it. Why not?" I fashioned a rod for myself, as I had seen the diviner did the other day, and I was slowly walking off, waiting for any signal it might want to send me. Paul joined up with me again:

PAUL: Whether that forked twig, which they called "*furcelle*" in the old days, points the way out to you or not, I'm taking you close to a spring.

I ignored this ancient name for a "divining rod," which in fact is not a "rod," but a little forked stick, a little divided branch. Paul said he was drawing on his knowledge of the works of Yves Rocard* on dowsers, which he had consulted after meeting with his diviner. He spoke to me of this physicist's passion for phenomena

---

* Yves Rocard (1903–1992) was a famous French physicist known as the father of the French A-Bomb and the French H-Bomb. For 28 years he was the director of the physics laboratory at the École *Normale Ssupérieure*. Later in his career he became interested in divining or dowsing, which he explained according to the general principles of electromagnetism and biomagnetism. He devoted his last published work to this topic: *Le Science et les Sourciers* (Paris: Dunot, 1996)—originally published in 1989.

DOI: 10.4324/9781003437451-13

that are magical, invisible to classical science. Then he asked me if Theodore had seen my "spooky friends."

FD:	I would have sworn to it. But that was secondary. I regretted above all having let him get away, and having run the risk, among others, of his being involuntarily committed. I saw him already being run in by the cops, and taken to the police infirmary . . . And those two advice-givers, neither one of whom had moved to stop him from leaving . . . I began by attacking Sullivan, rather satisfied that Theodore had put him in his place about the diagnosis.
SULLIVAN:	With experience, I lost hope for a long time of one day finding clear nosological entities . . .[1] Your patient brings to mind two I knew, who were among the most talented members of our society. Their number is legion; the social loss is immense . . . [2]
FD:	Tell me, between us, is this story of demons true or false?
WITTGENSTEIN:	The words "true" or "false" may be among the constituent parts of the language-game he's playing with the word "demon," but they do not fit it.[3]
FD:	You're evading.
WITTGENSTEIN:	And if, as matters stand, we were to ask ourselves the question about the "subject" of this sentence: "I am surrounded by demons." Who is this 'I'?"
FD:	Theodore has a strange conception of this "I"; he has neither an "ego," nor a "self," nor a "personality," nor even the least private life. Already as a child, he went into tantrums upon seeing, on the mantelpiece, a picture of a baby he didn't know. He yelled out that it was "he," his "ego."
SULLIVAN:	Crises of this kind are often linked to pieces of information which have been lost or cut out by the parents, which the child explores, stating their existence—not so much as something repressed.[4]
FD:	Yes, I heard the child analyst Françoise Dolto say that children were "sleepwalkers in the dream of the other." But these demons that trouble him, can they still be explained by the repression of local practices? I should perhaps get interested in his village, his region.
SULLIVAN:	No need to go so far. I'm sure that psychiatry actually includes more magic than all those villages. Take, for example, notions like "symbiosis," "narcissistic neurosis"—don't you think they're magical? They're the "open-sesames" of useless explanations.[5]

FD:	All the same, one can't deny the existence of mental disorders.
SULLIVAN:	Well, in that case, let us come back to the old notion of demonic possession, until fairly recently an accepted explanation of mental disorders, and still a potent magical notion among the body of citizens. Not that there are many Americans today who will admit or recognize that they believe in evil spirits— certainly not as interlopers into the human body, with mental disorders as a result. But, the ancient horror of leprosy is not so exaggerated an analogy to this aversion for the "insane" by the "normal."[6]

I was having trouble following, preoccupied with what I was going to say to Theodore. Ignoring my signs of impatience, Sullivan went on:

SULLIVAN:	It's a shame to see the sums of money given out to advertising campaigns that favor research in many possible directions: the physical, physicochemical, biochemical, chemical; anatomical, histopathological, neuropathological, endocrinopathological, cardiovasculopathological or metabolic physiological.[7] Psychiatry, meanwhile, is still floundering on such exciting discoveries as "narcissistic withdrawal" and the Oedipus Complex, or on the disorder of I don't know what gland.[8] There's always a discovery of etiology. After the discovery, the enthusiast sees nothing but evidence of his correctness thenceforth. You might say their "discoveries" are the production of dilettantes who have the same contact with their patients as prejudiced missionaries have with primitive cultures, or even as I myself have with equine conceptualizations.[9]
FD:	Still, there are the psychoanalysts . . .
SULLIVAN:	. . . Who, with respect to psychosis, use a lot of notions only to justify the failures of their day-to-day therapeutic work.[10]
FD:	You're not helping me a lot, and Theodore is coming here at any moment.
SULLIVAN:	Once again, observe which social relation you are involved in with him. Find the situation that lost its meaning.[11] In all the stories I've come to know, there's been a disaster-point, a collapse in self-esteem, and the discovery of incoherences transmitted through the parents.[12]
FD:	Suddenly I thought again of that lump that seemed to me to be growing by the hour. But apparently, no one was interested in what I had in my stomach, and in "the situation that had lost its meaning" for me. Wittgenstein was debating with Sullivan without paying the least attention to me.

WITTGENSTEIN: Then you too cast stones at the parents?

SULLIVAN: No, you don't have to look for causal factors. These people have been caught up by certain events and by such incoherent social situations that they have been able to transmit only cultural distortions to their children.[13]

At that moment only I was aware of Theodore's presence. Had he been present for this discussion? By placing a finger on his lips, he signaled to me not to interrupt them.

SULLIVAN: Consequently, these same children could very well see us, us other normal people, as caricatures or as carnival masks, engaging in bizarre activities more or less injurious, as far as they're concerned.[14]

WITTGENSTEIN: I sometimes imagine that people are automata, lacking consciousness, even though they behave in the same way as usual . . . [15]

SULLIVAN: In that type of situation, the cosmos becomes uncertain. There's a total loss of confidence in the integrity of the universe, and in our cultural values.[16]

WITTGENSTEIN: Indeed, everything topples over. Suppose there's a chair and suddenly it disappears from sight. I then say: "So, it wasn't a chair but some kind of illusion." But in a few moments we see it again. "Very well," I say, "the chair was there after all; its disappearance was some kind of illusion." But suppose that after some time it disappears again, or seems to disappear. What are we to say now? Have your rules ready for such cases?[17]

Bringing his index finger to his temple, Theodore gave me a sign, putting on a knowing look, indicating that he knew that he had the diagnosis ready for that sort of thing. Wittgenstein himself seemed very excited.

WITTGENSTEIN: Better still: imagine someone who is always doubting before opening his front door, wondering whether an abyss did not yawn behind it. He goes so far as to reassure himself before passing through the doorway. Couldn't it be that on certain occasions he might be right to do that?[18]

This was too much. I asked him if he often amused himself with these little tricks. He seemed caught off guard by this, and he justified himself:

WITTGENSTEIN: To doubt and to imagine a doubt are not the same thing.[19]

Then he pushed the matter:

WITTGENSTEIN: And if I were to ask you if the exactness of your watch is ideal exactness?[20]

Theodore jumped at the chance to tease me again.

THEODORE: Good question! What assures me that the time on your watch is the correct time?

Now I had all three of them against me. I flatly answered Theodore:

FD: My watch clearly shows the same time as yours. It's two o'clock; you're exact. You had told me you would return at the end of a half hour.

THEODORE: But what can make me sure that your watch is working? Who can guarantee for me that it's not two o'clock in the morning? So many strange things happen . . . While you were chattering, I went to type on my computer in the hope of finding an answer there. I'm uneasy. At the other end there's an evil genius who deliberately deceives me. I have proof of it. When I typed out the code, he answered me only with absurdities. If I were to trust myself, I would have some reason to panic. I wake up every morning as if it were the end of the world. Don't you see that we're living under attack? And how to know if you're not all specters that are going to disappear?

Both of them lowered their heads, quite embarrassed. This nod did not escape Theodore's notice at all, but he went on with a strong hint of sincerity:

THEODORE: I am cut out of biological time. You were speaking, a while ago, of the mind. Mine is made of bits and pieces. Where to find some kind of coherence? I must have got the film wrong.
WITTGENSTEIN: Which film?
THEODORE: A power pushes me to perform; it pulls me to trespass the frontiers, to go beyond boundaries. I am permanently acting out.
WITTGENSTEIN: What do you do when you have the impression of being guided along in this way?[21]
THEODORE: It's indescribable.
WITTGENSTEIN: That word tells me nothing.
THEODORE: Since you insist . . . I perform like an actor in a film whose script I don't know, and yet I play it perfectly; all the spotlights are pointed at me.

WITTGENSTEIN: Aren't you like the man, for example, who could read a text fluently, while under the influence of a drug, and would have the feeling that he knew it by heart, but yet had never seen it before?[22]

THEODORE: That happens to you too? But, alas, I don't take drugs, except my meds.

WITTGENSTEIN: It actually happens to me in dreams, and I wake up with the impression that I've read a script, although there had been no writing at all. What, in your opinion, does this reading consist of?[23]

THEODORE: To answer you I'd have to have access to the text that inspires me. Well, I have no idea. Each time I rush to grasp it, I bump up against nonsense—with the result of a huge mental bump, a mental hematoma.

WITTGENSTEIN: So it is with philosophy. It makes us uncover one or another piece of plain nonsense and of bumps which understanding has got by running its head up against the limits of language. These bumps make us see the value of the discovery.[24]

THEODORE: You're an optimist; mine have rather discredited me.

WITTGENSTEIN: I'd like to take a walk. Let's continue this conversation outside.

I saw all three of them get up and get ready to leave. I didn't have the strength to hold back Theodore, and I only said to Wittgenstein, as he left: "Take it easy." "Leave it to me," he answered mysteriously. Basically, I wasn't sorry at letting Theodore go in their company. On the doorstep, I told him about my surgical operation, and I gave him an appointment for the following month.

Chapter 14

The Fly-Bottle

A walk in the woods.

PAUL, FD

The hospital where the analyst is hospitalized.

FD, WITTGENSTEIN

Paul asked me if I knew what script I was involved in myself while leaving for the hospital.

FD: After the operation, the diagnosis of cancer was almost brushed
            aside. I was declared "borderline," and the physician waited
            for a year to make his decision. The time of this hospitalization
            was paradoxically welcome. Finally, to be able to stop! I was
            euphoric at having no responsibility, since the therapist was
            someone else—the surgeon who had operated on me was in
            charge. I said to myself: "What a strange business!" Having
            made this entire journey—crossed seas, plains, and mountains,
            hoping to find the formula for "psychotic transference," and to
            end up in a hospital bed . . .

PAUL: Weren't you following Otto Will's lesson to the letter?

FD: Indeed I was, but I realized above all that all these travels were
            bringing me back to square one. Or better, into the prison in the
            game of goose, without any wish that someone would come
            and free me from it. I particularly dreaded seeing Theodore
            again, judging that the last meeting had led nowhere.

PAUL: Especially since you bragged about doing your work without
            mixing your private life into it, and without falling ill . . .

FD: Yet this time I was really cautious not to let the least affect
            appear. When I informed him about it, I had used a profes-
            sional tone of voice. Now, my discharge from the hospital was

DOI: 10.4324/9781003437451-14

	dangerously approaching, and with it the prospect of having to confront his demons and his visions once again.
PAUL:	Had you forgotten the Sioux people, who don't have our prejudice against this kind of experience?
FD:	But here, that kind of know-how has been lost in the sand . . .
PAUL:	On which you again had the impression of rowing—to take up the image of the galley, to which Lacan seems to have condemned us . . . Then Wittgenstein paid you a visit.
FD:	How do you know?
PAUL:	I am beginning to get used to it; he has a therapist's vocation.

That day Wittgenstein was in a playful mood.

WITTGENSTEIN:	So, you're unable to show the fly the way out of the fly-bottle?[1]
FD:	I don't know what happened; I can't move anymore.
WITTGENSTEIN:	Actually, you are the victim of grammatical illusions . . . Why are you looking at me like that? I have already told you philosophy is a kind of therapy.[2] And the philosopher's treatment of a question is like the treatment of an illness.[3]
PAUL:	Do you really think that statement can be taken literally?
FD:	For Wittgenstein, at least, I believe it to have been an actual practice. I confessed my fear to him that in going through the hospital gate, I could fall into a void and, anyhow, that nothing would be as it was before. So, I was entangled in my own language rules.[4] He added:
WITTGENSTEIN:	That abyss is only an image, and inside that abyss is the inside of that image. Undoubtedly, you must change your way of looking at things, but not at everything. If the rule becomes exception and exception rule, this would make our normal language-games lose their point.[5] Find, then, with Theodore, a point of agreement removed from the influence of demons, an agreement to start from, which it would not be possible to doubt. At this point, you're like an engine idling—not doing work.[6]

I could not see at all what he was referring to. Before taking his leave, he looked for an example that was on my level:

WITTGENSTEIN:	When you buy a cheese, the weighing and pricing procedure that follows would lose its point if the cheese, before weighing, suddenly started to grow or shrink for no apparent reason.[7]
PAUL:	When I think of hospital menus . . . He seems to have wanted to make you salivate . . .

FD: The following night, I dreamed of pieces of cheese that were growing like the mushrooms in Tintin's *The Shooting Star*.* I woke up with Theodore's *idée fixe*: The end of the world . . . I realized how much the laws of logic had, with breathtaking swiftness, shrunk for him. Left alone to fight for the survival of his reason, he had panicked at seeing it put in doubt. Well, it was he whom we accused of insanity, when around him the cosmos was turning upside down and he had to find a way, like Descartes, of staying on his feet.

The next day, I found myself again at the hospital door, without having had the time to say "phew." I got ready to take up my work again, pondering Wittgenstein's instructions. First of all: "Use ordinary, everyday language"—a rule which Descartes, writing The Discourse on Method in French, had imposed on himself, so that he could be read by "women," who are, as he said, after all, half of the world.** Second: "Be done with explanations."[8] "Internal experience adds nothing." You should stop conceiving of mental disorders in terms of archaic, primitive drives, coming from the depths of a psychic or neuronal apparatus. Finally: "Trust in your impressions."

Indeed, my impression had been of letting myself be enclosed in a huge fly-bottle with Theodore. Even more so, during my convalescence. I had the time to turn this situation over and over in my mind, in every possible way.

In the first place, the fly-bottle had worked against Theodore, caught inside the closed doors of the hospital, because he was agitated. By then, my position was on the outside, concluding that Theodore's suffering was incommunicable. It seemed to arise from a private language, like a secret code to which he alone had the key.

Paul sat down again, against an oak tree, and concluded:

PAUL: One could indeed observe the behavioral tribulations of the fly, in the fly-bottle, even propose some tranquillizers, according to the variations in its mood—in turn agitated or prostrated—until it falls into the sugar-water.

FD: I had no expertise on this path where Theodore was dragging me. He knew how to be a pitiless observer of himself, counting

---

* Cf. Hergé, *The Adventures of TinTin: The Shooting Star* (New York: Little, Brown Young Readers, 1978). This volume of *The Adventures of Tintin* was first published in France in 1942, and had the title, *L'Étoile mysterieuse*.

** Cf. René Descartes, "Letter to Vatier, 22 February 1638," in C. Adam and P. Tannery (EDS) *Oeuvres de Descartes*, Volume 1 (Paris: Vrin, 1964–1972), 559.

and measuring the cyclic repetition of his crises, whispering to me, like Casimir, the appropriate diagnosis, and observing the effects of his meds with the docility of a guinea pig.

I therefore had given up the attempt to penetrate Theodore's psyche, and was going to declare analysis impossible, when I became aware—in the second place—of looking at this fly-bottle from a different angle. As if I too were "imprisoned" on the outside of this wall of glass—which brings up exactly a problem of interior and exterior, since the exterior turned back on itself is the interior.

To understand that new way of seeing things, I had to be healed, and to be, in my turn, enclosed in a hospital ward. Fearing to find myself in the open air, I had received the impression of experiencing what Theodore had described to me: isolation, doubt, a suspended sentence—leading to immobility. In wishing too strongly to play the clever fly, fatigue came quickly, and with it the temptation to fall to the bottom of the bottle that had gulped me down.

Chapter 15

The Girl

A walk in the woods.

PAUL, FD

The psychiatric hospital.

FD, THE GIRL

The analyst's office.

FD, WITTGENSTEIN, THEODORE

Resuming his walk, Paul remained thoughtful. I was cross with myself for having stirred up some recent memories for him. Better to stop this narrative. Abruptly, he branched off from the wide path we were on, and resolutely started off into the thicket. We had to fight against thorns until we entered a grove of ancient oak trees. All the time, Paul was enigmatically silent, not responding to any of my attempts to talk about something else. He eventually asked:

PAUL: And what was your condition after the hospitalization, when you started working again?

FD: I remembered having seen my patients again a month later, and asking Wittgenstein to come for Theodore's appointment. That day, I was coming back from the psychiatric hospital where I hadn't gone since my operation. Still tottering a little, I wanted to resume contact with a girl, who also was labeled "border-line," and whom I had seen regularly for a year. She had spent the previous day in the isolation room after having struck some "grandmothers" on the ward, who, she said, she couldn't stand any longer. She was all curled up in her bed when I entered, and she welcomed me with these words: "She is magnificent, the

DOI: 10.4324/9781003437451-15

	sick girl, when she enters the hospital. Now look at the pitiful thing she's become!" I told Wittgenstein about this meeting:
FD:	I didn't know whether she was speaking for herself or for me. Strange, isn't it?
WITTGENSTEIN:	It sounds strange only when we imagine a language-game different from the one that was really going on between you.[1]
FD:	A language-game in which the "I" and the other would be undecidable? Perhaps. I had that impression. And what do you think of the attribute "magnificent"? That word struck me, as if, in a flash, I understood it. Yet, she started to yell louder and louder: Get out of here!
WITTGENSTEIN:	You grasped this word in a flash, and yet its meaning is in the use you made of it.[2]
FD:	The initiative was hers. Instead of getting out of there, as she invited me to, I stayed, without knowing much of what to say or do. To my surprise, she got up, took me by the hand, and led me into a treatment room where she told the nurse: "We're going for a walk in the park."

From the nurse's hesitation, I understood that the "sick girl," as they say there, "was not allowed in the park." Allowing me the risk of this outing, the nurse only recorded both our names in her log. The "sick girl"—since this is the name she gave herself—directed our steps toward the exit. I expected to see her sprint the hundred meters to freedom, and I was still wondering about how to react, when she abruptly broke off in the opposite direction, toward the park that's situated in the back of the hospital. She led me to the foot of a magnificent tree, where she decreed: "It's a cedar of Lebanon."

I tried to get her to free associate with the word "Lebanon." Instead, she began a rapid discourse, scattered with unintelligible words, which—for want of a better idea, or for want of a "game," you might say—are called neologisms. I guessed about the medicinal properties of the sap and membranes of that tree. She pricked me on the wrist with a needle of that conifer, in order to heal me, she said. In order to drug me, I thought, for injecting herself had once been one of her favorite pastimes. But I said nothing to her, and I remained under the influence of this silent impression, while, without saying a word, she was taking me back to the ward.

WITTGENSTEIN:	And then?
FD:	Then, that's all. I thought she had shown me the magnificence of the "sick girl" in the form of a magnificent tree, still green in autumn, and more than a hundred years old. I believe I have shared with you my mental process during that entire episode.

WITTGENSTEIN:	Try not to think of understanding as a mental process at all. For that's the expression which confuses you.[3]
FD:	I followed your advice. I trusted the impression that the word "magnificent" made on me, when I received it, as in a flash.

Wittgenstein lost patience: "But the application is the criterion of understanding. What did you do with that intuition? How have you applied it?"[4]

FD:	Be logical! While you tell me that I should trust my impression, you repeat that to know a language is to master a technique, and then you need on the contrary to wait for the application of this technique, or the practice of this impression, if that still means something.[5]
WITTGENSTEIN:	We'll return to that paradox. You can very well seize upon a formula, and yet apply it differently, according to the traditions or the education you have received . . .[6]
FD:	What are you hinting at? That I have let myself be led by my education, when I thought I understood the word "magnificent"? Yes, maybe I preferred staying with a culturally acceptable impression of "magnificence," rather than letting myself be led along by playing at drugs with her. But how to know if I had indeed guessed what she was making me do?
	Besides, what to say of that drug? I don't use drugs. Although . . . I must confess to you, the most pleasant part of my hospitalization was the morphine they injected me with when I woke up. I found life wonderful, and I asked for more. Unfortunately, the nurse said no. That brings me back to the question I wanted to ask you at the start: Don't you find the knack that these borderline patients have of guessing about us, and even of caring for us, quite strange?
WITTGENSTEIN:	You assume they guess about you. In that case, why not ask them the question, and they'll answer you.[7]
FD:	I'm afraid of confirming them in their delirium, if I tell them they're right. That's not my role.
WITTGENSTEIN:	You have a preconceived idea of your role, which comes from the formulas that have formed you, and from the techniques you've been trained in. You forget the essential.
FD:	What, then, does this essential consist of?
WITTGENSTEIN:	It's a question of agreement among human beings.[8]

I was not expecting such a simple answer.

FD:	So, you're saying that human agreement will decide what's true and what's false?

WITTGENSTEIN: It's what humans say that is true and false, and they agree in the language they use.[9]

FD: This is extremely useful. On the one hand, we won't be obliged to stick to what the delusional say. On the other hand, we only have to discover in what language-game what they're saying makes sense, and would eventually be true. Moreover, it would be enough to find an agreement on the formulations that would authenticate the truth of their delusions among human beings—outside the logic of the true and the false, since that agreement is the condition of the possibility of such a logic.

WITTGENSTEIN: That agreement is the basis of the notion of paradigm, which I told you about after our stay in South Dakota, when we were looking for a general principle. But this applies also to what works in the act of "obeying a rule," in everyday life.[10] If the agreement were made straightaway, our normal language-games would have no reliability at all.

FD: So abnormal language-games would be the condition for normal language-games?

WITTGENSTEIN: Indeed, that's the paradox. If everything could be made out to accord with the rule, then it could also be made out to conflict with it. So, there would be neither accord nor conflict.[11]

FD: I bet Popper whispered this one in your ear. It's his charge against psychoanalysis. He condemns it in the name of what you've just been saying. All psychoanalytic interpretation seems to support its own principles. Psychoanalysis is unfalsifiable.* Whether a patient agrees with or objects to an interpretation amounts to the same thing. If he agrees, the interpretation is true; if he's in conflict with it, it's still true—for the patient is resisting, and the symbolizing machine of the analyst is always right.[12]

WITTGENSTEIN: The misunderstanding here comes from the mere fact that in the course of your argument you give one interpretation after the other, as if each one contented you at least for a moment, until you think of yet another standing behind the first one.[13]

FD: So, when the patient accepts, and then, just afterward, rejects his diagnosis of psychosis, his rebellion is all the more proof of his disturbance.

---

* Cf. Karl Popper, *The Logic of Scientific Discovery* (New York: Routledge, 2002). This very famous and influential work in the philosophy of science was first published in German as *Der Logic der Forschung* (Vienna: Verlag von Julius Springer, 1935).

WITTGENSTEIN: This shows in a totally simple way that what we call "obeying a rule," or "going against it" is exhibited through actual cases, not from interpretations.[14]

FD: If Popper had taken the trouble to examine actual cases, to sit in the analyst's chair, instead of confining himself to their successive interpretations, he would perhaps have noticed that in spite of their analysts' rationalizations, patients have a way of grasping the rule and of going against it, which doesn't pertain to any interpretation, and which announces some change in the fundamental rule. On this point, analysts fight with one another. They have to find a new language for those true statements that have been rejected in the name of delusion or error. Folly's in the air; some even give up . . . Do you remember Casimir who never wanted to free associate, or lie down, or remember the past? Now, here's this girl who takes a hand in caring for me; the world is upside down.

WITTGENSTEIN: Logic seems to be abolished. But not at all . . . Take a machine symbolizing its own action. The machine's action seems to be there from the start.[15]

FD: Oh, you know me and machines . . .

At that moment Theodore rang, on time for his appointment; I let him in, and without paying more attention to his presence, I continued the discussion.

WITTGENSTEIN: Your patient is there . . .

FD: I know . . . But what do you mean with these machines?

WITTGENSTEIN: I mean that if we know the machine, all the rest, that is to say, all its movement seems already completely determined, like those interpretations you cited.

FD: Up to that point, it's easy to follow.

WITTGENSTEIN: But don't forget, in this case, that there is a possible play between socket and pin, that a pin breaks, bends, or melts down, etc.[16]

FD: I also won't forget that—for that's what generally happens when I use a machine.

WITTGENSTEIN: Well, when the language-game machine breaks, or comes into conflict with existing symbolizing machines, you have to find another paradigm.

FD: So, delirium would be the expression of a rule that's lost its paradigm. From which comes its tone that asserts and orders, and admits of no reply. By sheer solitude, and forced holidays, that language loses the habit of "agreement among human beings," and will end up speaking to the walls, saying frozen words to them.

WITTGENSTEIN:	Whom are you still thinking about?
FD:	Still that girl from the hospital. She had a way of grasping the analytic rule and of subverting it, which is not a resistance, and evidently does not have to be interpreted . . . We know very well, since the work of Searles,[17] that our patients take care of us, but it's a whole other thing when we ourselves are in a situation of being taken care of. I should have told her something about the new rules of the game we're playing. I'm vexed with myself for remaining silent.
WITTGENSTEIN:	Here is the whole problem: obeying a rule is a practice. And to think one is obeying a rule is not to obey a rule. Hence, it is not possible to obey a rule "privately"; otherwise thinking one was obeying a rule would be the same thing as obeying it.[18]
FD:	Apropos of practice, Joseph Needham, a scientist, says that Chinese mystics and magicians were real scientists, since they themselves did experiments with their hands, while at the same time, in the West, rationalist theologians refused to look through Galileo's telescope . . .[19]
THEODORE:	And if you looked a little through my telescope?
FD:	I'm listening to you.
THEODORE:	Nothing has changed in a month. I always have the impression that I'm acting in a film whose script I don't know. The spotlights and cameras are focused on me. I'm the hero in a role that I am performing by heart, without having ever learned it . . .[20]
FD:	And what does this hero bring to mind?
THEODORE:	You pretend to ask me seemingly unbiased questions, but I see you coming with your Oedipus. You're trying to make me swallow the psychoanalytic code. Mind you, I've tried hard to be the Oedipus; I've told myself I should have wished to sleep with my mother. It doesn't go anywhere.
FD:	Why would I tell you something other than what I'm telling you? Have I interpreted anything whatsoever in this way? Besides, you don't even allow me the time; you ask and answer the questions.
THEODORE:	Because I distrust myself. You wouldn't act any other way if you confused dream and reality, as I do. But let's stop there. You make me want to return to the hospital.

I hesitated for a long time before confessing to him:

FD:	I sometimes wish for that too. It's true that this time we both went to the hospital. I have the impression that each of us had a narrow escape.

THEODORE:	When you told me that you couldn't see me for a month, being hospitalized yourself, I thought immediately that they were operating on your stomach. In June, I had found you completely exhausted and didn't dare tell you for fear of alarming you. At the end you seemed to be forcing yourself to receive me out of duty. It was unbearable, because you didn't seem to be aware of it in yourself.
FD:	That's true; I noticed only later that something was abnormal.
THEODORE:	And I was delusional about there being something hidden—demons, black men, giving themselves over to some occult practices towards me. That racism horrified me. At present, all my dreams are broken. I have fucked up so much that I've been discredited.
FD:	How uncanny it is! When I found out that things went wrong, I myself dreamt of a demon attempting to take me away. I was trying to resist him but I had no strength—just a kind of inertia that sometimes happens in nightmares. On awakening, I knew it was death.
THEODORE:	At least on that point we could perhaps agree.
FD (TO PAUL):	When he had left, I stayed silent for a moment, as if to let resonate the harmonic of the chord he had just struck.

I told Wittgenstein such a discovery:

(To WITTGENSTEIN):	He had therefore indeed read a script that wasn't written, which he didn't know, and it was in my life, which I thought did not concern him. He stated then that things were being plotted behind his back, works of death . . . We would have known nothing about it if the idea hadn't suddenly occurred to me of informing him of the coincidence that had, at a one-month interval, taken each of us to the hospital.
WITTGENSTEIN:	The common behavior of mankind is the system of references by means of which we interpret an unknown language . . .[21]
FD:	In China, my older son had also panicked in the same manner as Theodore, pointing, through his monsters, at a terror I barely felt. In the language-game that I was sharing with Theodore, I perceived this dread after the danger, at the moment of crossing the hospital doorstep. What do I fear in the outward reality? To tell you the truth, I am scarcely at rest. For the present, Theodore seems to have recovered his spirit. He will no longer need to go wandering around

everywhere, displaying the imprints left on him by the absent script. Nor will he need to act out a message that's impossible to inscribe, since I recognized the legitimacy of his interpretation. But don't you find it disturbing that I trigger for my patient delusional themes from shapeless things that I'm not aware of?

WITTGENSTEIN: Speak frankly. So you fear triggering off demons? Why not use the mythological expression "demon"?[22] It gives a good account of the experience of any mathematician working on his equations, when he's surprised, for example, that a solution has been whispered to him during the night. The expression is correct; it doesn't need any kind of causality. It would be a mistake at this point to confuse a causal and a logical determination. That which trigger a language-game for what cannot be imagined.[23]

Then after a period of silence, he added:

WITTGENSTEIN: Can we go so far as to try to use language to get between pain and its expression?[24]

PAUL: At this point, I was going to ask you again Cooperman's question: What had happened for you to put into play, in the analysis, that unnamable thing that mattered to your stomach?

We had reached the foot of a magnificent oak tree many hundreds of years old, the most ancient in the forest. They call it "the Twins," Paul told me, for at the height of a man, its giant trunk divided into two trees dominating all the surrounding tree tops. An ancient, sacred tree—now a geodesic marker for survey maps. This mark of predilection brought to mind the Sioux rite of the Sun Dance, which Stanley Red Bird had made me attend. I told Paul how that rite began with the picking of a divided tree—"like man," they say—and then setting it up in the center of the circle, adorned with pieces of colored cloth. The medicine man had tied some young men to this tree, by the skin of their chests. Crowned with sage, girded in red cloth, they made a vow of fasting and dancing facing the sun, then by abruptly pulling away, they offered this bit of flesh as a sacrifice for others, related to them, in the community.

Chapter 16

The "Far Away" Look

A walk in the woods.

PAUL, FD

The analyst's office.

FD, WITTGENSTEIN, CONSTANCE

After having pointed out that giant forked tree, Paul headed off straight through the underbrush. Then he stopped to fashion himself a walking stick out of a shrub that had been twisted by clematis growing around it. "Trust in my recent experience," he said, while working with his pocketknife. "The limits of pain and the limits of language are difficult to draw. Especially for pains that aren't felt, like those that Theodore had detected in you. But you haven't answered my question: What did he show you to interpret, in giving himself such a hard time?"

FD:	Wittgenstein asked me the same question over and over. When I was in a state of uncertainty and still had to wait a year to be reassured about my health, he made some cryptic remarks to me *à propos* "of interpretations that do not determine meaning, but hang in the air somehow, without any support, seeking something to interpret."[1] As if my patients were in possession of a formula, and were looking to me as the object to apply it to.
PAUL:	And that interpretation?
FD:	You're asking me?—who was the object or the terrain the interpretation was applied to! It is usually the case that the field or the terrain is the other one . . . So, would you like the object of the interpretation to give its opinion on the formula that's applied to it? Physicists aren't able to locate their particles while they're moving, but you would expect the particle also to provide a commentary . . .

DOI: 10.4324/9781003437451-16

PAUL: Actually, you had been a thing to take care of and observe—a thing that didn't even know something was going wrong. The interpretation he was talking about was not so complicated. Once again, it's clear that you were going through an experience similar to Otto Will's. You too had found yourself in bed one fine morning, stripped of your professional skills, with a formidable neighbor beside you, pointing out to everyone what you didn't even know about. Remember the soldier, appearing for Otto Will as somebody between life and death, who had vanished from his early childhood. Didn't the same happen with Theodore? Hadn't he shown you that in your story too the tool of words had been broken?

FD: He had explained his act of divination in his own way, in terms of a child's scrutinizing stare at the sufferings of his mother. But as far as the part I had played in that story, I was—you can believe me—not aware of it. I had stepped head-on into his famous ghost-scenario, and it was my turn to wonder what I was doing there. Otto Will, by becoming sick and going to bed at his analyst's, had shown Sullivan this father with TB, who had been conjured away, when Otto was a baby. But I, once confined to bed, didn't see anything particularly significant in that.

PAUL: Well, nothing to declare at the site of your stomach?

FD: I was trying to keep that place a private one, remaining thereby a private person who had a cyst that was surgically removed. I was not, therefore, an analyst, and it was not, *a fortiori*, a public place where others discuss their business.

PAUL: If I understand correctly what you call "psychotic transference," you would have done better to wonder which of you two was the subject to be analyzed. I bet it was neither you nor he. Perhaps it was that being without qualities Lin Tsi speaks about, which was only waiting for this experience to begin to speak . . .

FD: You win. But to learn that, I had to wait for another patient, Constance, who made me realize it through a dream I had, which was, in fact, quite a vision . . .

PAUL: I see. Not only medicine men work with their dreams and their visions . . .

FD: I had trouble admitting it. This dream and its interpretation were very disturbing. Everything happened as though, in her bewilderment, Constance had been guardian of an interpretation that came out of her own experience, but which, for lack of validation, had remained hanging in the air without any support, until it applied to this dream of mine. During her analysis,

	this suspended formula took aim at my own story, as in a scenario that unfolded little by little. After having displayed a pregnant woman to Casimir, and then to Theodore a woman with stomach pains, this time I was going to put on stage a baby threatened in his mother's womb.
PAUL:	In short, a true tracking plan!
FD:	War was always the backdrop, with a foreground of madness and its procession of monsters. The kind which sometimes come out of women's bellies. At the interference of the Big History with those individual histories, terror happened, and broke the tool with the name "N".
PAUL:	And what about getting to the heart of the matter?
FD:	When Constance made her appointment, her voice on the phone hadn't let me foresee that she would look as groggy as those for whom an earthquake or a hurricane had destroyed everything—both family and belongings. She told me she had kept my address in her pocket for several months, and had made the decision only recently to come to see me on the sly from the psychiatric hospital, where she had been confined for some more or less lengthy stays. She didn't know what was pushing her to return there periodically. Probably a demon. She didn't believe in it for a second, but it made her suddenly indifferent to all her loved ones, and uninterested in her work, which she had normally enjoyed, for it was otherwise very exciting. She added: "I don't even know if I'm in pain or not; you can't figure out what I'm feeling." Then she stopped speaking and became motionless, like a statue. I was seeing on her face a look of extreme pain, which perhaps she was not feeling; and moreover, neither was I. For the umpteenth time, I was not equal to the task.

Naturally Wittgenstein got involved. For some time, he had been walking straight into my office. He tended, more and more boorishly, to take my place. I resisted him only weakly, as happens when one is unable to stop an intrusion in time.

This day, he drew his inspiration from his "Notes on Private Experience and Sense Data," a text in which he analyzes some situations of going mad.[2] From the first line, the reader lands right in the middle of a dialogue between a philosopher and a voice that's silent. The philosopher in the dialogue is stubborn. Far from dismissing that "faraway look" and that "dreamy voice" as incurable negativism, and without dulling them with tranquilizers, he wonders "what puzzles him about the matter,"[3]—he, the philosopher, supposed not to have any nerve.

PAUL:	You could only agree with that.

FD: With only one objection: In this text he set himself up against the notion of private experience. It became a point of contention between us. Since these recent events I was committed to protecting my private life, while he argued radically against the very idea of it. So I was not taken in by his agenda. Addressing himself directly to Constance, he wanted to lecture me as usual:

WITTGENSTEIN: You say you have an intangible impression. I am not doubting what you say. But I question whether you have said anything by it—that is, what was the point of uttering these words, in what game?[4]

His blunt tone shocked me, and I prayed to heaven that Constance didn't hear him. But she seemed armored against incongruities and she answered without swerving from her indifference: "You're asking too much of me." He insisted:

WITTGENSTEIN: Whether or not you want to, you're talking about your experience in my presence.[5]

I pressed him to leave Constance in peace, since she had said to him that her sensations could not be described. He turned his back to us and headed for the door, all the while grumbling that private experience was a degenerate construction of our grammar.[6]

WITTGENSTEIN: It's as if you were saying that your right hand can give money to your left hand,[7] or that to measure yourself you lay your hand on top of your head . . .[8]

I couldn't help retorting:

FD: So, according to you, private experience doesn't exist! And we wouldn't have the right to "lose it" without you getting mixed up in it—without you treating what we feel deep within our very selves, and unknowable for you, as a degenerate construction.

WITTGENSTEIN: There we are! You have let yourself be possessed by this grammatical monstrosity, so it seems to you I'm denying the existence of an experience. . .To deny the experience of pain![9] That means nothing, any more than denying the private experience behind the smile of an unweaned baby . . .[10]

FD (TO PAUL):   At that point, visibly at the end of his tether, he left the room. Calm returned. I apologized to Constance for this interruption, which hadn't yet seemed to disturb her. So, I asked her about the context of her successive hospitalizations, which she said she hadn't understood at all. She gave an account that was as precise and detailed as possible, but I saw it no more clearly than she did. I was preparing to end the session there, sorry about not having been sufficiently present, when, as I was getting up, I heard myself declare, like jack coming out of his box, in an absolutely peremptory tone: "Resistance is making you crazy." With these words, her cheeks began to turn pink . . .

PAUL: Miracle!

FD: I had picked up this word without thinking about it. Just to say something. It was recurring, in very diverse senses, throughout the account of each of her hospitalizations: at one point she had had to "resist" a friend's manipulations; at another, she had passed out after the failure of a "resistance" in an electrical appliance. There was also the question, when she was going to the hospital, of her having reached the end of her physical "resistance," and of encountering there strong "resistances" to psychoanalysis.

That was all for that day. After her blushing, she hastened to get up to end our interview. Although doubtful she would return, I gave her another appointment. Yet she came back the following week. Meanwhile she had officially left the hospital. The medical director had decided that she was improving. She had resumed her work, and returned home to her children. I was the one to look bewildered. She provided me with details about this "resistance," which had functioned between her and me like a "broken tool of a name." The tool of the name "resistance" had been broken for her between the Resistance her family had been involved in, and the arrest of her mother, which had never been clarified, for it was surrounded with a pious silence.

PAUL: Still, madness and war.

FD: The three-year-old Constance had been the only witness of that arrest, the only one to know that her mother had been arrested **and deported** as a Jew. The child was not told that she was dead, but that she would not be coming back. Constance concluded, therefore, that her mother could possibly return, and she waited for her, beyond hope. Besides, for her, her mother was no longer her "mommy," but rather **an unreachable** heroine, memorialized in official ceremonies. She continued to search for her among the living-dead of the hospital, with no tears, nor affect.

PAUL: So, she got out of the asylum through the magic of a single signifier.

FD:	That theory was certainly enough for me. I was almost satisfied with it when, a little afterward, I had a strange dream—one of those that persists after waking up, like a vision. In the dream I saw, with horror, one of my sons as a baby, drowned. He was in front of me, his arms outstretched, in the shallow water of a little pool inside a house. This detail struck me: the pool should have been outside. My baby was deathly pale, expressionless. I took him in my arms to give him mouth-to-mouth resuscitation; the pink color came back to his cheeks.
PAUL:	You dreamed of your patient at the age when they came to arrest her mother, and you were bringing that entire period back to life.
FD:	Yes, but that interpretation was not enough; the dream continued to worry me. To such an extent that I couldn't help consulting Wittgenstein. After all, it was his fault—bringing up the smile of the unweaned baby, in the first place. With no hard feelings, he took on a rather pedagogical tone.
WITTGENSTEIN:	Let's begin by describing the situation of that dream, without being tempted to say that you believe she has what you have, that she feels the same thing as you. In other words, without talking about her consciousness and your consciousness. The idea should not occur to you that you could only be conscious of your own consciousness.[11]
FD:	Because you imagine that I have been tempted to believe that we feel the same thing, that I was conscious of anything whatever . . . You miss the point. I was so far from thinking about feeling her pain that I almost submitted to the psychiatrist's verdict that analysis in her case was contraindicated. Besides, I'm not the one to be told that the dream depends neither on her consciousness nor on mine, but on the unconscious.
PAUL:	Your transference to Wittgenstein was in the process of shifting, like a weather-vane.
FD:	Or like milk turning sour, which was my feeling. Even so, he risked an interpretation:
WITTGENSTEIN:	Perhaps your dream made you see better what she saw.
FD:	I beg your pardon! You're not going to assume that I should know what she sees better than she does.
WITTGENSTEIN:	Yes, we can also do this. Likewise, one could very well imagine two people who would feel pain in the "same" place . . . I am not saying the same pain.
FD:	Because to be in pain in the same place is not to feel the same pain?
WITTGENSTEIN:	No. One cannot know, but one can easily point to that "same" place. It would be the case—for example, with two Siamese

brothers. In that sense, it is possible to feel pain in the body of another person. The idea of the ego inhabiting a body must be abolished.[12]

FD: Then, according to you, Otto Will's soldier would have been like a double, having pain in the same place . . . Would that baby of my dream be like a twin brother for Constance, with the same cheek turning pink, revived with the same breath?

A preposterous idea occurred to me: "That Siamese baby, could it be me?"[13] Wittgenstein didn't answer.

PAUL: I don't understand—that baby was you?

FD: . . . Because of the uncanny detail of that inside pool. Remember the confidence I had given to Otto Will in spite of myself. I was only realizing, although I always knew it, that I had been a fetus in my mother's womb/pool,* at the time of her arrest, when she was secretly crossing the demarcation line, carrying papers for the Resistance. Unlike Constance, I had indeed been obliged myself to go into prison with her into one of those crowded cells, designated each night for hostages, in case of a Resistance action against the Nazis. Each night resounded with cries of torture; each day began with the wait for an execution or for the departure in one of those trains, bound for concentration camps, that Constance's mother had taken, no more to return. In the dream, I resuscitated the unborn baby that I was, threatened with drowning in my mother's womb/pool—bearing witness—unseen, to the same atrocities, the same howling . . .

PAUL: Wittgenstein was really taking on the role of your analyst . . .

FD: Thanks to him I was beginning to understand Otto Will's teaching. Like Otto, and perhaps like Wittgenstein too, I was working on unspeakable matters in my own story. To begin this language-game, I was using words and images that pointed, in Constance's story, to that she, as a bemused or stupefied child could not name either. Such was the nod I gave her this time, to begin a language-game there where the tool of the name had been broken for each of us.

PAUL: That famous "meeting" Frieda Fromm-Reichmann talked about[14] . . . had been taking shape here while you were talking about it to Wittgenstein. Likewise, Otto's meeting with the soldier had taken shape from the moment he began a language-game with his analyst.

---

* The French word "*bassin*" means "pool," and it also means "womb."

FD: Precisely. With respect to Wittgenstein, I had become as recalcitrant as Otto had been toward Sullivan. I called him. I needed to talk to him. When he was there I wanted him to go away. I asked advice from him, and I didn't let him intervene. I decided to open myself up to a real analyst and, exchanging ghost for ghost, I planned to take the train to Vienna the next weekend. At least Freud's advice would be authorized, and I knew that ghost stories wouldn't scare him. I had visited his house in London where the accumulation of funerary statuettes around the famous couch must have evoked "the beyond," even in his day. I intended to talk to him about my breaking the rule of "benevolent neutrality," to ask for supervision on the spot, and to hear at its very source that voice which, like a basso continuo, accompanied my work. And then—who knows?—as the *Berggasse* was not, for a tourist, so far away from the *Kundmangasse*, I'd also like to wander over toward the house built by Wittgenstein for his sister Gretl, in the hope of discovering some secret there.

Chapter 17

19 Berggasse

A walk in the woods.

PAUL, FD

Vienna, Freud's house.

FD, FREUD, WITTGENSTEIN

While we were talking, we came upon a grove of young trees. Paul laid out the picnic near a spring sheltered by a very old stone vault. The place was just right for me to tell him about my trip to the country of Freud's "Manes."* "Were you intending to sway the gods above, or indeed to move the world below?"[1] he asked, while brushing aside, with the back of his hand, a black beetle, which was on its bumpy way to make a raid on our provisions. Knocked over on its back, the insect revealed an abdomen iridescent with shades of metallic blue-violet, between legs desperately flailing about. Taking pity on it, I put it back on its feet.

FD:	I had the impression of crossing the Rubicon, incurring the wrath of the father of psychoanalysis, if I approached subjects taboo to the establishment.
PAUL:	You were imagining things. The clinical treatment of the psychoses is all the rage at conferences now.
FD:	Frankly, I was preoccupied mostly with getting my bearings in that transference with Wittgenstein, which smacked of heresy. When I rang the doorbell on the second floor of Freud's house, 19 Berggasse, I was deeply moved. A woman welcomed me; she was all smiles, as if she knew me, or was perhaps expecting me . . .

---

* In ancient Rome, the *"Manes"* were the deified spirits of the dead, which were often venerated by the living through graveside sacrifices.

DOI: 10.4324/9781003437451-17

PAUL: You didn't notice that she expects everyone?

FD: It mattered little to me then. She entrusted me with a cata-
                   logue that contained commentary on what remained in the
                   apartment, which had been devastated by the Nazis. I quickly
                   walked through the waiting room—the only one furnished—to
                   enter what had been his office. On the walls, sepia photographs
                   depicted the master's couch, in life-size, surrounded by por-
                   traits of the great family of psychoanalysis. Higher up, a cast
                   of Gradiva. On the right, the room that housed the library, also
                   depicted in a photograph. I lingered on the threshold, fasci-
                   nated by those ghostly furnishings. There, the catalogue said,
                   Freud often took his patients off the couch to the next room,
                   in order to show them parts of theory he was elaborating with
                   them, with the help of the archeological relics on the shelves.

I resumed walking, stopping for a moment in front of a little photograph of the
portrait, by Klimt, of Margaret Stoneborough, one of Wittgenstein's sisters, nicknamed Gretl. She had been Freud's patient and his interpreter for her brother. Then
heading toward the exit, I hesitated for a moment. Looking furtively around to
see if anyone saw me, I sat down in one of the chairs in the waiting room, hoping
to remain unnoticed. On the table next to me were Freud's tarot cards, similar to
those my grandmother also liked to play with. The muffled and thoughtful hub-
bub of psychoanalytic pilgrims coming and going gradually died down. To keep
my composure, I took Freud's "Gradiva" out of my bag, and also his "Negation,"
which I had brought along for the trip. A few minutes later, I was inadvertently in
full conversation with their author.

FD (TO FREUD): Wittgenstein tells me that madness is a matter of grammar;
                what do you think? You yourself say that it poses problems of
                negation, first in its fierce denial of itself as a problem, then
                in its systematic attempts to ruin all therapeutic efforts in its
                regard. It seems to me that it also raises questions about the
                sequence of tenses. The famous "negativism of some psychot-
                ics," which you describe on that page that I have in front of
                me,[2] perhaps doesn't represent only the vestige of a pathologi-
                cal regression to early stages. On the contrary, what if it was
                necessary for a creative functioning in the present time of what
                you call "the genesis of judgment," for those who were pre-
                vented from exercising their judgment? In a word, aren't you
                confusing an archeological site with a construction site?

Look where your passion for archeology has led us! Because of it, it has become
impossible to conclude anything about the treatment of psychosis, for we strain to
analyze psychotics as remnants of a bygone time. We dig them up from so-called

archaic periods, and then we regard them with respect due to old monuments. A "super-delirium," as described by old timers, or a fine psychotic structure—a superb foreclosure of the Name-of-the-Father, on some patri- or matri-linear line. That anteriority of origins leads to a dead end!

PAUL: You forget that Winnicott tried to theorize the function of time in another way, in his last article, "Fear of Breakdown," written just before he died. He talked there of an unconscious that was not that of repression.[3]

FD: Freud told me he had anticipated that discovery.

FREUD: Re-read my "Gradiva." I myself wrote that everything that is repressed is unconscious, but that we cannot assert that everything unconscious is repressed.[4]

FD: So this unrepressed unconscious would no more know time than the repressed unconscious does. But since it's not repressed, it is not related to the past, and would produce **timeless** effects in the present. You referred to it, moreover, with respect to traumatic dreams. Those dreams repeat a catastrophe in the present, which happened in the past, but has never been inscribed as past. It has, therefore, to be conjugated in the present tense, as if nothing of the past had occurred. That's why, in such a case, an analytic interpretation referred to the past can't work—for it must be applied here and now, between the present interlocutors. You have indeed indicated that the way out of this sort of repetition is to play it out the way children do.

Wouldn't that be the purpose of negativism? To try to play out a catastrophe in the present, first by showing it, then by naming it and clearing it away, while inscribing it in a language-game that can from then on be conjugated in the past? Impossible, as an analyst, to stay on the sidelines. That's really where it gets difficult, for we have become quite guarded since the time when you were doing your own analysis with your patients . . .

The fact remains that in the absence of analysts ready for this game, the famous negativists must unravel it all by themselves, by provoking catastrophe upon catastrophe in reality, for want of a witness. Sometimes they take themselves for the famous wooden reel, and end up by throwing it away.

There's the problem: how to make use of one's judgment all alone, about phenomena that in the first place have been taken away from judgment? In the *fort-da* game, imagine that not only is the mother not returning, but also that the string breaks—the string of the wooden reel, that is, the string of names. I mean that no one is able to speak about the mother's disappearance. Imagine that the grandfather in your story were also absent himself, unable to pay even the least attention to his grandson. Do you still say that the child will have perceived nothing at all of this disappearance? Will he not still have registered it, passively?

FREUD: Perception is not a purely passive phenomenon, indeed on the contrary. It was also one of Mach's ideas. The ego periodically sends out small amounts of cathexis into the perceptual system by means of which it samples the external stimuli, and then after every such tentative advance it draws back again.[5] The aim is to introject into itself everything that is good and to eject from itself everything that is bad . . . In order to understand this step forward we must recollect that all representations originate from perception and are repetitions of them. Thus originally the mere existence of a representation is a guarantee of the reality of what is represented.[6]

FD: But what happens when that guarantee blows up, when nothing vouches for the first perceptions? What becomes of those perceptions disconnected from the presentations, to which they should be linked?

FREUD: Well, the first and immediate aim of the reality-testing is, not to find an object in real perception that corresponds to the one presented, but to re-find such an object, to convince oneself that it is still there.[7]

FD: You're not hearing me. How can one re-find that object when no presentation attests that it has indeed been perceived? An impression remains but without any support to tie it to. When there's no one to recognize the cry or the smile, you know well that that smile ends by freezing up, that even the crying is silenced, and that babies become too nice, too quiet, too good at not being able to trust what they have felt . . .

It seems to me that our patients complain less of traumas than of the illogicality in which they have spent their childhoods. As if essential information had been concealed from them, in their so-called interest: "Indeed, it's not serious;" "You're imagining it;" "You're too little;" "You don't understand." Don't understand what? Death, betrayal, social decline, dishonor, shame, evil? And if what's horrible isn't serious, then everything at every moment becomes horrible. In that context, we understand that time and judgment are hanging on that unlikely perception. Hence the perplexity. Impossible to settle whether it's good or bad. In fact, the worst has happened. Doubt about its very existence has taken hold. Has it only been a dream? And if it's only a dream, why does it come back, over and over, in the present as reality?

FREUD: In the beginning the antithesis between subjective and objective does not exist, any more than that between inner and outer.[8] For that we have to wait for the creation of the symbol of negation.[9]

FD: So, it's impossible for the analyst to stay outside such an experience . . . And this beginning you're talking about would not be in chronological time, but in logical time marking the beginning of the function of judgment. Therefore, that beginning can happen at every moment . . .

Sometimes I tell myself that the craziest among us are also the most Cartesian, and that madness is an enterprise of rationality. Negativism is primarily used as a means to produce a tabula rasa, wiping out all certitudes. Then the time comes when it's necessary to show what indeed has been registered even while we have been unable to talk about it; and finally the time for establishing, with some other, the objectivity of those dodged perceptions, while verifying that they can be shared in a common language.

What do you think? I call those non-repressed dodgings of the truth "cut-out impressions," and this verification device for authenticating those impressions in a language, I call "psychotic transference." We analysts are tempted to slip away from it, and we should be excused for that. Who would willingly want to be confronted with those unnamable things? Yet, that's what we've been paid for. Like the citizens in Athens—those too broke to attend the famous tragedies—who were paid to see on stage the unleashing of fate.

I had noticed for some time that Paul's eyes were beginning to close. Now his eyelids were shut and he was sleeping the sleep of the just. However, I didn't care. I continued my conversation in thought with Freud. It had been such a long time since "I had a conversation with him,"—which is what Descartes said about reading.* I stretched out flat on my stomach near the spring, in the hope of surprising some of its denizens. After an instant, I could distinguish through the bluish water some miniature dinosaurs, tritons or salamanders moving around slowly in the mud on the bottom. I too had been slowly taking a lot of time in Vienna to broach the real subject that had brought me to Freud's apartment. I had preferred to wander prudently about on theoretical ground before jumping and suddenly asking him:

FD: And what happens when shapes appear—uncanny, spooky shapes?

FREUD: Like a double? Don't bother; it happened also to Mach, and even to me . . . I wondered then whether this kind of phenomenon was related to repression.

---

* Cf. René Descartes, *Discourse on Method*, Translated by Lawrence J. Lafleur (New York: Bobbs Merrill Company, Inc., 1956), 4.

FD: But there again, I have indeed thought to employ that term beyond the limits that one can legitimately assign to it. It would be more correct, for all these phenomena—spirits or demons—to talk of the return of animistic convictions which among civilized men have not really been surmounted. I analyze precisely that experience in "The Uncanny."[10]

FD: Exactly, but I seem to be a vivid application of your text. You have heard, I believe, of Ludwig Wittgenstein . . . Would you be surprised by my telling you that he appears to me each time I converse in my private language? In order to turn it into a public matter, so to speak, I would like to resume the habit of talking to myself without anyone meddling. But he never misses an occasion to drum into me that's it's a monstrosity. Perhaps he's pursuing an aim on the sly . . .

I suddenly stopped my complaining as I noticed Wittgenstein's silhouette among the group of visitors, and I tried to look natural:

FD (TO WITTGENSTEIN):   Were you there? I didn't see you this morning at the house that bears your name. Besides I found it closed. Did you also dawdle at the door, or pass through the wall, as usual?

Without looking at me, he shuffled the pack of tarot cards while muttering something about private language being like playing patience by oneself,[11] and then he headed toward the door, saying that he could not tolerate staying another minute in that city. I followed him to the railroad station. When the train set out, I saw his face cloud over and melancholy overtake him, as they say it did each time he returned to **Vienna**. *What could I do about it? I hadn't asked him to take the trip with me. So I immersed myself in "Gradiva," and acted as if he weren't there. When I looked up, we were crossing the Salzkammergut Mountains. I remembered that one day, on vacation at his uncle's house in Hallein, Wittgenstein had gone into those mountains with the intention of killing himself. I felt his gaze heavy on me. What was he thinking about among those pastures, those chalets? Did he want to read over my shoulder, or into my thoughts? Little by little, I was overcome with torpor. On coming out of the Arlberg tunnel, he asked me a funny question:*

WITTGENSTEIN: Now then, do you still believe that another person can't have my pains?[12]

I was far from suspecting that one day, by letting myself be intrigued by his pain, I would feel its effects in his place, and so I pretended to fall asleep again. He answered the question himself:

WITTGENSTEIN: When we meet another who feels nothing, we can feel his pains in his place, exactly in the same place, without knowing anymore whether it is we or the other who is the subject of that pain. But according to you—what about the language that describes these experiences?

I answered that it was a private language we all made use of, more or less. He replied dryly that if we all made use of it, such a language could not be private.[13] I nodded in agreement, for the sake of peace, and I made a decision that I would drag him along the next day to the asylum where I was working, in order to see if he could still maintain that idea in front of those specialists in private language who are confined there.

Chapter 18

Ready-Mades

A walk in the woods.

PAUL, FD

The psychiatric hospital.

FD, WITTGENSTEIN, MADAME DURAND,
NURSE, MEDICAL
DIRECTOR, INTERN, ANSELM

We spent the afternoon going all around the grove, trimming young wild cherry trees and cutting down some birches that dominated the weakest ones. That part of the woods was very sunny. As we made our way along, without hurrying, Paul recounted a dream he had had during his nap. In the dream, he had returned to the psychiatric hospital where he had been an intern, and a patient had thrown her arms around his neck to hug him. He remembered this woman very well, a "chronic" patient with whom he had worked, aiming toward her discharge. Then he had left and he had always regretted not knowing what had become of her. Curiously, Paul awoke nostalgic for the psychiatric hospital—or rather, for the patients he had left there. He wanted to hear about my experience of that place.

FD: During our trip back home I got the idea of taking Wittgenstein with me to visit what today we call, with political correctness, a "Specialized Hospital Center." He raised no objection, for he wanted to get to know my ward.

PAUL: No kidding. Did you intend to leave him there?

FD: Who knows? At times, I wished to argue with him; at other times, to get rid of him; and when he was there, I couldn't help arguing. As we crossed the hospital grounds, I challenged his denial of the existence of private languages, especially in that place. But he refused to let go of it:

DOI: 10.4324/9781003437451-18

WITTGENSTEIN:	What would it be like if human beings showed no outward signs of pain (did not groan, grimace, etc.)?[1] Suppose there's a child among them.
FD:	Let's suppose there is.
WITTGENSTEIN:	He would have only sensations, but no natural expression for his sensations.[2] You agree that it would be impossible to teach him, for example, the use of the word "toothache." Good, let's suppose that the child is a genius, and himself invents a name for his sensation![3]
FD:	The hospital is full of ex-geniuses of that kind.
WITTGENSTEIN:	But then, of course, he couldn't make himself understood when he used the word.[4]
FD:	Probably not.
WITTGENSTEIN:	So does that child understand the name without being able to explain its meaning to anyone? What does it mean to say that he has 'named his pain'?[5]
FD:	Well, you will soon meet people who, like that child, are in pain, but unable to explain it to anyone. Still, they name their pain with words understandable only to themselves.
WITTGENSTEIN:	Be that as it may, what is their purpose? You seem to forget that a great deal of stage-setting in the language is presupposed if the mere act of naming is to make sense.[6]
FD:	If you like stage-settings, you're going to get some!

While opening the door to the ward, I noticed Madame Durand seated with a nurse, in the entrance-area that was used as a waiting room for the medical director. I had worked with her for a long time in the ward where she had been placed among the chronic patients. Then she had left and had stayed outside for several years. I was not aware of the state she was in when she returned, and I was expecting some theatrical improvisation, which was customary for her. But she remained motionless, visibly anxious about being received by the doctor. I told her of my surprise at finding her there, since she hadn't been seeing me at the clinic for some time.

MADAME DURAND:	That sensation is coming back. FD: Which sensation?
MADAME DURAND:	Telepathy. They connect with me every night; it's diabolical. They make me work. Tonight, I had to restore a woman's bone marrow to health. They wanted me to hold a cancer for someone else. I refused. It's exploitation; I can't do it anymore. Put yourself in my place. They are going too far . . . How do you expect me to get rest? The operator ordering me was all worked up, behaving like a madman. And still, I'm used to it. What torments me most is that now they want to take my grandson, and make him work on the same things.

FD:	Are you sure it's the same thing?
MADAME DURAND:	I'm telling you. My grandson will be taken like me. In the public park, he made another little boy fall off the slide; he threw sand in his eyes. It couldn't have come from him. He's been pulled into psychiatry. The whole family's been carried off. I told you about it. Even my daughters . . .
NURSE:	You're saying that because you haven't raised boys. They're devils. They love fighting. You can't get a little upset without seeing loony bins everywhere.

Wittgenstein was following this conversation with unconcealed interest. Madame Durand pointed to him.

MADAME DURAND:	And how do you know that they're not talking to him in his head too?
WITTGENSTEIN:	I also happened to notice the recurrence of a sensation that intrigued me as odd. On the days I had the sensation, I therefore wrote the sign S, for sensation, in my diary. The only problem was that I couldn't formulate any definition for that sign . . .[7]
MADAME DURAND:	But I can always define this "telepathy" to myself. It comes from a machine I'm connected to. At the other end, an operator sends me work to do, depending on his needs.
WITTGENSTEIN:	After all, you are giving this definition to us—not only to yourself. But let's say you are giving that ostensive definition to yourself. How do you proceed? Can you point to that sensation? Do you concentrate your attention on that sensation, and so, as it were, point to it inwardly?[8]
MADAME DURAND:	You're splitting hairs! When that sensation occurs, I know it won't be long before they're talking to me in my head. That's telepathy. I make a link. I impress on myself the connection between telepathy and that sensation.
WITTGENSTEIN:	But what does that mean: "I impress on myself?"[9]
MADAME DURAND:	It means that it's recorded and that I'll remember it for the next time. At least, it makes sense for me . . .

Turning toward me, she said "Your friend is quite complicated." Madame Durand was just delivering this diagnosis when the medical director appeared and invited us to come into his office. In the presence of some staff, he was greeting new patients, who were present. He began with a question:

MEDICAL DIRECTOR:	Well, Madame Durand, what is happening?
MADAME DURAND:	I'm waiting for relief from duty.

MEDICAL DIRECTOR: Relief? What relief?

MADAME DURAND: Well, even the dead get relieved.* I want to be relieved of my functions.

MEDICAL DIRECTOR: Could you explain yourself?

MADAME DURAND: First, I insist on being given my psychiatrist's diploma. I've waited too long for it, while holding the illnesses of others forever . . . Don't take it personally, but the medical director before you loaded me down with his whole family. Obviously, they all weighed so much on him, poor man. His mother was so burdensome. Do you understand? Now I have them all on my hands. Look, tonight, as I was saying a little while ago, I held leukemias. Still, I'm lucky. It's been ages since they've given me any mental illnesses.

MEDICAL DIRECTOR: Madame Durand, you see very well that you're talking nonsense. You've never studied psychiatry.

MADAME DURAND: And when I've been hospitalized, not only here with you, but before you, and even before before-you, how many interns have I helped to do their theses? And all that, without the least little thanks. Do you think that's normal? So, I am wasting my time, waiting. Mind you, I am dealing with eternity. I don't mind waiting. It's not a big deal.

MEDICAL DIRECTOR: Eternity? My gosh! Come; tell us— how old are you?

MADAME DURAND: Five hundred years old.

MEDICAL DIRECTOR: Look, you see you're exaggerating.

MADAME DURAND: When each second can last several centuries, I'm more than five hundred years old by now.

MEDICAL DIRECTOR: Well, you're in great shape. You'll be able to go home soon.

Turning toward the head nurse, he asked her to make preparations for Madame Durand's discharge. There was nothing more for her to do here. When she had left, he asked us all what we thought.

FD: You haven't given her diploma in psychiatry.

MEDICAL DIRECTOR: But she can live very well on the outside with her delusion.

FD: One can look at it as a delusion. On the other hand, she's not mistaken in making a claim on that therapist's diploma.

---

* A pun on the French verb "*relever*," which means "to relieve," or "toget up," but it also refers to the practice of removing the dead from their original coffins after a period of time, and relocating them to smaller caskets, to be buried again in the same place.

MEDICAL DIRECTOR: Congratulations! You too are joining in her delusion.

FD: It took me time to join her. Do you remember the time when she imagined herself to be Pétain's granddaughter?

A NURSE: She had baptized a white-haired gentleman "Pétain." He didn't stay very long. She said he was there secretly, and that they had clandestine conversations, which shouldn't be known . . . She talked about that underhanded proceeding with us for quite a while.

FD: That's how she approached me when I came to the ward. I played her game.

MEDICAL DIRECTOR: She even complained to me that you were pushing her into a delusion.

FD: In fact, in listening to her, I was acting "as if" I believed in it. One day, she greeted me furiously: "That story about Pétain is false, totally false. You made me believe it." It was all my fault. Moreover, she pointed out that I was not a psychiatrist, and that I did not have her experience.

I was forced to admit that she was not entirely mistaken. I had indulged in these stories for the sake of talking with her. I loved her corrosive sense of humor and her implacable logic. I also acknowledged that she had more experience than I had in the hospital, and with different therapies. She looked at me doubtfully and left the room without saying a word. I thought that was the end of our meetings. I felt so little like an analyst with her, and she was so much of a psychiatrist . . .

MEDICAL DIRECTOR: But what does being an analyst with her amount to, exactly?

FD: I was about to find out. The following week, to my surprise, she showed up for an appointment. Little by little, she told me a story that was strange and common at the same time, of a hospital during the war, in Normandy, near the beaches of D-Day, where the boats were unloading. Her mother, a lace maker, was there, dying of tuberculosis. The hospital was full of wounded soldiers. She knew every nook and cranny of it, for it was home for her: the orphanage, where the children of the dying woman were committed, was housed in the same building. Although a few steps from their mother, they were not allowed to pay her a visit, for fear of contagion. The wounded were pouring in, and she was still there, oscillating between long periods of boredom and spending time caring for the sick. When some nurse had used her as a helper for the wounded, she didn't mind seeing so many people suffering—and, even if she did . . . At the mention of that—40 years after—her eyes filled up with tears.

Not that she had felt nothing. Far from it. But as she was unable to decide between her pain and that of others, she had forged a language for herself in the way children do. And in her total loneliness among so many people, this language had been so vital to her that she never renounced it.

NURSE: Everyone here is accustomed to listening to her delusions. We usually smile: yes, yes, you're right . . . She tosses out her expressions with such conviction that we're almost forced to agree with them.

WITTGENSTEIN: It's a case of abrogation of the normal language concerning the expression of a sensation—from which arises the illusion of a private language, including hers.

PAUL: Wasn't anyone stunned by the presence of your host?

FD: He himself had been a dispensary porter at St. Guy's Hospital in London during the Second World War, and he was behaving totally naturally there. Besides, I was in the habit of occasionally bringing some foreign analysts into the ward. He continued:

WITTGENSTEIN: But the rules of that private language-game—are they really rules, or indeed do you act "as if" they were rules, without anyhow sharing them? The balance on which impressions are weighed is not the impression of a balance . . .[10]

FD: There lies the whole problem: between playing *a* game of pretending, and playing *the* game, implying that one has a stake in it. Without this preliminary agreement, this "we" that's the basis for a shared reality, nothing can begin. In so far as I seemed to stick to her private language, nothing happened. Until I noticed that Madame Durand's telepathy and the whole setting of nocturnal care meant taking care of me.

WITTGENSTEIN: Therefore, the monstrosity was neither her bizarre sensation nor her errors, but indeed the grammar that aimed at confining them in a private language.

FD: I don't know whether I changed grammar once and for all, but it is a fact, "the telepathic effect" started one day to function between us, while becoming curiously intertwined with an element of my own private life. Here was that "intertwining of irrational and unthought first elements that comprise reason," which Socrates talked about with the young Theatetus.[11]

MEDICAL DIRECTOR: What are you alluding to? Frankly you're becoming impenetrable. Remember you're not among analysts here.

FD: First I have to tell you how that odd telepathy took us to such a critical threshold that the analytic work almost stopped. One day, during one of our more and more absurd appointments, despite the apathy into which I found myself sinking, I noticed that her machine was taking my place. I was becoming that diabolical being relentlessly exploiting her therapeutic powers, for which she was not paid. I was now giving her my illnesses to hold.

That day, her features were drawn, her face weary, her body worn out. She complained that her stomach was swollen. Since I was of no use to her, she again gave me a holiday. As I wasn't budging, she added: "That's enough of that! It's a shame to make me work so much. What's the use of talking to you? Now it's my daughters' turn. I saw them on Sunday. They look ghastly. We're all on a tightrope. They suit your own pleasure. You've begun to burden them too. At their age! If that's not appalling! You're insatiable; you need young women. The work I do for you is not enough then . . . I held old people all night . . . "

In the face of such an assault, I remained dazed. In my defense, I had just lost my grandmother after a long hospitalization. I had gone regularly, each weekend, to her province to see her, except that one weekend when she had chosen to pass away. So, the words "hold old people" rang out as if they had suddenly found their stage-setting in the hollowness of the empty space my grandmother had left behind.

WITTGENSTEIN: . . . and the post where that expression is stationed.

FD: That post signaled the entrance into the field "between two deaths," where both of us had found ourselves so close to, and so far away from, a loved one dying. While pondering whether I should disclose this coincidence, I asked her a question, which at the moment appeared to be surrealistic: Could it be that for weeks Madame Durand had, so to speak, borne this burden of holding my old grandmother?

MEDICAL DIRECTOR: Good gracious! You believed it?

FD: Madame Durand was discharged from the hospital without my knowledge (Just after that application of her private language to my case) only to return here today, several years later.

Well, what had I done other than confirm her own words, by stating that she had guessed exactly, and correctly named, that holding of the old? But at that time I could not acknowledge that it had been such a heavy burden for me. I had, however, verified that her imaginary machine, that impression of a machine, was a very real one meant for measuring cutout impressions. Similar to an extremely sensitive reading head, it had been able to record unidentified variations at my place—a potential difference, a potential drop in tension. Simply for lack of interest in jointly decoding her recordings, Madame Durand's machine always ended by losing contact and panicking.

WITTGENSTEIN: All that pertains to a particular language-game that asks only to be described. Take the apparently privately used word "telepathy." Is it to be assumed that you invent the technique for using the word, or that you found it ready-made?[12]

INTERN: Ready-Made . . . Are you alluding to Marcel Duchamp and his bicycle wheel, which he fixed one day on a kitchen stool, for the sole purpose of seeing it turn?[13]

WITTGENSTEIN: That wheel that can be turned though nothing else moves with it is not part of any mechanism.[14]

INTERN: Duchamp described those "ready-mades" under a special rubric of "The Conditions of the Language: The Search for Prime Words Divisible only by Themselves and by One." It was the very question, I think, that was raised in Plato's *Theaetetus*. Duchamp talks of it as a meeting, in a state of visual indifference, of complete anesthesia, of total absence of good and bad taste. What counts for him is the meeting, created by a "particular time-process." But all the same, if we had to lose our grandmothers each time we want to discharge a sick person from the hospital with the idea that she's not delusional . . .

WITTGENSTEIN: What strikes you is that there seem to be a few useful applications of the idea of the other person's having pain without knowing it, and a vast number of useless applications, applications which look as though they were no applications at all.[15]

Suppose I say: I see blood, unaccountably sometimes one sometimes another color, and the people around me make different statements. But couldn't I in all this chaos retain my meaning of 'red,' although I couldn't now make myself understood to anyone? "Now am I mad or did I really call this 'red' yesterday?[16]

MEDICAL DIRECTOR: Frankly, you could ask that; however, I'm afraid . . .

WITTGENSTEIN: That you ought to hospitalize me on your ward . . . Your psychoanalyst has had that idea at the back of her mind since this morning. I'm beginning to feel superfluous in this world. That's the old sensation that comes back . . . that

I'm good for nothing; that I don't have the right to live.[17] How many times I've wondered whether I'm going mad . . . The atmosphere surrounding this problem is terrible. Dense mists of our language are situated about this crucial point. It is almost impossible to get through it . . . [18]

The medical director turned to me: "Your German colleague looks exhausted to me. You should help him get a little rest . . . "

Paul stopped to take a swig of water and gave me the flask. After walking about for some time among the rows of trees, he let himself fall on the grass of the path that runs alongside the grove. That story brought up a memory that had taken his breath away:

PAUL:	At that time I was an assistant director, and I held meetings with the staff in my office—similar to the meeting you just mentioned. One day, we were interrupted by shouts of a voice at the door. It was the voice of ANSELM, a longtime patient in the ward. "Let me in," he cried, "I have to see the doctor. It's extremely urgent." Breaking through a barrier of nurses, who told him I was very busy, he entered the room, moved by one of those uncanny "time-processes" so frequent in psychiatric institutions. Just like Donald at Austen Riggs Center, such patients, though kept out of those meetings, seem irresistibly pushed to meddle in what's concocted outside of their presence. "And what's so urgent?" I asked ANSELM.
ANSELM:	That I'm pregnant.
PAUL:	Come on! You're talking nonsense. Look at yourself; you're as skinny as a rail.

Walking around the room, ANSELM threw out his flat stomach and arched his slim silhouette in full view of those present, so that all could take note of that absent pregnancy. To this exhibition, I insisted:

PAUL:	Look, that's crazy. First of all, you're not a woman (*une femme*).
ANSELM:	How do you know? You're really infamous (*infame*)!*

---

* In French there is a pun being played out, based on the similar sounds of "*infame*" (infamous) and "*une femme*" (a woman).

And he left, eyeing us scornfully, without waiting for a response. I asked around to see whether anyone had an idea about that pregnancy. Some were empathic, claiming he was anxious. Others were blasé and claimed that he must be suffering from a nervous pregnancy. At that point, a young nurse trainee spoke up to recall a simple fact. The psychiatrist in charge of ANSELM *was expecting a child and, having to take an unexpected leave at the beginning of the week, she had neglected to inform him of her pregnancy. It was clear that* ANSELM *had shown us the information which his psychiatrist had considered it her duty to omit. An impression of pregnancy had been disconnected from the mechanism of language, and he had to point out to all of us, ostensively, the presentation corresponding to that cut-out impression.*

Chapter 19

The Philosopher Comes Back

A walk in the woods.

Paul, FD

The clinic.

THE INTERN—FAN OF DUCHAMPS, MADAME DURAND'S **VISITING NURSE** SOCIAL WORKER WITTGENSTEIN, FD

The analyst's office

FD, THE PHILOSOPHER, WITTGENSTEIN

PAUL:	I'm really stunned that your medical director wasn't more intrigued by Wittgenstein's tone.
FD:	I was as puzzled as you. But that day, while leaving the hospital, I wasn't interested anymore in all that. My fascination had disappeared. For no apparent reason, I was feeling indifferent.
	On arriving at the clinic, I heard roars of laughter. The team was commenting on the morning's events.
MADAME DURAND'S VISITING NURSE:	Speaking of "ready-made," do you know about the lawnmower patented in England? The scene is set in a doctor's office.
MR. MURPHY:	I don't understand, doctor. My wife thinks she's a lawnmower.

DOI: 10.4324/9781003437451-19

DOCTOR:

A lawnmower? Send her to me, Mr. Murphy. I'm sure I can help her.

MR. MURPHY:

But without her, how am I going to mow my lawn?

Wittgenstein was quick to laugh:

WITTGENSTEIN:

You said it! "I don't choose the mouth that says I have a toothache." Along the same line, one day I thought of a rose with teeth in the mouth of a cow that was grazing.[1]

THE INTERN—FAN OF DUCHAMP:

Better yet, a patient recently told me about pipes that have mouths and ears.

NURSE:

Organ pipes?

INTERN:

Much more commonplace—plumbing pipes. By the way, Duchamp advertised them as "singing ready-mades": "Among our lazy pieces of hardware, we recommend a faucet that stops running when nobody is listening to it."[2] This young woman was telling me the other day that she wanted to talk to me about a phenomenon that hadn't occurred in a good while. The pipes in her bathroom and in her kitchen used to modulate their sounds in response to her worries. They quieted down when she no longer paid attention to them. This happened especially when she was a bit out of sorts. "You really can't claim," she said, "that the noises in my pipes are the fruit of my imagination . . ." Indeed, why would I have questioned her precious appointment with her pipes, the only things able to respond to her in those moments when she was feeling out of sorts? What do you think of it? Should we assume that her pipes are ventriloquists, or, that someone at the other end is sending her Morse code,

	as prisoners do, in order to talk to each other? Should I play her game, pretending it's true?
WITTGENSTEIN:	That would be like buying several copies of the morning paper in order to assure yourself that what it says is true,[3] or like moving the hands on your clock to the position that strikes you as right—to pretend that it's on time.[4]
INTERN:	What are you suggesting?
SOCIAL WORKER:	Perhaps she's just pipe-dreaming. You needn't think she's loony. Pipe-tuning has illustrious predecessors. Proust, for example, used that piece of plumbing in *Time Regained.* Some time after the First World War, he went to a musical evening at the home of the Prince de Guermantes. While in the library, where he had to wait for the end of a musical piece played in the lounge, a shrill sound of water running through a pipe transported him for a fraction of a second into another time that he called "a piece of time in its pure state."[5] There he got the idea for his search. He wasn't locked up for that.
INTERN:	Not everyone has Proust's intimacy with plumbing. For sure, if that young woman spreads the news about the pipes to people on her floor, as she has when she's been fidgeting—saying that a mysterious correspondent is speaking to her through the pipes, somebody confined, like her, in the prison of life—her neighbors will call the police right away . . .
WITTGENSTEIN:	Once again, if you don't manage to connect those noises to your listening, and through your listening, to what she is saying to you, then here's the trouble: it's as if she had turned a knob as though it could be used to turn on

some part of a machine; but, in fact, it was a mere ornament, not connected with the mechanism at all.[6]

At that moment, one of my patients popped in, and we went into my office without hearing any more. By the time I left, the secretary's office had calmed down. Without rushing, I took the bus to go home where another patient was waiting for me. I already mentioned him to you. He's the Philosopher who had introduced me to Wittgenstein. He had come back for some weeks, just to verify whether I had made any progress. But on that particular day, I was dragging my feet going to the session. Wittgenstein's remark wouldn't stop going around in my head. All those mechanisms of his—with their connections, and their disconnections—were connecting me to some other, bull-shitting machine.

PAUL:	Madame Durand's?
FD:	Another one, more concrete. I mean a sophisticated antenna disrupted by interferences, which the Bell Company engineers thought had to be cleaned. They imagined it polluted by bird shit. Until the point when, taking it seriously at last, through a series of delicate measures, they discovered at the other end, no extraterrestrial coming to communicate, but a signal they called "fossil radiation." Those researchers received the Nobel Prize.
PAUL:	They deserved it. What's the problem?
FD:	That without going so far as the Nobel Prize, no recognition of any sort, but rather a most shameful degradation confirms the recording with a delusion of persistent noises, bearing witness to a fossil phenomenon evading the degradation of time.

Daydreaming, I remembered the Philosopher as I was approaching the house. Since his return, he insisted that he heard a static interference that he had never been able to quiet. The number 14 was unexpectedly popping up in his face. So he had come back again, to clear up this mystery, after having dropped me, as he said, like an old doll.

PAUL:	In the *fort-da* game, he had thrown you overboard . . .
FD:	This time, obviously, he had been able to get rid of my fake wooden reel, and to bring it back. But what element of language stood, in his case, for "*fort*"? However, by dawdling, I made myself late. He was already there waiting for me.
THE PHILOSOPHER:	There you are at last! You analysts have it easy. Sitting, daydreaming all day long! That's not work, compared to

psychiatrists. They at least bother a great deal; they militate in favor of reality. The stubborn number 14, a real shibboleth, continues to haunt me. I meet it everywhere. Again this morning, since the metro didn't come, I took bus number 94, (in French Ninety fourteen),* in order to get to the XIVth district and your address. My neighbor in the bus was reading a book on the War of 1914, and you were late by 14 minutes exactly. You're going to wonder once again if I'm going crazy . . .

FD: No more and no less than Freud . . .

THE PHILOSOPHER: Hm . . . The famous letter to Jung, I know. Freud was sure that he would die between 61 and 62 years of age, and he tried to calculate his way out of that fateful day.[7] So much the better for him. Still, I've heard that an American psychiatrist, playing the same game, didn't have that kind of luck.

FD: Boy! You've heard about Harry Stack Sullivan? When he was in his thirties, he had indeed imagined the case of a man who would die of a ruptured aneurysm at 55 years old. Eventually, the number caught up with him: he died at the hotel Ritz in Paris, in 1949, at the age he had foreseen.[8]

THE PHILOSOPHER: It wasn't only Freud or Sullivan who were nuts. Take a little look at yourself. For a week, I've been thinking that you've fallen into a routine, that you're getting old and lackadaisical. I blame you for it. So here I am, as a result, prevented from writing and creating. Don't you find this a strange coincidence? Here we are. This session will be a short one. I'm expecting an answer next time.

Lackadaisical! He found me lackadaisical! I was offended and tried unsuccessfully to interpret this projection in terms of his past: his mother had died when he was a child, on Bastille Day, July 14th. A year earlier, when he had seen her waiting for him at the exit of the school, she had looked exhausted and old. He had been ashamed in front of his buddies, and ashamed of his shame. And then he was wondering what, during the 1914 war, had happened to the contacts that the family had traditionally maintained in Germany.

PAUL: Did you tell him about your interpretations?

FD: I didn't have time to. The following week, waiting for him, I was thinking about everything but his session.

---

* In French, 94 is *quatre-vingt quatorze*, which translates literally asfour-twenty fourteen.

I was in particularly good shape, having just discovered the reasons for my levity, as well as for the torpor that had preceded it. An important date had recently passed—the day on which I had been scheduled to have a second operation, in case of a recurrence. This scheduling had been done a year in advance, and—although the doctor had, in the meantime, reassured me—that fateful day, mechanically programmed, had continued to haunt me unwittingly, as a danger from which I had just escaped.

The Philosopher, however, arrived at that moment, and greeted me with a resounding "How are you today?" Which was quite uncanny of him. I answered him in the same tone: "Very well, thank you," as if we were filming a cliché scene about a handshake, subtitled: "How-are-you-very-well, thank you." The appointment, the timing, the absence of affect: all were there. That resounding "ready-made" resulted in my remembering at once my bad move of the previous week. Right away I connected his greeting to his concern about my health during the last session.

FD: It's indeed possible that I've gone through a strange and probably lackadaisical state, without actually realizing it. This week, I was probably worried about the possibility of an operation I had been tentatively scheduled for. I was in that bizarre state where one could await a possibly fatal outcome, without feeling the least anxiety. I would perhaps never have realized it without your offensive remark.

THE PHILOSOPHER: You understand now what I've told you over and over. This really kills me. At home, contrary to what you and other psychoanalysts relish, there hadn't been any drama. Only this stupor and this absence of anxiety—for I was not supposed to know about my mother's disease and its fateful outcome. But there was also this lack of energy that I've experienced since my childhood, before and after my mother's death.

PAUL: So, "lackadaisical" had taken the place of "*fort.*"

FD: I realized only then his loneliness, as a child, waiting for that fateful day—a wait bathed in the love his mother had for him, a love without a wrinkle, aside from those that an unspeakable weariness was drawing on her features. My strange fatigue and his strange invalid-state had combined to create for him an image of a sick woman who had set herself up in my place as a living tableau of the months that preceded her death. Then, after he had been able to talk to her and blame her for having dropped him, she very softly left the stage of our session in order to go back to the past.

Meanwhile, Wittgenstein had arrived. The Philosopher, aware of Wittgenstein's objections to psychoanalysis, soon made him a witness to what had just happened. They seemed delighted to meet each other again, and they mocked my penchant for dramatization.

FD: Laugh all you want. All the same, I just gave my voice to a pain that wasn't felt.

For Wittgenstein, that was obvious:

WITTGENSTEIN: Pain-behavior may point to a painful place—but the subject of the pain is the person who gives it expression.[9]

At that moment, something got triggered on my side. I wanted to ask Wittgenstein if that famous subject was brought about by that strange identification—the one mentioned by Frieda Fromm-Reichmann—through which the analyst can understand the patient and his emotional reactions without becoming involved in them.[10] But nothing came out of my mouth, as if the flow of words had dried up. A shell of indifference enveloped me. I looked at the two accomplices, wondering what I was doing there. Wittgenstein spoke up:

WITTGENSTEIN: I turn to stone and my pain goes on.[11] Well, how do I know, if I shut my eyes, whether I have not turned into a stone? And if that has happened, in what sense will the stone have the pains? In what sense will they be ascribable to the stone?[12]

But I'm not suffering, I thought, not giving a damn about his comments. Only the string had broken and the spell had ended.

With a clinical glance at my condition, Wittgenstein began a story that he said he got from Sullivan. He wanted to tell it to the Philosopher, for it concerned catatonics of all sorts. Sullivan had confided to him that he knew that condition. Having been committed in his adolescence for obscure reasons, Sullivan had remained intrigued by people turning into stone. Later, while in military service, he decided to clarify this—and so he stuck a friend's buttocks with a pin (in order to bring the matter into the open). The friend was not a catatonic, but a marksman concentrating on his invisible target when Harry stuck him. Throughout the process of aiming, the marksman did not react. Only after having fired his shot did the friend feel the sting and give Harry the devil.[13] Sullivan drew some decisive conclusions about targets invisible to us, which all those so-called numb people are aiming at for a very long time, concentrating on an invisible somewhere where no one can reach them. And Wittgenstein concluded:

WITTGENSTEIN:	Then, if he had kept his cool, the rifleman would have been able to say: "Oh, of course I know what 'pain' means; what I didn't know is whether the sensation that I had while I was shooting was pain."[14]
FD:	During that whole story, my only concern was to return Wittgenstein to the Great Beyond. Suddenly I had an impulse. "Hold it," I said to the Philosopher, while giving him the great man's books, "take your Wittgenstein back. For a long time I have allowed him to animate my own personal movie. Now he's no longer of use to me." The Philosopher took back the books without looking surprised.
PAUL:	It was your turn to play *fort-da* . . .
FD:	Wittgenstein didn't seem troubled either by my rude dismissal.
WITTGENSTEIN:	Above all, don't forget to trust your impressions.
FD:	He said that to me as a good-bye. Then they both disappeared.

"For good?" said Paul, while getting up again and pointing with his finger to two kites that were circling around above us, making short meow-like cries.

FD:	As you've already noticed, the problem with ghosts is that it's difficult to stop them from coming back.

Chapter 20

Beetles

The house in the woods.

PAUL, FD

The analyst's office.

FD, A COCKROACH, WITTGENSTEIN

The shadows of the trees had grown longer when I noticed the log cabin a few yards away from us. It was dark inside; the fire had died out. Instinctively I looked for the electric switch, and I found it near the door, but it wasn't connected to anything. I sat down, not knowing what to do, listening for noises, which until then hadn't struck me: squeals, scratching—were there mice or insects? Then, from outside came what I thought to be howling and barking. Was the diviner's wolf prowling around? In no time, Paul lit the candles and the gas lamps, stoked the embers, and started up the fire. While I still remained completely unable to move, the water for the soup and pasta was already singing and hissing. Paul soon served them on steaming plates. I was as hungry as a wolf. He touched almost nothing; he seemed to be waiting. I resumed my story while I was wolfing down my last piece of bread.

FD:	Of course, I saw Wittgenstein again. I noticed gradually that he had not really disappeared. He was living his life in his own way. His logical theories fascinated everyone . . . But that aspect of his work escaped me—and moreover, it didn't interest me at all.
PAUL:	"The grapes were too green . . ."*

---

* The common English expression derived from this line of Aesop's "The Fox and the Bunch of Grapes," is: "Sour Grapes." Olivia and Robert Temple, in their 1998 translation of Aesop's fables, point out that while the Greek word "*Omphakes*" can mean "sour," a more accurate translation is "unripe." The emphasis is on how the grapes appear and not on how they taste. "Too green" is a translation of "*tropverts*," and points to the unripe appearance of the grapes. Cf: *Aesop: The Complete*

DOI: 10.4324/9781003437451-20

FD:	Make fun, if you want. I'm entirely ready to acknowledge that Wittgenstein I thought I understood had nothing to do with the real Wittgenstein. I must have been mistaken about him. It happens. Don't think I was longing for him. On the contrary . . . I felt more at peace; my work was unfolding in a normal, neutral way.
PAUL:	And how did he come back then?
FD:	I don't really know anymore. It was probably a false move.
PAUL:	You're not going to tell me that it's you who . . .
FD:	Indeed, rather foolishly. One morning I calmly went into my office: the day was shaping up beautifully; my first appointment was no problem—or so I thought: a young man who had come once, urged by a buddy, just to see. I was heading toward my chair, when I was stopped short.
	Right in the middle of the room an enormous, flat insect, with light brown armor, and about as long as my thumb, was calmly waiting for me. Seeing it, I cried: "*maman!*"—which was my grandmother's alarm cry when she was surprised by a mouse. In response to the panic it set off, the insect pretended to be dead. I pulled back behind the door. Was I going to crush it with horrible crunches, or grab hold of it with some paper, and throw it out the window? . . . And what if it struggles? Not knowing what to do, I called on Wittgenstein the way I had called on "*maman,*" without at all expecting him to come. But instantly, as always, he rose to the occasion.
WITTGENSTEIN:	What is it now?
FD:	That enormous cockroach there, looking at me right now. Where had it slipped in? I didn't dream it.
WITTGENSTEIN:	No matter. Can you describe it for me?
FD:	Impossible. I hardly looked at it; it was filthy . . .
WITTGENSTEIN:	Then, why call me and talk just to say nothing? You're not giving me any information.
FD:	I told you there was a horrible beast. I was awfully scared. That's what matters to me.
WITTGENSTEIN:	What matters is whom you're informing of it, and on what occasion.[1]
FD:	Whom I'm informing? Well, great gods, you! And get rid of that sententious tone of yours. You could guess what's going on in me without my describing it to you . . . In order to make you

Fables, Translated by Olivia and Robert Temple (New York: Penguin, 1998). The French verse, "*Ils sont trop verts,*" comes from the La Fontaine (1621–1695) version of the fable ("*Le Renard et les raisins*"). Which is the actual source of this line in the text. Cf. Jean de la Fontaine, *Fables* (Le Livre de poche—Classique, 2002), 124.

happy, you would probably have liked me to take the beetle in
my own fingers, and enclose it in a box—just the way children
do, with mini cicadas in Japan, May bugs in England, cucara-
chas in Mexico—so that I could show it to you. I still know
how to do that, but I no longer have that courage. I'm too old
for that .

. . and besides you can't understand!

Wittgenstein made as if to head for the door.

FD: You're upset.
WITTGENSTEIN: Of course, you're really inclined to say something that gives
                         no information.[2] I'm asking you on what occasions you noticed
                         that insect, and you exclaim that only you know what you
                         experience . . .
FD: Is that sensation of fear something for you or is it nothing?
WITTGENSTEIN: It is not a *something*, but not a *nothing* either! . . . Besides, a
                         nothing would serve just as well as a something about which
                         nothing could be said. I have only rejected the grammar that
                         tries to force itself on us here.[3]
FD: Too bad, I would really have liked for you to tell me what that
                         troublesome visitor was doing here. You must think I've made
                         up this story to make you come back, and that I made up this
                         insect as a fiction, since I can't show it to you. Right?
WITTGENSTEIN: If you do speak of a fiction, then it is of a grammatical fiction.[4]
FD: Good gracious! I talk to him about a big, monstrous insect, and
                         he tells me it's grammatical!
WITTGENSTEIN: Well, once again, tell me about the occasions of his appear-
                         ance. That's all I'm asking of you.
FD: I was waiting for someone who had a second appointment,
                         that's all. Someone who said he didn't want an analysis because
                         he has no problems. But on the other hand, what he said he did
                         have was a holy horror of opening up. Well, I had no intention
                         of forcing him to. What would you have done in my place?
                         Perhaps I should have crushed the insect. I was afraid to hurt it.
                         It was there, exactly where you are, not budging anymore than
                         a stone—no more nor less than that patient.
WITTGENSTEIN: Did you wonder this time in what sense the stones have pains?[5]
FD: Your usual question. Well, they suffer probably from the bom-
                         bardment of all those particles, which can gradually speed
                         up their erosion, or perhaps from a petrified pain, like Niobe*

---

* Niobe, one of the most tragic figures of Greek mythology, saw her 14 children killed by Apollo and
  Artemis in a matter of minutes, just after she had bragged about her children and made fun of Leto
  (the mother of Apollo and Artemis), who had only two children.

	after she had witnessed with her own eyes the murder of her children.
WITTGENSTEIN:	And what's the point of telling me that?
FD:	To pass the time and to forget that dire cockroach, keeping it magically at bay . . . Who knows, perhaps to tame it so that it would appear only at my call.
WITTGENSTEIN:	As you've called me?
FD:	And if it were sneaking in without making any noise? Wouldn't you look for it, please, under the furniture? It could come back at the worst time, when I'm with this patient.
WITTGENSTEIN:	Don't be such a coward. I enclosed it in a box a long time ago. Look at paragraph 293 in my *Investigations*.
FD:	I don't have your book anymore.
WITTGENSTEIN:	No matter—I know it by heart: "Suppose everyone had a box with something in it: we will call it a 'beetle.'"[6]
FD:	Is it a beautiful light brown one, like mine—or is it green, black, shiny, or perhaps bronze?
WITTGENSTEIN:	"No one can look into anyone else's box, and everyone says that he knows what a beetle is, only by looking at *his* beetle."[7]
FD:	I especially hope that their boxes are well sealed.
WITTGENSTEIN:	Don't worry, everyone has a beetle.
FD:	Yes, but theirs don't look like mine, underneath the furniture, with evil eyes.
WITTGENSTEIN:	You don't get it at all—but no matter. "It would be quite possible for everyone to have something different in his box. One might even imagine such a thing constantly changing."[8]
FD:	I get you. You just want to reassure me. It could be that the bats in our belfries are somehow changing into magnificent butterflies . . . You see, I do understand . . . But suppose the word "beetle" had a use in this people's language.[9]
WITTGENSTEIN:	If so, it would not be used as the name of a thing. The thing in the box has no place in the language-game at all—not even as a something: for the box might even be empty.—No, one can 'divide through' by the thing in the box; it cancels out, whatever it is.[10]
FD:	Will the beetle have escaped?
WITTGENSTEIN:	You're still not following. I told you the box might be empty; the thing, whatever it is, might be cancelled out.
FD:	I liked it better when you told me that we didn't have to open the box. Our great French jester, Raymond Devos (who died in June, 2006), gave that advice. He warned us against letting non-existent butterflies go free in nature, for fear they create phantasms.[11] But what happens to the beetles that escape? For

me, it's too late; the thing has indeed been let out of the language game. I don't just cancel it out, as you say, by "dividing through."

PAUL: Raymond Devos, if I correctly remember his sketch, advised us to catch these non-existent butterflies and flatly obliterate them. What about Wittgenstein?

FD: He didn't want to answer, as if he didn't care at all about this insect's comings and goings between his book and my reality. He left me at the moment when the young man arrived. So I couldn't clear up the nature of this troublesome guest, which had forced me to open my mouth and make Wittgenstein come back.

The scratches had started up again, somewhere in the log cabin's roof, stronger this time, regular and methodical . . . I gave Paul a questioning and vaguely unsettled look.

PAUL: A spirit, undoubtedly a grammatical subject of some message still impossible to express between Wittgenstein and you. But tell me, how did you finally take the risk to open your box, and your mouth, and give an account of what I missed by being late the day of your presentation?

Chapter 21

The Deaf-Mutes

The house in the woods.

FD, Paul

The House of the sciences of man.

THE YOUNG DEAF WOMAN, WITTGENSTEIN,
A PSYCHOLOGIST, BERNARD MOTTEZ, AN
AMERICAN SOCIOLOGIST, FD

I had completely forgotten the unpleasant memory of my presentation on "Trans-
ference and Psychosis," though it had brought about my visit here, so I tried hard
to remember how that preposterous idea had occurred to me.

FD: After the adventure of the beetle, I intensified my uni-
          versity activities and took part in various work groups,
          in order to get back on firmer, rational ground. At that
          point, some unrealistic enthusiasm pushed me to pro-
          pose that I make this presentation to analysts.

I remember having gone one day to the House of the Sciences of Man* to attend a
seminar on Robert Wilson's play, "Deafman Glance, "**to which the sociologist Ber-
nard Mottez***—whose work had contributed to the development of sign language in

---

* The *Fondation maison des sciences de l'homme* (FMSH) is an institu tion dedicated to research in the
human and social sciences. (There are many "Maisons" located throughout France.) It is "housed"
in the same building as the École *des Hautes* Etudes *en Sciences Sociales* (EHESS), where FD, along
with Jean-Max Gaudillière, runs a weekly seminar on "Madness and the Social Link."

** This play was first performed in Iowa in 1970, moving to New York, and later to Paris, and to many
cities throughout the world. It was particularly well received in Paris, where it became the subject of
some serious study and critical analysis.

*** Bernard Mottez, the author of many texts on deafness, on deaf- mutes, and on institutions for the
deaf both in the United States and in France, was a researcher in sociology in the same center as FD,
CEMS. Cf. footnote, p. 75.

DOI: 10.4324/9781003437451-21

France—had invited me. I was surprised to discover Wittgenstein there, among the participants, having an intense conversation with some deaf-mutes, with the aid of an interpreter. Everyone in the seminar seemed to know him well; some appeared visibly flattered by this familiarity. After having quieted down the vocal and gestural chatter, that day Mottez introduced the texts of a deaf-mute named Desloges,* who was a defender in the eighteenth century of the sign language and method initiated by the Abbé de l'Épée (1712–1789).

A young deaf woman was the first to ask for the floor. Mottez introduced her. She took care of deaf children, who were labeled "psychotic," because they ran up against the bounds of an normal language, which they definitely can't use. Instead of looking for "mental defects," she was second to none in developing and helping to spread the use of a gestural language-game, in which these children could express their anger. Seldom had I seen more expressive language and so much passion for communication. Far from being mute, this deaf psychotherapist repeated her gestures as many times as necessary, when the interpreter had trouble grasping what she was saying. Then, the interpreter translated for us:

YOUNG DEAF WOMAN: I knew a deaf child who was forbidden for a long time to have contact with other deaf people. Whether it was to protect him from his handicap, or to pretend that he wasn't deaf, he had never met those people whose gesticulations seem zany to those who can hear. So, imagine his exultation when one day he discovered a world where he belonged. To be deaf was no longer a problem, as soon as he no longer had to strive to produce articulate sounds, whose sonority would be forever denied to him. He had finally discovered a language in which he could speak, and therefore desire.

WITTGENSTEIN: Sign language is the place where thinking is not incorporeal. It shows that thinking is not an abstract process which lends life and sense to speaking, and which it would be possible to detach from speaking, rather as the Devil took the shadow of Schlemiel** from the ground.[1]

---

* Pierre Desloges (1747–1799?), *Observations d'un sourd-muet* (Paris: Mottin, 1799).
** Adelbert von Chamisso, *Peter Schlemiel: The Man Who Sold His Shadow.* Translated by Peter Wortsman (Fromm International Publishers, 1993). This German classic, written by a French émigré who left for Germany during the French Revolution, was published in 1814.

The word "devil" startled me. This same morning, all the signs written in black on white by my word processor had been erased right in front of my dumbfounded eyes. It was impossible to attribute this amazing disappearance to a power failure or to a mistake. Desperate, I had tapped away at the keyboard, seeking its mercy, but it stayed insensitive, mute, and deaf to my supplications. So my entire text had vanished without a trace, with the outline of my presentation, which I had labored over so much. I even wondered whether this text had ever existed, for it had been impossible for me to put it back together. Some wicked "other" inside the box, had erased all those letters—and with the same blow had sucked up the text of my own memory, which remained as white as that shadowless screen.

PAUL:	In short, the perfect crime.
FD:	Paying no attention to the discussion that was developing in the seminar, I was absorbed by my detective investigation. What could this apparatus have in mind? Did I happen to buy a text-killer machine? It was able to grasp my language, while its own, **was** enclosed in its box, and remained totally impenetrable to me. How to face this infernal logic that was likely talking to itself with a synthetic voice, and ostensibly refusing to communicate with me . . . I was pulled away from my reverie by a psychologist's question.
THE PSYCHOLOGIST:	But in assuming that the deaf have only learned a language of gestures, you can't actually deny that each of them talks to himself inwardly, with our words, in a vocal language . . . You seem staggered by this obvious fact. Don't you understand?
WITTGENSTEIN:	What is there to understand? What can we do with your observation, if that's what it is? This whole idea of understanding smells fishy here, as the English say . . .[2]
THE PSYCHOLOGIST:	Yet I'm talking in plain language.
WITTGENSTEIN:	Evidently, it's an English sentence, apparently in order, but anyone who has not been calloused by doing psychology or philosophy would notice that there is something wrong here.[3]
THE PSYCHOLOGIST:	And what's wrong?
MOTTEZ:	Your stubbornness in thinking that sign language is only a stopgap. You're deaf to hearing that the deaf speak through gestures. That

it's a true language, with its poetry, its plays on words, even its music. You absolutely want to force the deaf to cry out. For want of that, you insist that they speak as we do, but inwardly.

WITTGENSTEIN: The explanation by means of identity doesn't work here.[4]

THE PSYCHOLOGIST: Don't you know William James's account of the reminiscences of Mr. Ballard, a deaf-mute? In order to show that thought is possible without speech, Ballard wrote that in his early youth, even before he could speak, he had had thoughts about God and the world. Indeed, that period preceded his initiation into the rudiments of written language.[5] This goes against the thesis that was just being defended by Mottez. On the one hand, Ballard claimed he could have speculative thoughts on a high level without the help of language; on the other hand, access to our verbal language and not to sign language allowed him to develop those thoughts.

WITTGENSTEIN: Are you sure that this was a correct translation of wordless thought into words?[6]

MOTTEZ: The words taken from this smattering of written language carry no information about thought before that acquisition. We **are** less informed about what Ballard was thinking before talking than about the way he had been brought up, and thus about the violence of hearing people, when they demand that the deaf speak a vocal language.

THE PSYCHOLOGIST: But obviously people say things to themselves that they don't want to disclose, and even when they have never spoken an audible language, it's easy to suppose that they still say some things to themselves in their own imagination.[7]

WITTGENSTEIN: If they always say things only to themselves, then they would merely be doing what in reality we do sometimes. . . One need only make the easy transition from some to all.[8]

MOTTEZ: Humanity's benefactors are often totally disgusted at the sight of places cut off from our common bearings: communities of gesturing deaf people, psychiatric institutions, all sorts of spaces where they're not so sure of being like their fellow human beings, seeing that there are other ways of speaking.

THE PSYCHOLOGIST: Even so, you can't help wondering what they're saying to themselves in their heads.

WITTGENSTEIN: Will you at last catch on that our criterion for someone's saying something to himself, is what he tells us, and also the rest of his behavior.[9] Through his words, but also through what he shows. Take my word for it: there aren't "meanings" going through your mind in addition to verbal expressions; the language is itself the vehicle of thought.[10] And we only say that someone speaks to himself if, in the ordinary sense of the words, he can speak. And we don't say it of a parrot; nor of a record player.[11]

FD: Why not of a parrot? What do you know about it?

WITTGENSTEIN: Why not? Couldn't we imagine God's suddenly giving a parrot understanding, and it's now saying things to itself? But here it is an important fact that I imagined a deity in order to imagine this.[12] To mean something, you must have mastery of a language.[13]

FD: And when one no longer wants to mean something, one ends up developing a psychiatric condition. I think of that gorilla in the Garden of Plants* which ostensibly turns its backside towards the visitors who would very much like to see it monkey about. How to know what's going on in its head? And what do wild geese say to themselves when they pass over in a triangle with a great noise of wings, honking above our heads? Are they holding a seminar in the sky all the while as they fly? Too bad Konrad Lorentz is dead; I would have liked to ask him what he used to say to them— as they were flying over the looping turn in the Danube—to make their land near his house.[14]

---

* Le Jardin des Plantes was founded in Paris in the eighteenth century by the naturalists, Cuvier and Buffon, to keep plants, minerals and fossils.

AN AMERICAN SOCIOLOGIST: Don't think that he had broken into their secret thought through some magic. He was talking to them in a gestural and sonorous language built up as soon as they hatched and caught sight of that bearded man, whom they took for their "mommy." Likewise Vicky Hearne, in the United States, trained animals, dogs and horses, inspired by Wittgenstein's philosophy. She wrote a book entitled *Adam's Task: Calling Animals by Names*,[15] where she quotes *The Investigations*. For her, training amounts to creating a language-game (worked out on each side) between human and animal. There's no need for them to attempt to read one another's thoughts. If the animals read our minds more than we do theirs, it's because they're swift at marking what we say unwittingly to them, which builds itself as a language-game between them and us. But this language game also has its pernicious grammar. She cites cases where she had to be the therapist for horses and dogs driven crazy by the double language of their masters.

FD: Would this lady also train computers?

MOTTEZ: Why? Has yours become stubborn?

FD: It's stolen a text from me. I wonder what it keeps turning over in its memory—perhaps an old grudge . . . you never know. I have indeed tried to talk to it, to cajole it. It remains impervious to all the languages I try, verbal, gestural, whatever. I have even wanted to type forcefully in order to improve our contact . . .

Mottez got up and signaled the end of the seminar:

MOTTEZ: Don't despair. Perhaps it will someday give back your text, with its own commentaries on what it recorded. That day, you will have finally found the screw that's loose in your computer.

He laughed while saying these words and he glanced at Wittgenstein who answered him in what I thought was a secret code:

WITTGENSTEIN: The fluctuation in her grammar between criteria and symptoms makes it look as if there were nothing at all but symptoms.[16]

Judging this remark offensive, I pretended to ignore it, and showed Mottez a text of Sullivan's that I had brought along, but had forgotten to talk about. He suggested that I introduce it at the next seminar. Then, amid the noise of chairs, we all hurried for the exit. I was, for an instant, tempted to ask Wittgenstein to come with me, but he was surrounded by many people, so I set off by myself toward the hospital.

Chapter 22

The Private Life of Dogs

The house in the woods.

FD, Paul

The psychiatric hospital.

THE MEDICAL DIRECTOR'S DOG, THE INTERN, MAN,
THE MEDICAL DIRECTOR, THE MAN IN THE HOODED
PARKA, THE HEAD NURSE, MADAME DURAND

It was beginning to get late. I asked Paul if he was listening to me. With his hands wrapped around his enameled mug, which was filled with mulled wine, he was sipping slowly, with a far away look in his eyes. He mumbled some "hmm," "hmm," sounds, which I translated into the international language of oral culture, shared by analysts and South Dakota Sioux medicine-men, when they want to encourage you to go on speaking. I understood that I would have no rest until I came to the point of his clumsy entry during my presentation.

FD: Assailed by doubt, I hesitated at the entrance to the hospital. In that place too, an evil genius seemed to be relentlessly set on defeating everything I was doing, and on bringing to despair everything I had hoped for. "How not to see symptoms everywhere, in such a place?" I was saying to myself. Patients come back as if pushed by a demon, and even so—as hopeless as they may seem—these returns may very well lead to recovery.

I was addressing part of this reflection to the medical director's dog, all the while petting him through the fence of the garden where he was waiting for his master. His favorite pastime was barking at the patients who were afraid of dogs. Then, regretfully, I decided to go into the building.

DOI: 10.4324/9781003437451-22

A huge man was waiting. The medical director showed him into his office and I rushed in so I could get to know this newcomer. The intern started the questioning.

INTERN: So what's going on? (he asked kindly) Why have the police brought you here?

The man answered in a stentorian voice.

MAN: I didn't want to screw up, but the outcome is the same.
INTERN: And why?
MAN: I don't know.
INTERN: What are your thoughts about it?
MAN: Nothing. When I'm screwing up, it's automatic; I'm not thinking.
INTERN: We can try to understand.

The man got up, furious.

MAN: There's nothing more to understand. That's all. That's enough. Shut up.

The medical director ordered that he be taken to his room. While the man was following the nurse without looking around, the head nurse told me that Madame Durand had come back. She refused to come to see me at the outpatient clinic; she only wanted to see me in the hospital, even if it meant a short stay.

The medical director asked our opinion on what we had just heard. The intern thought that a suicidal rapture was to be feared. When my turn came to speak, I quoted what I had heard that morning:

FD: This is the time to notice that talking is not an incorporeal process.[1]
THE MEDICAL DIRECTOR: What's that again?
FD: It's like your dog. He barks at us who are afraid of him.
INTERN: Be careful of what you may say. He's not a dog! Honestly!
THE MEDICAL DIRECTOR: We're going to wait a little to see how he behaves on the ward.

I took out my Sullivan book, which I had carried to the seminar on sign language. I wanted to share with them Sullivan's analysis of the private life of dogs, which I thought was suitable to this case. But everyone got up quickly in the same hub-bub of chairs, and left to attend to their affairs. My book in hand, I made my way upstairs toward Madame Durand's room.

On the way I was thinking about the mysterious beetle, which that man, according to the intern, was keeping to himself—so like the bug that I had imagined concealed behind my screen. I feared for him that a time bomb, an infernal machine, whose mechanism would unwind like a spring, without being slowed down by words, would turn against him. Wittgenstein would have known what to answer to these images of a deadly inside. The grammar that drives one crazy had struck again. However, the man's refusal to answer (with which he opposed our good intentions)—was it really a symptom, or was it, on the contrary, the criterion indicating that nothing had to be extracted from the depths of his psyche? Moreover, everything had to be invented as a language-game, with his voice that made the walls tremble.

Madame Durand was not in her room. I assumed she was in the cafeteria. In order to go back down, I unlocked the door to the landing. Stealthily, a young man took advantage of the half-open door to slip through, while murmuring some pretext. One more patient I had let escape. Obviously, I wasn't even able to play watchdog. When I returned to the front of the garden, the medical director's dog jumped up to meet me. I interpreted the dog's thought ("Long live freedom") without being able to decide whether it was mine, the patient's, or his own.

I should have insisted that Madame Durand come to the clinic—not surrendered to her reasons. She wanted to drop psychiatry, to have a private life, without me sticking my nose into it. I said this to myself in an almost loud voice as I opened the door to the cafeteria. The room was nearly empty. The sad young man was thoughtfully drinking a cup of coffee. A girl was trying unsuccessfully to start a conversation with him, and she eventually started talking to the glasses, being energetically dried by the nurse in charge. I stood planted there, in the middle of the room—and then I went out again, wandering, without purpose, along the paths on the hospital grounds.

The weather was rainy. In front of the wall of one of the wards, a man, wearing a hooded parka, was pacing up and down, having taken on a kind of crab walk, moving forward in his own way, as he had for years at that hour—a faithful sentinel at his post, but who guarded what? Unless too visibly he was pacing to and fro, the length and breadth of an invisible cage. I crossed his path for the umpteenth time, and he looked askance at me, with one eye—the eye the hood was not covering. For once, I didn't take that determined attitude, which, in such a place, the possession of the keys allows you to have. That day, like most of the people locked inside, I knew neither what to do nor where to go. So I said hello to him for the first time, and heard a clear voice thrown back ("Hello, Madame") from under the parka. Finding myself again in the head nurse's office, which was empty, I sat down and plunged into the Sullivan book. The nurse pushed open the door:

HEAD NURSE: The man who was admitted a short while ago is shut up in his room. He refuses all contact. The boss has forbidden him to leave, and he wants us to leave him in peace. The intern says it's inhuman. What can you do!

Then she asked me about my reading. Sullivan had interested her ever since I had informed her of his curious way of recruiting his staff. The legend was still circulating: not only was his

    ward limited to a very small number of beds—a sign that there shouldn't be too-long stays—but more seriously, his nurses were chosen according to criteria opposed to common professional standards. Today it's said that every other psychiatrist would have recruited them also—but as patients. He considered their apparent symptoms—shyness, reserve and sensitivity—as criteria of their capacity to make contact with young schizophrenics. The model nurse could only make them run away when she brandished the motto: "Duty above all," a refrain heard too much in their own families.[2] At least, I had finally found an obliging ear for the Sullivan passage I had been trying to share since the morning:

FD:	Here's another of his provocations. The scene takes place at Chestnut Lodge. Sullivan held weekly meetings there with a team of doctors and nurses, and his Great Dane. The debate concerned respect for the human person.[3] In the days after the Second World War, Sullivan had already given a conference entitled, "The Illusion of Personal Individuality," which he had been dissuaded from publishing, because it seemed scandalous in that period after the War. Here he persists with the same theme,[4] especially as the following dilemma occurs in every psychiatric place: Where to mark the limits of personal individuality?
THE HEAD NURSE:	Indeed, that's the problem with the new admission: Should we allow him to screw up by suicide, as he asks, or to die by inches of a life he doesn't want? He's claiming a private life. What does that mean in his case?
FD (TO PAUL):	I read for her Sullivan's response which I still remember.
SULLIVAN:	"That there are particular lives each with a unique career line, I no more deny than do I the fact that I am a particular person who has a particular dog. I can say that I act in two modes: my public mode, and my private mode, in which I feel my inviolate isolation from my fellows. So, doubtless does my dog; the transformations of energy, which he manifests in living his canine life, often transcend being-my-dog, in the culturally patterned world of dogs and people, which is his life-space. He doubtless acts much more frequently in the private mode than I

could I think that I do, and I doubtless act much less frequently in the private mode than it is easy to think that I do. The immutably private in my dog and in me escapes and will always escape the methods of science, however absorbing I may once have found the latter. Without digressing on the value of the comparative approach in formulating non-cultural and especially non-language aspects of living, I seek here to stress the central fact that the true or absolute individuality of a person is always beyond scientific grasp and invariably much less significant in the person's living than he has been thought to believe" (December 31, 1946).[5]

That reading was interrupted by cries and a hubbub that made both of us rush out of the office. It was Madame Durand, out of her wits.

MADAME DURAND: That psychiatrist is completely cast out. He sees everything from his window. He sees only symptoms. He takes me for a nutcase. He thinks I do medical work. Me—I am reclaiming from him my due for past services: to be authenticated. I am through with that dirty work of taking care of others. Now I want to live in luxury and normality.

I greeted her and asked her to come with me to another room. The others returned to their business. She told me then, in the same tone:

MADAME DURAND: As far as symptoms are concerned, I've given enough. Consider that I no longer have either marrow, or spleen, or liver. The swine worked on me all night.

Then, assuming a confidential manner, she leaned over toward me, as if we were going to exchange the recipe for lamb stew (of which she knew I was very fond):

MADAME DURAND: There's something that especially bothers me. Let me ask you. Perhaps you can answer me: "What does 'raise the dead' mean?" They drum it for me, in telepathy. Does it mean that the dead come back to life? I don't know whether my imagination deceives me, but I sometimes have the impression it does.

That question wasn't new, and it came back periodically. I asked her then about what had happened on the days that preceded the immediacy of such a question.

MADAMD DURAND:	After our last meeting, I went to my country, to meditate on my father's grave. I didn't find it ....
FD:	In cemeteries, we talk about "raising the dead," when they have to remove the bones from the grave or the coffin, to give more space to newcomers.
MADAME DURAND:	to put them in the common grave; I know, for my mother, they had to do that. It's old; I was nine years old. My father died, you know, not so long ago. But it's my mother whom I sense, so to speak, physically. Time plays tricks on me. I came here to be authenticated. Can't you tell them?
PAUL:	So she had come to the hospital, as you had gone to Freud's house in Vienna, in order to be authenticated.
FD:	But this time I didn't see at all about what. She cleared it up for me.
MADAME DURAND:	Since our last meeting, a lot of things have happened. I wanted to replace my I.D., which was lost for a long time. Well, they made a mistake and wrote my name in two parts: "du"—then separately, "Rand." Here I am with a particle, like a noble lady! Then you can imagine (she concluded, laughing) what kind of delusion would be mine, thinking that the castle in that village belonged to my parents ...
FD (TO PAUL):	You see, then, what she wanted to authenticate by coming back to the ward. She had indeed made a normal pious gesture. She was not identifying herself with a landlady born of a spelling mistake on her father's grave. Now her face was perfectly calm when she went out of her room. She asked immediately to go back home. I decided to do the same.

Chapter 23

The Machine

The house in the woods.

FD, PAUL, DESCARTES

The analyst's office.

FD, WITTGENSTEIN, DESCARTES, DIDEROT
WITH HIS HARPSICHORD, THE MAN WITH THE WAGON

In the traffic jams on the way back home, I was thinking about Erasmus composing his Praise of Folly, *while on horseback. "I know of no one who knows me better than I do myself,"[1] says Folly, who had once more proved this in offering Madame Durand a true youth cure. The change in her face had been so sudden that I could scarcely get over it. But she first had to have had her organs disappear in one night. That symptom has a name in psychiatry. . . .*

PAUL: Cotard's syndrome—which, in its typical form, consists of ideas of negation: "The sick person denies the existence of his organs, and comes even to deny the existence of his body, of his parents, of his friends, of death, of places, of time, of the world."[2]

FD: What are you trotting out for me?

PAUL: Henry Ey's *Manual of Psychiatry.*

FD: I thought I recognized Descartes' symptom in his First Meditation: "I shall consider myself as not having hands, not eyes, not flesh, not blood, not any senses, but rather falsely opining that I have all these things."[3]

Indeed, when she had come out into the corridor, calling upon the audience as her witness, Madame Durand had weary features, sucked up by some internal void. Her complexion was very pale, her eyes expressionless; words didn't seem to reach her anymore. Her organs were disappearing. A little more and she would have

DOI: 10.4324/9781003437451-23

entered a state as improbable as that of a Cheshire cat who could no more even smile at Alice. Well, so little time was enough for her machine to connect her to another talking machine, mine in this case—so that her blood started circulating again, her skin began to relax, and its color returned. . . .

I would love to tell you more about it, but I remember almost nothing of that conversation: one cheek turning pink, a look starting to glow, a sigh of relaxation, a youthful expression that came like a breath. All the rest would be reconstruction afterwards. In spite of her thinking herself a perfect dummy, she was aware of being a good deal less so than her supposed caregivers. She still knew that she was unwittingly recording information about us that we had no awareness of, and that, as a duty, she had to take care of it. Like Erasmus's Folly, no one knew more than she how to describe her condition. She asked only that her work be authenticated. Just as I had to authenticate Theodore, at the moment when he had known, better than I, that I was not so sure either of my internal organs.[*]

PAUL:	That's what's disturbing; the analyst can't play her role— defined by Lacan—as the "subject supposed to know."[4] Since in the presence of madness, it's she (Folly) who knows.
FD:	Once back home, I collapsed, sinking into a progressively numb state, as I often did upon returning from the hospital. On the shelf, a book by Diderot was left half open. Who could have wanted to read that today? When I opened my eyes again, the morning clouds had broken up. Wittgenstein was seated facing me, with the Diderot book open next to him. I thought he looked faintly worried, but I didn't have time to linger on this impression, for I realized we were right in the middle of a discussion.
WITTGENSTEIN:	Yes. In ordinary circumstances, those words and this picture have an application with which we are familiar.

But if we suppose a case in which this application falls apart we become, as it were, conscious for the first time of the nakedness of the words and the picture.[5]

On the off chance, I tried submitting to him the picture of the "machine" and the words "raise the dead," whose application had fallen apart, until we found another one for them. I would have preferred to quote Madame Durand's words literally, with her inimitable style. All I could do was to summarize them for him rather flatly.

FD:	You've already met her. You know that she, like you, understands philosophy as a therapy. In order to do it, she connects

---

[*] Cf. Chapter 15.

herself to a thinking and talking machine. Her telepathy machine is also an apparatus for philosophical dialysis, which knows how to sort out criteria and symptoms, which you think I'm incapable of doing. The same goes for her village's chateau. Madame Durand told me that, when she was very young, she saw, with her own eyes, her mother opening the shutters. Frozen like a snap-shot, that memory gave birth to a chimera. Was her mother the lady of the manor, or a peasant woman married to a prince, in the style of the pastorals of the seventeenth century, with genuine sheep grazing on the lawn?

WITTGENSTEIN: Her sense-impressions may have deceived her, but that false appearance is nevertheless founded on a definition.[6]

FD: She had actually based that false impression on the "redefinition" of her name by the registry office.

WITTGENSTEIN: The idea is already found in Descartes: "Whether I would imagine a goat or a chimera, it is no less true that I imagine the one than the other. Moreover, no falsity is to be feared in the will itself or in the emotions. For although I could wish for depraved things, and although I could even wish for those things which nowhere are, it is still not therefore not true that I wish for them."[7]

FD: Well, what does Madame Durand wish for? A slight spelling change in her name—an article changed to a particle—confers a rank upon her, as a revenge for her humiliations.

WITTGENSTEIN: The point here is not that her sense impressions have lied to her; but that she has understood their language.[8]

FD: By the way, I don't know right now whether or not my impression is deceiving me, but you seem worried.

WITTGENSTEIN: Isn't there something private that you keep tracking down, an intangible something . . .[9]

FD: I can't help it; it's rather ludicrous.

WITTGENSTEIN: Why ludicrous? Your reaction is normal. It is, as it were, a dream of our language . . .[10]

"An angel passed"—we no longer knew what to say. I instinctively took up the Diderot book, skimmed through to where it was open, and tried to fill the silence:

FD: Listen, it's about your leitmotiv: what sort of sensibility can stones be affected by? Diderot offers his friend D'Alembert a philosophical tool that Madame Durand would have enjoyed: "Suppose there's a harpsichord with sensibility and memory, and tell me if it won't repeat for itself the pieces you would have played on its keys?"[11] The following is even more surrealistic: "There's a moment of delirium when the sensing harpsichord thought it was the only harpsichord in the world, and that all harmony in the universe came through it."[12] That harpsichord is certainly an ancestor to Madame Durand's machine, in charge of repairing the disharmonies of the world with the vibrations that go through it.

WITTGENSTEIN: Well, in your opinion, could a machine think? Could it be in pain?[13]

FD: In pain? Why not? I sometimes make the machines I use suffer. But thinking is another question . . . though this morning there was that machine that abused my text. I had fears about it starting to think. Do you suppose it could have been delusional?

WITTGENSTEIN: That doesn't bother me.

FD: But a machine surely can't think or be delusional.[14]

WITTGENSTEIN: Is that an empirical statement? No. We only say of a human being and what is like one that it thinks. We also say it of dolls and no doubt of spirits too.[15]

FD: Then it's not absurd to say it about my machine; even so, I'm not crazy When you come back to the hospital, I'll show you another thinking machine, whose job is never to get out of the way of cars. I meet it often, but I've never thought to ask it what it's showing to passers-by. There's this children's wooden wagon, which an ageless little man, in blue uniform and slippers, pulls by a rope. One meets him on walkways, looking serious, and toddling along, pulling his wagon. Unless it's the wagon that leads him along—for as each car comes past there's the wagon, in front of the wheels. And the little man, without batting an eyelid, waits for the driver to confront him, by crushing his innocent toy. Unless it's the other way around, and in spite of how small it is, the wagon had the fantasy of assaulting the automobile. However, the wagon always has the upper hand—for the car regularly makes a big swerve, and at the risk of wrapping around one of the hospital's trees, avoids the catastrophe by running bumpily up onto the pavement. Then the little man eyes it up and down, and, imperturbable, following it going away, says with a glance that speaks volumes: "What do you know about that?"

WITTGENSTEIN: Of course you've just evoked several possibilities about what you know about it. You might have told him your impressions, describing for him the picture he's showing you, the sensations that wagon experiences . . . But you seem worried . . .

FD: I'm thinking about the presentation I promised to make to some analysts . . . Do you think that I can tell them about the method

	you're suggesting to me? It's really quite risky . . . Imagine that I describe, as you suggest, my impressions during the unfolding of a session, giving in some way an impressionistic picture of what happened . . . I'm heading right for a catastrophe.
WITTGENSTEIN:	What's the risk?
FD:	Put yourself in the place of my audience, or even of my patients. Imagine, for example, a session as a room I'd like to paint for them. What would you say, as a patient, if, having described things to me in green, I rendered them in dark red, or where I paint in yellow, what you had shown me as blue?[16]
WITTGENSTEIN:	Well, I would say: Quite right! That's what it's like.[17]
FD:	Rubbish!
WITTGENSTEIN:	Your reaction is the same as that of Henry James to the Exposition of the premier impressionists in 1876. Hardly more inspired, by the way, with that painting than his brother was by deaf-mutes, he thought those painters were devoid of any talent, and he considered them to be singularly lacking in imagination.[18]
FD:	You hit the nail on the head. The imaginary is something, say the Lacanians, that I must be suspicious of, and avoid like a plague. The analysts who will hear me hold it in holy horror. An analyst must work with the signifiers of language; he can only become mystified by images . . .
WITTGENSTEIN:	I don't see why it wouldn't be necessary sometimes to yield to the temptation to use some images, even if it means to give up looking for their diverse applications, including mystifying ones. Why have you so little confidence in yourself and in your impressions? I didn't think of you as relying on the agreement of others.[19]
FD:	But, at last, how can we know whether the reproduction that I will make of it is faithful or pure invention?
WITTGENSTEIN:	That's like my asking: how do you know that this color is red? It would be an answer to say: Because you have learned English.[20] Don't be so fearful! An interesting question to ask them would be, for example: could one imagine a stone having consciousness?[21]
FD:	There's the statue of the Commander again! But why don't you take it for granted, after Descartes,[22] that we are things that think (consciously or unconsciously), while, on the contrary, the stone is an extended thing and it doesn't think at all? What fly is still biting you? Is it the one you have helped to escape from the fly-bottle? Is it necessary to start all over again from scratch? You'd think you really were in a psychoanalysis.

Wittgenstein had stood up. He headed toward the window and went out on the balcony. He was talking to himself outside.

WITTGENSTEIN: And if anyone could imagine that a stone is conscious, why should that not merely prove that such image-mongery is of no interest to us?[23]

From my chair, I shot back at him:

FD: Well, let's not think of it anymore. Since that image-mongery is of no interest at all, let's leave it alone.

I saw him then lean over the balcony; he was making me dizzy.

FD: A little more and you're going to ask, as Descartes did, whether the hats and coats you see from that window aren't covering ghosts or dummies that are only moving by springs.[24]

WITTGENSTEIN: I can perhaps even imagine (though it is not easy) that each of the people whom I see in the street is in frightful pain, but is artfully concealing it. And it is important that I have to imagine an artful concealment here. That I do not simply say to myself: "Well his soul is in pain: but what has that to do with his body?"[25]

Seeing him lean over more and more dangerously, I in turn worried and went out onto the balcony.

WITTGENSTEIN: Look at that one laughing. It must be difficult to laugh when one is in such pain.[26]

From the height where we stood, it was impossible for me to distinguish faces. Feeling the anxiety rise, I tried to joke:

FD: The tools of philosophical optics since Descartes have improved. Do you use a zoom lens?

At that moment, Wittgenstein went back in. I stepped back too, for fear he was going to be angry. But his eyes weren't seeing me. His look was elsewhere; he was staring at the window casement. Intimidated by the expression on his face, I wondered whether he wasn't concealing an intense suffering. We couldn't remain like that. So, on the spot, I invented something to do outside—a visit to the ophthalmologist's, which I announced without thinking—and with no further delay we went downstairs and outside to the boulevard.

Chapter 24

The Window

The house in the woods.

FD, PAUL

Boulevard Monparnasse.

THE WOMAN ON THE SIDEWALK, FD, WITTGENSTEIN

The lively activity downstairs seemed to perk him up. Opposite at the post office we passed by one of my old acquaintances, a woman standing motionless on the edge of the sidewalk. A figure from central Europe, she was wearing a scarf, peering down the boulevard, standing like a babushka. She smiled at me and said with a strong Yiddish accent: "The Germans have occupied the Polish embassy. Get ready."

The Big History was once again getting mixed up with our little history. We were, effectively, in a period when East Germans had taken refuge in the Polish embassy in Berlin. I had expected our walk would get Wittgenstein to take his mind off things, but it didn't work. I greeted her in my turn, and went on my way. He started up again with renewed vigor.

WITTGENSTEIN: When I imagine that someone who is laughing is really in pain I don't imagine any pain-behavior, for I see just the opposite. So, what do I imagine? And I do not necessarily imagine my being in pain.[1]

FD: What if we talked about something else I'm done with my analytic work for today.

WITTGENSTEIN: What do we need an analyst for? What we especially need here is someone to play a theatrical part, to whom we would say: "Here you must imagine that this woman is in pain and concealing it." We give her no directions, do not tell her what she is actually to do. For this reason the suggested analysis is not to the point either. We must watch the actress who is imagining the situation.[2]

DOI: 10.4324/9781003437451-24

*I nodded in agreement, without trying to understand, and I hurried on. I was begin-
ning to feel sick, probably an effect of the dizziness before, but I didn't want him
to notice.*

PAUL:	Why is that?
FD:	Because this whole show was his business. I no longer wanted to be mixed up in it, especially since the date for my presentation was approaching and I still had nothing prepared. Besides, he didn't seem to want to help me. He persisted.
WITTGENSTEIN:	In what sort of circumstances should we ask anyone: "What actually went on in you as you imagined this?"[3]
FD:	Why not ask yourself? In what sort of circumstances does one imagine that the man in the street is concealing horrifying pains beneath a stone face, and beneath his laughter, a deadly anguish? Into what scenario do you want to drag me? *Night and Fog?** *Mother Courage*** during the Thirty Years War? Your prison camp at Monte Cassino?***

To get over this queasy feeling, I kept talking.

FD:	You don't want to answer me. Good. Well, if you like, I can tell you what went on in me and what I imagined by reason of my meetings with that woman, whom we have just passed by on the boulevard. We've been passing each other on the sidewalk for a good dozen years. In the beginning, I met her nearly every day while taking my children to school. Sometimes she followed close on my heels to the bus stop, to the window at the post office, through the Luxembourg Gardens, and I listened to her with only half an ear. But I couldn't ignore her pleading with me to watch out for these children, that they don't get snatched away. "She's imagining things," I would say to myself. That's what one says to oneself in such a situation. My only concern then was to escape, to find a polite way to end this discourse that had no commas and no periods. I tried, therefore, to get away from her when the tone of her voice got lower, but she had the knack of starting up again before I could get away. I imagined her to be a teacher—Jewish, either Russian or Polish. From observing her always on the look-out,

* *Night and Fog* [*Nuit et broullard (1956)*] by Alain Resnais is a short documentary film of the devasta-
tion and horror of the concentration camps of the Second World War.
** *Mother Courage* is probably Berthold Brecht's masterpiece. He wrote it in five months, in 1939, after
fleeing Germany for Sweden. The plot is set during the Thirty Years War (1618–1648).
*** Wittgenstein was a prisoner of war in 1918 at Monte Casino.

| | at the hours when the sidewalk is filled with the comings and goings of kids bent under the weight of their school bags, I eventually understood that for her children, this way to school must have been a path of no return. That's all. Is that all you want to know? |

WITTGENSTEIN: Go on.

FD: One fine day she stopped me, imperiously. It was in the month of June. "You're skinny; it's frightening," she told me. "Hide, they're going to come for you." I hurried on, forcing an awkward smile. To the devil with prophesying folly! How can I be at risk on this clear morning? Two months later, however, I entered the hospital, to have my operation. Like Theodore, she had guessed. Do you remember?

WITTGENSTEIN: And what next?

FD: The following school year, she had again taken up her look-out the post for the new children who, hand in hand with their mothers', went in their turn down the boulevard, butterflies in their stomachs, saying to themselves that they couldn't possibly soon let go of that hand. And she hurled at them her usual warning: "Pay attention to those children." And we passed by her, busy with our kids and our schoolbags, as sure of our square meters of asphalt as of those hands gripping ours. A little later that autumn there was an attack in a neighboring street,* blowing to pieces some of the children, ripping off the arms with which they held hands. You spoke of theater, yes, but "theater of cruelty."[4]

Since then, when the "look-out" and I pass each other, we smile; we know each other. She is a steadfast effigy of time. Recently she recommended that I organize the underground ("You never know"). Her words sound more and more familiar to me. Who talks through her mouth? Are they the poet's "dear voices which have fallen silent"**—talking through her mouth? At the time when I was of the age of those new little ones on the way to nursery school, the only talk at home was about those stories of escapes—of secret walled-up hiding places under curves in the roof—uttered in the same tone: "They have come, looking for the blond lady, my mother."

Then there was D Day, June 6, 1944; flags were put up. But the war was not over for everyone—not in the Alps; the Germans were retreating through the Vercors.***

---

* In 1981, a bomb went off at a discount store, Tati, in the Rue de Rennes, in the area between the district of Montparnasse and Saint Germain des Prés.

** This is the last line of *"Mon Rêve familier,"* in *Les Poèmes saturniens* of Paul Verlaine, written in 1866 and published by Gallimard in 1948. Cf. Paul Verlaine and Norman Shapiro, *One hundred and One Poems: A Bilingual Edition* (Chicago: University of Chicago Press, 2001), 4.

*** Vercors is a plateau in the Alps, where resisters were massacred in July 1944.

They were berserk; they knew they were done for. They locked men inside the barracks, who weren't seen again, until their mass grave was discovered later at the Little St. Bernard Pass. And the cries of the pharmacist whom they buried alive—and some weeks later, the German soldiers, who were being kicked in the ass, as they went up the main street to the football field, where they were shot. "They were kids:" said my father, "fifteen year old soldiers." Are these all part of the theater you were talking about? Is it always the same story that we've seen on TV between our entrée and the dessert? You seem tired. What if we go for a coffee?

Comfortably settled in on the terrace, I felt more in the mood to listen to him.

WITTGENSTEIN:	Can you still say after that, that you have images of your own, which your neighbor doesn't have?[5]
FD:	Of course, my story is made up of images that are my own.
WITTGENSTEIN:	How can you still qualify as your own, images that that woman also has—and, as a matter of fact, that others have too?
FD:	You're always drumming to me the same thing, that there is no private sphere. When I ponder it, I agree. But spontaneously, I think the opposite. So, I think she's slightly off, that Cassandra of the street, while her neighbors are not. Well, not in the same way—not quite so much.
WITTGENSTEIN:	You therefore don't understand that there is here no question of a "seeing"—and therefore none of a "having"—nor of a subject, nor therefore of "I" either. May I ask you: In what sense have you got what you are talking about and saying that only you have got it?[6] What are these words for? They serve no purpose.

I swallowed my burning coffee in order to give myself time, and I devoured croissant after croissant:

FD:	Don't hurry. Take again the example of our neighbor on the boulevard. Earthly possessions don't seem to overburden her. Another thing possesses her—if that's what you mean—but she doesn't keep it to herself either, since she pours it out in the public square on whoever happens to cross her path, her eyes, her destiny. Like Cassandra, "with the scent of a hound, she'll search out the blood . . . "[7]
WITTGENSTEIN:	I can go on: "What god, what power, forces you to this? Where is it from? Cries, shrieks, tuneless melodies of terror and horror. What set you on this path of horror?"[8] That modern Cassandra makes you see a new way of speaking, a new comparison; it might even be called a new sensation.[9]
FD:	So what? If it's more than two thousand years that the same sketch of Aeschylus is still running without intermission—what novelty do you find in it? Is it because ancient crimes

periodically vanish in amnesties? Because we no longer know about gods?* Must we re-discover them each time we brush against a catastrophe? In 1918 you wrote: "Whereof we cannot speak, we must pass over in silence."[10] Did you change your way of seeing things, and decide, in the '30's, that inevitably we could not pass over in silence what we could not speak about? What is this method of representation? A theater beyond good and evil? In which stones with consciousness have parts to play, whatever effort has been made to pound them down? Sometimes I wonder whether there are good crimes and evil crimes. Some exterminations are marked with three stars in ideological tour guides, while others don't merit the detour, and still others don't even receive the honor of being endorsed. By the way, what did you see in my window frame?

He stayed silent.

FD: You still don't want to tell me what you saw up there on my balcony? Is it something you've got and others haven't? See! You're relishing that image yourself, in your own dark room like something that belongs to you and to no one else.

WITTGENSTEIN: But what thing are you talking about?

FD: It's for you to tell me . . . *Das Ding*, why not?[11] The Freudian thing, taken out of language-games, which stinks and is rotting, like the body of Polynices (since you're keen on theater) deprived of burial, thrown out like garbage.[12] That thing is everyone's. I agree—but you, who give me a lecture, pull back when I ask you about it.

WITTGENSTEIN: You're wrong. The "visual" room has no master, outside or in. It need not have any owner. Inasmuch as it cannot be anyone else's, it is not mine either.[13]

FD: Then since you decree the suppression of private property for the "visual" room, why not simply say what you saw, and what I have seen you see?

He didn't answer. The basket of croissants was empty, and I asked the waiter for the check.

---

* Cf. Jacques Lacan, *The Ethics of Psychoanalysis, 1959–1960, The Seminar of Jacques Lacan, Book VII*, edited by Jacques-Alain Miller, translated by Dennis Porter (New York: W.W. Norton, 1997), 259–260: "Weno longer have any idea who the gods are and in order to recall what the gods are, we have to engage in a little ethnography."

Chapter 25

The Puppets

The house in the woods.

FD, PAUL

A Medical Center.

FD, WITTGENSTEIN

The Luxembourg Garden.

FD, WITTGENSTEIN, DESCARTES

Walking along, we reached the front of the medical center, where I was supposed to get a consultation. I hesitated before the list of various specialties, forgot all about the ophthalmologist, and finally decided on a dietetic consultation. I was feeling sick again. Without blaming the half dozen croissants I had just gorged on, I hoped that a healthy and balanced diet would bring my discomfort to an end, and solve the problem of my suddenly too tight belt. While on our way through a waiting room, Wittgenstein drew me out of this meditation, by asking me: "Who is this I who is in pain?"[1] Sensing I was being alluded to, I didn't answer him.

WITTGENSTEIN: When I say "I am in pain," I do not point to a person who is in pain, since in a certain sense I have no idea who is."[2]
FD: Because you're in pain?
WITTGENSTEIN: No, in saying this, I don't name any person. Just as I don't name any person when I groan with pain. Though someone else sees who is in pain from the groaning.[3]

In order to grab on to something, I concentrated on the game of tracking the arrows marking the way to the dietetic consultation. But he was blindly going along, following. This medical place must have inspired him.

WITTGENSTEIN: What does it mean to know who is in pain? For example to know who is in pain in this room? Is it the man who is sitting

DOI: 10.4324/9781003437451-25

over there, or the one who is standing in that corner, or the tall one over there with the fair hair, and so on . . .?[4]

FD: What are you getting at?

WITTGENSTEIN: At the fact that there is a great variety of criteria for personal "identity." Now which of them determines my saying that "I" am in pain? None.[5]

FD: Don't shout so loud; everyone is looking at us. Besides, I haven't told you I am in pain.

WITTGENSTEIN: You didn't say it, but you pointed to it by bringing me here.

FD: You mean I want to draw attention to myself?

WITTGENSTEIN: Surely what you want to do is to distinguish between yourself and other people. But are you sure you want to distinguish between your pain and another's? For example, Ludwig Wittgenstein's pain?[6]

I looked at him, stunned. But only then did it come to mind that this unpleasant state could also be his . . . It was ridiculous . . . We had come to a secretary's desk. We had to get in line.

FD: When I go into the common room at the psychiatric hospital, I often wonder how to know who is in pain—when I see that guy seated there, always in the same place, near the radiator, or the woman always looking out the same window, or still that tall young man with piercing blue eyes, who has the slow movements of a Japanese Butô dancer.

WITTGENSTEIN: It would be possible to imagine someone groaning out: "Someone is in pain—I don't know who!"—and then our hurrying to help him, the one who groaned.[7]

FD: That's what they often say. They have had themselves committed in order to sound an alarm, but the one who truly is in pain and should have his pain relieved is still at home.

Suddenly, it no longer seemed to matter so much for me to see a doctor, and I abruptly left the waiting line. While tearing down the stairs, I again asked him: "By the way, what did you see in my window?" Without waiting for an answer, I headed to the Luxembourg Garden, which was very nearby. The weather had gotten milder after the morning rain, and the sun stirred up a spring-like desire for a stroll.

WITTGENSTEIN: You seem better.

FD: It's not unusual. When a patient gets better, some relative of his often has to be hospitalized in a psychiatric or medical ward. As if we were connected by invisible threads to a thing waiting to give us a jolt of pain, one after the other.

WITTGENSTEIN: Imagine several people standing in a ring, and me among them. One of us—sometimes this one, sometimes that one—is connected to the poles of an electrical machine, without which he is unable to see. I observe the faces of the others and try to guess which of us has been electrified.—Then I say: "Now I know who it is; for it's myself." In this sense I could also say: "Now I know who is feeling the shocks; for it's myself." Don't you think this would be a rather queer way of speaking.[8]

FD: Sure, it would be simpler to say: "Ouch!" Curious—your story of the machine for torturing prisoners . . . Are you electrifying Dr. Bordeu's network in The Dream of D'Alembert,[9] which you were reading a short while ago. He too upheld the view to Mademoiselle de Lepinasse that man is not limited by the surface of his skin, but participates in a network constituted by many invisible strings. At the center of the web—a spider, located in the meninges (your beetle, in a way) which the good doctor uses to frighten the young lady. But she doesn't allow herself to be impressed and tells him that he has a marvelous fondness for madness.[10] I would indeed say as much to you.

While speaking, we had arrived at the puppet theater in the Luxembourg Garden. "Pinnochio" was on the bill—at last a tale with a moral!

WITTGENSTEIN: But if I make the supposition that I can feel the shock even when someone else is electrified, then the expression "Now I know who" becomes quite unsuitable. It does not belong to this game.
FD: What if we change the subject? You're telling me cock-and-bull theories.

I dragged Wittgenstein toward the merry-go-round, with its white elephant, celebrated by Rilke.* Then he wanted to explore the garden, while I sat down on a chair at the edge of the playground, where a bustling gang of kids was squealing. Moved by an old reflex, I took out a book from my bag, and set myself to reading it—one eye on the page, the other on the children who were throwing themselves headfirst down the big slide.

PAUL: And what did you happen to read, squinting in that way?
FD: As you probably noticed, books for me are talismans against the unknown. Before leaving, I had grabbed up my copy of Descartes in order to find the sentence about fools and chimeras which Wittgenstein had quoted to Madame Durand. In looking for it, I came upon the page where Descartes admits that he is not located in his body as a pilot in his ship.[11] He

---

* "*Das Karussell*" ("The Merry-Go-Round"), in *Rainer Maria Rilke: Selected Poems*. Translated by Ernest Flemming (New York: Routledge, 1990), 114–115.

then wonders about the "beyond" of the pleasure principle, in stressing the case of those sick people who usually know how to flee from what hurts them, and to look for what gives pleasure, but who still wish to eat and drink things which may be harmful.[12] I felt concerned by this page—especially about eating. Descartes was tackling there the vine of my symptom in the morning, de-masting the ship in which my mind wanted to be the pilot, and which might well change into a ship of fools. My symptom looked like what Descartes described about people suffering from dropsy, who cannot stop drinking, although drinking is injurious to their health.[13] Then he raises the question of how it is that the goodness of God does not prevent human nature from being faulty and deceptive.[14]

If I were you, Paul, I would pick up a psychoanalytic lesson from this same passage. At first totally attributing dropsy to a mistake of nature, Descartes states that a comparison of a sick man to a badly made clock "depends entirely on his thought and designates nothing found in the thing he's talking about."[15] His analysis gravitates then toward another paradigm, another way of looking at things and explaining nature in a manner that finds some truth in the things he's mentioning. For "a badly made clock, which tells time inaccurately, is still made of wheels and counter-weights, which follow all the laws of nature no less closely than it does when it completely satisfies the wish of its maker."[16]

For demonstration, Descartes compares the body to a vibrating cord, which can be moved by the slightest motion in any of its parts. "As, for example, in the stretched cord, A B C D—if its last part D is moved and pulled, the first part A would not be moved in another way, as it could be if one of its middle parts, B or C, were moved, while the end part D remained unmoved. Likewise."[17]

PAUL:	*All my relatives!* I see emerging a wave theory of the relations among people who are confined to a corpuscular theory—that is, among "individuals," at least as we call them in the West.*
FD:	You've guessed it. At that moment, Wittgenstein, who had taken a stroll in the garden, reappeared, whistling to himself. I read him the following passage as if he had known the preceding pages by heart: I too remember it quite well:
ED (TO WITTGENSTEIN):	"Likewise, like stretched cords extending from the foot to the brain, any part of the nerve reaching from the foot to the brain may be

* Cf. Chapter 22 for a brief discussion of Sullivan's "The Illusion of Personal Individuality."

felt as a pain in the foot."[18] The same, wrote Descartes, for dryness in the throat.[19] In other words, one doesn't choose the place in the body that says "ouch," or "I'm thirsty," or "I'm hungry," or "my foot hurts." And if, as you suggest, one extends the distribution of the pain along the stretched and vibrating cord to other bodies contiguous with it, one comes upon your aphorism: "I don't choose the mouth that says I have a toothache." Therefore, if today I have been hungry without being hungry, and if I have gorged myself while my health called for a diet, it's perhaps that another nausea was found at the other end of the vibrating cord, in the body of another person who could only be you. You follow me?

WITTGENSTEIN: No.

FD: If you prefer to remain among Diderot's strings, one doesn't choose the key of the harpsichord that says: "My fingers hurt," nor the mouth of the harpsichord player who says: "I have pain in my keys." And even more, what if you electrify the philosopher-harpsichord . . .

I hoped to make him sick, but he didn't let himself be upset. He took up the game:

WITTGENSTEIN: My turn! Answer these questions for me.

1 Are these books *my* books?
2 Is this foot *my* foot?
3 Is this body *my* body?
4 Is this sensation *my* sensation?[20]

FD: How many points for each question? Wouldn't you prefer, as in the magazines, to play at: Are you: "obsessional," "hysterical," "schizophrenic," "crazy," dropped on the head?

WITTGENSTEIN: Each of these questions has practical non- philosophical applications.[21]

FD: Let's see . . . The secret to the answer certainly doesn't consist in the possession of books, or sensations, which one can very well do without . . . One can even do without the body. I know analysts who, by dint of neutralizing themselves behind the backs of their patients, have become pure spirits, limited to their breathing . . . No, I don't see. I can't guess. "The cat's got my tongue."

WITTGENSTEIN: Think of cases in which my foot is anesthetized or paralyzed. Under certain circumstances, the question could be settled by determining whether I can feel pain in this foot . . . Sometimes, one might be pointing to a mirror-image. Under certain circumstances, however, one might touch a body and ask the question: "Is this body my body?"[22] For "I" is not the name of a person, nor "here" of a place, and "this" is not a name. But they are connected to names . . .[23]

FD: And when this connection isn't made, I might wonder whether my sensation isn't that of another. Your game consists then of successively cutting all the stretched, vibrating cords, the strings of our puppet, in order to make evident the different functions of the other, to which the sensation is related: the other as Imaginary, Symbolic and Real, to again pick up on the Lacanian triad.

He didn't react, probably not having had the time to pay a tourist's visit to the heights of Lacanianism. I asked him if he still had some other psychiatric curiosities to point out to me.

WITTGENSTEIN: But can't I imagine that people around me are automata, lack consciousness, even though they behave in the same way as usual? Say to yourself, for example: "The children over there are mere automata: all their liveliness is mere automatism." And you will either find these words becoming quite meaningless; or you will produce in yourself some kind of uncanny feeling, or something of the sort *unheimlich*.[24]

FD: I'm beginning to get used to it.

WITTGENSTEIN: It's nothing special, actually. Seeing a living human being as an automaton is analogous to seeing one figure as a limiting case or variant of another . . .[25]

FD: For example?

WITTGENSTEIN: The cross-pieces of a window, for example, as a swastika.[26]

FD: A swastika! That's what it was! But why choose precisely my window to make that damned emblem appear? . . . Now I'm positive; it's you who transmitted that vertigo, that disgust to me.

WITTGENSTEIN: What I'm supplying are really remarks on the natural history of human beings; I'm not contributing curiosities, however, but observations which no one has doubted, but which have escaped remark only because they are always before our eyes.[27]

PAUL: It seems to me that the moment has come for finding whatever cord he had made vibrate for you.

Chapter 26

The Dame Jeanne*

The house in the woods.

FD, PAUL

The Fontainebleau Forest

LA DAME JEANNE, JEAN-JACQUES ROUSSEAU

Boulevard Saint Michel, Port Royal

FD, WITTGENSTEIN, KLEIST AND HIS NARRATOR

Since I was starving again, I stopped to buy various licorices, marshmallows, and chewing gum at the little house situated near the fountain in the Luxembourg Garden, and to chat with the lady who runs the stand. Then, still in Wittgenstein's company, I hurried along, chewing, quite determined to take the shortest way home.

WITTGENSTEIN: There are people who are blind to the aspect of things changing, and are actually incapable of letting themselves be affected by them.[1]

FD: We should say in their defense that, "affected" in this way, they risk ending up in a psychiatric hospital—where their therapist will have the knack of remaining cool, looking for a way to stop the cord from vibrating and spreading images to him, so as to let these images return to the possession of the one hallucinating, as that person's own private property. I wonder what Descartes would have done with your swastika. Would he have advised you to turn toward God, and examine how the

---

* The French title of this chapter has been largely retained, because it has several meanings that would be lost in translation. "*La Dame Jeanne*" refers to a large rock that is in the shape of a *Dame-jeanne* (demi-john—a large container for wine or other alcoholic beverages). There is also a reference to FD's paternal grandmother, Jeanne, implied by the title.

DOI: 10.4324/9781003437451-26

goodness of God doesn't prevent you from having this vision? Or indeed, would he have asked if you needed mental glasses, or mood regulators?

WITTGENSTEIN: The feeling of an unbridgeable gulf between consciousness and brain-process: how does it come about that this does not come into the considerations of our ordinary life? This idea of difference in kind is accompanied by a slight giddiness—which occurs when we are performing a piece of logical sleight-of-hand.[2]

FD: Speaking of giddiness, as a matter of fact, a little while ago, I had no consciousness at all of what happened (if it wasn't through vertigo, or nausea, or a cold sweat) before we sat down for coffee. At some point I was even afraid of passing out. Don't worry. I've never fallen into the apples,* in my whole life.

WITTGENSTEIN: It's less important whether you had or had not been conscious of what happened. What interests me is that you informed me of the fact that you had been on the point of losing consciousness. It would be still more interesting if, after you fainted, you had said, upon coming to: I am conscious again.[3]

Again absorbed in chewing my gumdrops, I eventually located that sensation of vertigo, which before had lasted for several years following an accident.

FD: "I'm conscious again," you say that sentence had made my ears burn on a nice afternoon in autumn, but I couldn't say it to anyone, for the good reason that I was stretched out on the sand in Fontainebleau Forest,** deprived of my senses, except my hearing, which was working perfectly. Some voices were talking above me: "Maybe she's dead; we should send for the ambulance." I couldn't open my eyes. Where was I? I didn't know yet that I had fallen to the bottom of the rock of The Dame Jeanne, which I had scaled a few minutes before. The intermittent honking of car horns, and some flashes of light were bombarding my head, calling me back to consciousness. In the darkness, I noticed a black man in a white shirt who was X-raying me.

FD: Am I going to die?

* A French idiom for "fainted."
** This is a forest, south of Paris, famous for rock-climbing because of its huge sandstone rocks.

"No," he answered, and I sank again into a happy unconsciousness. I had been climbing the tall rock in Fontainebleau Forest, called "The Dame Jeanne," as though I had been tied to it by an invisible thread. The thread must have broken at the moment when, putting my hand on a ledge (I remember up to that point), I had calmly let go of my grip, without the least panic. That's how come I was lying, an inanimate puppet, on the narrow beach of sand where I had chanced to fall between two rocks.

WITTGENSTEIN:	But what happened before you fell?
FD:	Nothing special.
WITTGENSTEIN:	You're not extending the least thread to me. Do you hope that after all, you can weave a piece of cloth: because you are sitting at a loom—even if it is empty—and by only going through the motions of weaving.[4]
FD:	I had found an analyst several months before, after having read Freud. Once discharged from the hospital in Fontaine bleau, I returned to see him, with a serious headache. He wanted me to pay him for the sessions I missed, while I was in bed, and evidently unable to come to see him. I was shocked.
WITTGENSTEIN:	More precisely—Tell me what had happened just before the accident.
FD:	The Sunday preceding my fall, I had gone for a walk in Ménilmontant.* On returning, I had read "The Second Walk" in *The Reveries of the Solitary Walker*, which departs from Ménilmontant. In that account, Rousseau tells how he was knocked over by a Great Dane and had lost consciousness— "feeling neither the blow, nor the fall, nor anything that followed," until the moment he came to. I had been struck by that precise moment when he had been able to say to himself: "I am conscious again." That first sensation had been a delicious moment. He was born to live in that instant, and he had no distinct notion of being an individual, not the least idea of what had just happened to him. He knew neither who he was, nor where he was, and he felt neither bad, nor fearful, nor concerned."[5]

With this text as a direction, I had entered another text—that of my own history—at the exact point where the tool with the name "N" had been broken for me. It had broken on the given name of "Jeanne," my other grandmother in Savoy, near Les

---

* *Ménilmontant* was once a hilly suburb of Paris, where Rousseau used to like to stroll. It has since become part of the City.

Charmettes. My mother never let me meet that grandmother. When she died, I was old enough to have asked questions, but not allowed to. I didn't ask them, since nobody talked about that grandmother to me.*

WITTGENSTEIN:	What, then, had happened?
FD:	Did I ask you such indiscreet questions before?

He answered that, yes, I had, but he recognized that he had not answered either. There was no longer an answer to them. We were all square, and I could get on with my story:

FD:	I had, then, made my assault on the celebrated rock near Larchant**—a predestined place, because its basilica, Saint Mathurin, during the Middle Ages, was the site of an important pilgrimage for the mad.
PAUL:	You mean those "dropped on their heads"?
FD:	My analyst had ignored everything about the history of that place. But, willy-nilly, he probably took the place of the now secularized saint. Naturally, I had climbed and then fallen from "The Dame Jeanne," with only a beginning analysis as a resource. When I returned to my analyst, I informed him I was conscious again. With that new consciousness, described by Rousseau as a new birth, I was able to give him the name of that Dame of Rock who had thrown me to the ground and had forced me to recognize her.

A lot later—the time it takes for working on the loom of the analysis, the woof and warp of which had just suddenly come together—that very traditional grandmother, from Savoy, so sweet to those who had known her, appeared to me in a dream, before a hearth, with a tender face and figure that, as a child, I had not been able to imagine. Then she said good-bye to me and went to place herself in the fireplace, from which she disappeared, returning to where she had come from.

PAUL:	Again a story of stone that speaks in the place of the broken tool with the name "N."
FD:	Wittgenstein stayed silent. As we were reaching the gate of the Luxembourg Garden, we turned onto the Boulevard

---

* *Les Charmettes* is a village near *Chambéry,* the capital of *Savoie,* where Rousseau spent many happy days with Madame de Warens—all of which he recounts in *Les Confessions,* translated by Maurice LeLoir (New York: Barnes and Noble, 2005).

** *Larchant* is a village on the outskirts of the forest. A cluster of rocks in the forest is named after it. *Larchant* is also the site of a beautiful old church—of St. Mathurin.

Saint-Michel, in the direction of Port Royal.* I had the idea of telling this story in my presentation. What if they were going to think that I believe in ghosts? How could I justify myself? No—impossible!

WITTGENSTEIN: You'll see quite well what they'll accept as justification through what they say to you, but above all through what they do, through their form of life! What am I believing in when I believe that men have souls, or that there are ghosts?

. . . .There is a picture in the foreground, but the sense lies in the background. Only I want to understand the application of the picture,[6] and not what other people think about it.

FD: The answer is easy from the story I just told you: finding one's soul, or indeed losing it, is linked only to a string, a puppet string that connects us to the names of our disappeared ancestors. And what if we described, as in a puppet theater, those extreme moments when a scene that has never been written is staged . . . What do you think? I'm afraid they will be suspicious of my using puppets as psychoanalysts.

WITTGENSTEIN: You're afraid that the actual use of that picture might seem like something muddied. That's why you're terrified at the idea of talking. But actually, these forms of expression are like pontificals which we may put on, but cannot do much with, since we lack the effective power that would give these vestments meaning and purpose.[7]

FD: You're totally mistaken. Come to such a meeting. I'll bet you would have the impression of going to Mass: silence, compunction, seriousness. Well, I wouldn't want them to get the impression that we're puppets, but simply that the strings that link us, one to the other, are so thin and so strong that a simple word or an absence of a word is enough to break them or to tie them together. By the way, it's you, isn't it, who put those pictures of automata in my head in the first place?

Saying that, I retraced my steps, for I had just recognized a book in the bookstore window. I went in to buy Kleist's Anecdotes and Short Writings,[8] and I came out

* Port Royal is a famous crossroad, named after the Jansenist abbey.

triumphantly pointing out to Wittgenstein the chapter titled: "The Puppet Theater."
The book was an omen. Now I know how to start my presentation.

PAUL: You had run into a *klèdôn*. A common type of divination in
              antiquity—such as a word heard by chance in the street, or
              out of the mouth of a passer-by, or heard from a children's
              game—which may or may not carry the day. Like the Spar-
              tan General who engaged a battle as he heard a child, playing
              "hop- scotch," shout, "I won." And he won.

FD: I was very close to that general's mood on the eve of that bat-
              tle. So I buried my nose in my book as a priest buries his in his
              breviary, without worrying more about Wittgenstein, who took
              the opportunity to slip away. There we are. Now you know
              everything.

PAUL: Everything except the dreaded presentation, which I missed,
              since I came in at the end.

FD: To talk about "psychotic transference," I had used Kleist's
              text. In that short story, the link between the operator and his
              subject turns into a nightmare. The narrator, one evening in
              a public garden, meets an extraordinarily successful dancer
              from the Opera. That meeting takes place not far from the Pup-
              pet Theater, where the dancer pretends to learn the essence of
              his art. To the narrator's astonishment, the dancer makes him
              aware of the invisible operator, "who finds the way that leads
              to the puppet's soul." Moreover, the dancer is confident that
              he is able to demonstrate the operator's technique of placing
              himself at the center of gravity of the puppet—which means
              "dancing."[9]

I then asked the psychoanalysts in the audience which movements we should make
in order to find the way that leads to the soul, or the center of gravity, of those
strange figures haunting the asylums which we psychoanalysts have deserted—the
people who have endured the soul-murder that President Schreber went through,
and wrote about.[*]

PAUL: Psychoanalysis compares itself, rather, to a more tragic and
              noble theater.

FD: You don't have a clue. Go into a puppet theater. Believe me—
              you'll see one of the last arts that still involves the spectator

---

[*] Cf. Sigmund Freud, "Psychoanalytic Notes on an Autobiography of a Case of Paranoia (Dementia
Paranoides)" (1911) in *The Standard Edition of the Complete Psychological Works of Sigmund Freud,
Vol. XII*(London: The Hogarth Press, 1991).

as an active partner in what is played out in front of him. The operator's hands must find not only the way to the soul of the puppets, but also to the soul of the demanding public, who act and dance with them, shouting and crying out. The children holler, "Watch out!", with eyes and ears mesmerized by the scene on the little stage where the energy reverberates back to the operator and puts him in movement, improvising, as in the *commedia dell'arte*. Thus the transference I was talking about comes to life, between patient and analyst, by movements of the vibrating cords, alternatively the puppet, the operator, the spectators, who are successively, one for the other, the analyst and his patient. For that analyst must not only interpret, nor echo some signifier, but also join the dance. Only then, perhaps, might a banished scenario come into existence and be inscribed in a story.

PAUL: You're kidding! To the analysts, you sang: "Enter the dance; see how one dances . . . "!* No wonder they stayed seated. Honestly, you didn't even wait for the applause!

FD: Kleist's narrator also objects to this so-called belittling comparison, but the dancer insists. A puppet constructed according to his directions would be able to dance with an art unrivalled by any living being. For, it would be without any affectation, and it would never put on airs. I alluded to a trait in our profession—especially when we do not find the other's center of gravity—which impels us to be pretentious. I wanted to illustrate it with a clinical case.

PAUL: A clinical case? Where did you think you were?

FD: Not one from my own practice. Before Parisian analysts, I wouldn't have dared—although during the discussion, at the moment when you came in, some examples might have leaked out No, the case I talked about was given by Kleist's narrator at the moment when he wanted to demonstrate to the dancer, through the reversal, the grounds of his paradox. After the dancer showed him how to find the soul of the puppet and to make it come to life, the narrator showed him how to lose it. For that soul, like that of violins,** is not immaterial, even if it's invisible; anything—a slight touch—almost nothing—can ruin it. The analyst may find the way to that soul through dancing his part, but he also can kill it, by refusing to play.

* This is a line from a well-known song, *"Sur le pont d'Avignon."*
** The French refer to the sound post as the "soul of the violin."

In the text, the scenery changes. We are in the baths, where the body of a young friend of the narrator moves with a marvelous grace. In the foreground—a "psyché."* In the background— a museum, where, shortly before, the young man and he had admired a reproduction of the "Boy with a thorn in his foot." In that scene, the older one—playing the mentor—hounds his young friend, wanting to free him from the narcissistic impasse in which, he thinks, his young friend risks becoming trapped. He will use that "psyché" as his educational tool, to prevent him from putting on airs. But in the whole psychotherapeutic enterprise, he despises his young friend's soul, and, unlike the puppet master, he crushes his stamina.[10] How does the catastrophe come about? By cutting out of an impression. You'll judge for yourself.

The young man casts a look in the large "psyché" at the instant he first steps on a stool to dry off. In a glance, he recognizes the movement of the statue. He smiles, and calls to his friend for confirmation. Under the pretext of remedying his self-consciousness, the other starts laughing and lies to him, telling him that he's having visions! That's exactly what I call the cutting out of an impression, followed by its disastrous consequences. "The young man flushes, lifts his foot a second time so that he could show me, fails. Disturbed, he does it again.

. . . and in vain. The movements he executed had something so comic about them that I couldn't help laughing."[11]

PAUL:	What a devil your narrator is!
FD:	As analysts, we may stand in that wicked place, and slam the door in the face of those whom we have encouraged to come knock on it. Thus, (I said to my audience) the vanity of the therapist can nip in the bud the theatrical game that someone is performing—a moment of grace, in contact with the gods. Kleist's conclusion is sinister: "From that day, from that instant, an incomprehensible change took place in that young man. First, he spent his days in front of that mirror; then his charms declined. It seemed that an invisible and elusive force, like a bronze net, locked up the free play of his limbs, and when a year had passed by, it was no longer possible to find the least trace of that grace that not long ago had brought joy to the eyes of those close to him."[12]

* A large, standing mirror, in a frame—a swing-glass, which the French call a *"psyche,"* which, in Greek means "soul." In Roman myth, "Psyche" is portrayed as a maiden so beautiful that men can only stand and stare at her. As a cult of her beauty develops around her, rivaling the worship of Venus herself, her beauty isolates her more and more. But eventually Cupid himself becomes her husband and Jupiter makes her immortal, so that Venus would not be offended that her son married beneath his station. Cf. Apuleius, *The Transformation of Lucius, Otherwise Known as the Golden Ass.* Translated from the Latin by Robert Graves (New York: Farrar Straus and Giroux, 1979), 96–143. This book was originally published in 1951.

PAUL:	Nice brainwashing machine.
FD:	The body had been hit by a simple sentence. Well a body seems a lot stronger than a sarcastic remark. Only when the tool with the name "N" breaks can the body become dislocated. Is that to say that the young man didn't have the psyché well fastened to the body in the mirror? Perhaps. But where to find his psyche, if not between him and the other, in the "in-between" where the threads of language are tied and untied, and where the battle in which the young man loses face has been engaged?

The limit of that example depends on the fixed distribution of roles between the good and the bad: in the psychotic transference, we are successively called, as analyst and patient, to occupy their roles alternately. Besides, is the dislocated young man so innocent, as he pursues Kleist's narrator with his jerky movement, so that he will never forget him again?

PAUL:	Hadn't you described to them, in your presentation, the jousting between host and visitor?
FD:	In great detail. To bring them onto the site of that battle, I had even cited an old T'Chan saying which should have seemed familiar to them: "Do not know him whom you meet; do not know the name of him with whom you converse."[13] Then I had described the confrontation of logical impasses and of impossible questions supposed to strip us analysts, gradually, of every bit of affectation. "Look," said Lin Tsi, "at the puppets, which perform on the platform; there's always a man inside."[14] What's at stake in an analysis, I concluded, is the coming on the stage of this subject, "the real man without qualities"*—the subject of stories foreclosed from history, whose soul, as well as the tool with the name "N," has been broken
PAUL:	Now I understand the pouting faces your listeners were making when I arrived. And also the silence that followed the end of your presentation—one of those analytic silences whose palpable density seemed proportionate to the number of analysts.

I had woven my yarn all the way to the end, and then I stayed silent. Some owls came by, tracking an animal in front of the log cabin. They shrieked with high-pitched cries. When we had rushed to the doorstep, the trees were peaceful again under the moon, and the hooting was already far away. Then everything once again fell back into silence.

* Cf. Chapter 7.

Chapter 27

The Little Boy

The psychiatric hospital.

MEDICAL DIRECTOR, FD, ALBERTINE

The clinic.

FD, WITTGENSTEIN, THE CHILD, SOCRATES, THEAETETUS

Early the next morning I was ready to be on my way, although I found it hard to leave the log cabin. Paul asked me to pass along to Wittgenstein, as a kind of good-bye, the words of Stanley Red Bird: "See you—one of these days—in hell!" Paul's paradise was made up of mountains. Against medical advice, he intended to go to Nepal. He was smiling as he said good-bye and his eyes told I'd never see him again.

Back in Paris, I also thought I wouldn't see Wittgenstein again, until that day I was waiting for the bus (as I do every week), which took me to the hospital. I had brought the Theaetetus with me, which I had taken at Paul's place that evening, now so long ago. Until then, I hadn't thought either of reading it, or of giving it back to Paul. I sat down under the bus shelter to glance at it, without being at all surprised that I was there alone, unaware that there was a transport strike that day. I hit on a passage, underlined by Paul, where Socrates asks the young mathematician whether it is possible for someone who knows, not to know the thing that he knows.[1] I continued to page through, reading along some underlined sentences, praying to heaven that the bus not arrive.

Socrates—Then knowledge is to be found not in the impressions but in the process of reasoning about them.

Theaetetus—So it appears . . .[2]

Socrates—Now I want you to suppose, for the sake of argument, that we have in our souls a block of wax, larger in one person, smaller in another.[3]

DOI: 10.4324/9781003437451-27

A car horn honked: From the car, the medical director was beckoning to me to get in. For once, he was in a mood to chat:

MEDICAL DIRECTOR: Did you forget about the strike? Last evening I went to see some NÔ theater. It's completely incomprehensible. You would like it. They say the scene takes place at "the crossroads of dreams."[4] Isn't that a little like your idea about the analysis of the psychoses—"at the crossroads of the dreams" of the analyst and the patient, where a story that can't be written can be represented?

But I was miles away. So, realizing that I was gathering my wits, he drove along in silence for a long while, then drew me out of my rêverie:

MEDICAL DIRECTOR: Albertine ran away this weekend; no one knows what became of her.

At this news I became gloomier. On her last escape she was found on the run, covered with knife wounds, by one of those casual friends she specialized in. Everyone, including myself, would say about her: "Albertine is hopeless; she'd be able to live outside, but she doesn't want to." All her attempts at leaving, officially or secretly, ended in disaster, with the police bringing her back to the asylum, or to a Parisian intensive care unit. I expressed my bitterness:

FD: What a whimsical idea to want to be interested in her! She's still someone for whom the psychoanalytic approach really seems to do no good at all. She never wants to see me. She runs away when she meets me; she insults me if I insist.

In the car, silence shrouded us again. It had all begun, several years before, when, on the advice of a nurse, Albertine had shown me a notebook filled with poems, in verse and in prose. They were marvelously crafted, with calligraphy and illuminations, like uncanny flowers in the ravaged countryside of her existence. We had seen each other; then, we talked about them. At that time I had gathered some bits and pieces about her. There was public assistance. There was a lot of foster-care. Too many people were unequal to the task. Her father died too early, and her mother had had to be mothered. Her own children had to be placed in protective care too. She evoked them with such understatement, that I felt they were her whole life. One day, notebook, belongings, had all inexplicably disappeared. Chaos had returned with renewed vigor, and the world was beginning to look like "a tale told by an idiot, full of sound and fury, signifying nothing."

I confided this to the medical director. "One isn't omnipotent," he stated, shrugging his shoulders, while clearing the hospital gates which, even though they were activated automatically, were also activated magically by a resident in a faded gray hospital uniform. He took his hat off to us.

Albertine was there, in the common room. She had returned in the early morning. Her aspect had changed. She seemed lost—embodying for the first time that madness which, until then, she had resisted so intensely. Today, her commitment didn't seem at all arbitrary. I said to her, without thinking: "Come, let's go talk." She followed me willingly. On the stairs, I unfortunately happened to turn around and ask her, without conviction: "So, what's happened?" She stopped short, and started shouting for anyone to hear: "No, I don't want to be psychoanalyzed! Help! She's forcing me! She's completely crazy!" Since I wasn't "burning with zeal" that day, I prepared once again to capitulate. Suddenly, she changed her mind, started to climb the stairs again, and explained:

ALBERTINE:　　　　　I'd like to know what I'm feeling. I don't understand. The others say I'm doing badly; they jab me with injections. Today, I have something for you to read. Open the door to my room.

I took out my key; she rifled through her wardrobe, and took out the famous notebook, which I didn't even know still existed. Then we headed together toward the small room across from the beauty parlor, where the hairdresser was occupied in setting a drowsy grandmother's hair. Albertine went to shake hands with her and then rejoined me.

ALBERTINE:　　　　　I had escaped to talk to Sidney, an old friend of mine who was not well, but didn't know it. I ring the doorbell; they let me in. They tell me: "Sidney just hanged himself." There he was, all red and blue, laid out on the bed. I take back my notebook, which I had let him have for safekeeping and go running back to the hospital. I'd like to know if I feel something, and what it is that I feel. I wonder what he was able to feel. I don't know what I want to know.

She handed me her notebook opened at the page of her new poems, written just before her escape. They were entitled "Des- tined,"* and they evoked in a superb

---

*   The French word here is *"Destinées."* As a noun the meaning is "Destinies." As a participle, it means "destined," in the feminineplural. The meanings are both present in the passage. "Destined" has the sense of "intended for," while "Destiny" has the meaning of "fate." Unfortunately, the two meanings are collapsed into one in the English translation.

style an obscure wall, crossed destinies, and a world in irons that she wanted to liber ate. I read them in a loud voice. She told me for the first time: "I'm not doing very well, I think." After a moment of silence, she continued:

ALBERTINE:	This morning, I played ghosts. Under my sheet, I went all through the hallways making the sound boo, boo . . . , I woke up the whole floor. After I got the injection, I don't know any more." She smiled.?
ALBERTINE:	They must have taken me for a nut.
FD:	You're not the only one here to chase after ghosts. And yours, under its sheet, what could it be feeling?
ALBERTINE:	Revenge! One year, we had been placed, my little brother and I, in the home of a sadistic, crazy woman. We wanted to kill her. We had put crushed glass in her food. It made no difference to her. That woman must have been armor-plated. Still, today, if I could get hold of her, she would have a bad time.

A nurse knocked at the door. She had just been looking for Albertine. The doctor wished to see her after her escape, so I let her go. At the end of the morning, I called a taxi to take me to the clinic. On arriving, I found the place deserted. Strange—no secretary and no one in the waiting room. Probably that transport workers' strike. Finally alone! I settled in to continue my reading:

Socrates—Can a man see something and yet see nothing?
    Theaetetus—Certainly not.
    Socrates—Then a man who is seeing something is seeing something which is?
    Theaetetus—Apparently.
    Socrates—It also follows that a man who is hearing anything is hearing someone thing and something which is.
    Theaetetus—Yes.
    Socrates—And a man who is touching anything is touching someone thing, and a thing which is (Plato, Theaetetus 188e)[5]

"So, that impression of strangeness corresponds quite well to something which is," I said to myself, half reassured. I came upon the passage about the wax where Socrates opposes, on the one hand, those in whom "the wax in the soul is deep and abundant, smooth and worked to the proper consistency; and when things that come through the senses are imprinted upon this 'heart' of the soul . . . the signs that are made in it are lasting, because they are clear and have sufficient depth But, it is a different matter, when a man's 'heart' is 'shaggy' or when it is sticky and encrusted with impure wax; or when it is very soft.

Persons in whom the wax is soft are quick to learn but quick to forget; when the wax is hard the opposite happens."[6]

Albertine had a soul made of deep and smooth wax, and what had come through her senses, had been well imprinted. This clear impression had set her off like a shot, in pursuit of old resentments, and she had brought back the ghost of a childhood given over to 'shaggy' and false hearts. "How does it happen," I said to myself, "that this way of knowing called "psychosis" is so regularly discredited?"

The telephone rang. The head nurse informed me that Albertine had found some work that very afternoon and was claiming she'd leave for good this time. She wanted an appointment in the outpatient clinic for the following week. After I hung up, I suddenly felt very lonely. The clinic seemed freezing cold to me and I got up to go and verify whether anyone was waiting in the waiting room. A known figure came to meet me.

WITTGENSTEIN:	Descartes died of the cold in Stockholm, and Gödel of hunger, not all that long ago in Princeton. Haven't you seen his ghost pass by, dragging the label "paranoid delirium" attached to his sheet?
FD:	Gödel? The one with the theorem?
WITTGENSTEIN:	He himself. My countryman. He didn't much like my philosophy, but he took a close interest in spirits. He let himself die of hunger in 1978, while in the hospital, believing "they" wanted to poison him with drugs.[7] So, obviously, he had more than one string in his bow— several language-games aiming at the unnamed —several sciences, caught in his aviary, as Socrates says in the Theaetetus.[8]
FD:	Why was he refused another way of access to knowledge than the one for which he had been so highly praised? In the hospital where he had let himself be shut in, with all his knowledge—could it be that they had used the wrong language-game, so inappropriate, in approaching him.
WITTGENSTEIN:	They were misled by the current parallel: psychology treats of processes in the psychical sphere, as does physics in the physical.[9]
FD:	That's precisely the mistake Socrates talked about: in the chase for the sciences that fly inside the aviary— thinking to take a dove, they caught a wooden pigeon.
WITTGENSTEIN:	Probably. Although, seeing, hearing, thinking, willing, are not the subject of psychology in the same sense in which the movements of bodies, the phenomena of electricity etc., are the subject of physics. You can see this from the fact that the physicist sees, hears, thinks about, and informs us of these phenomena, and the

psychologist observes the reactions of the subject as if he is detached from his senses.[10] Is there such a thing as "expert judgment" about the genuineness of expressions of feeling? More correct prognoses will generally issue from the judgments of those with better knowledge of mankind . . . Can one learn this knowledge? Yes, some can. Not, however, by taking a course in it, but through "experience."[11]

FD: What would your prognosis have been on the subject of his ghosts and extraterrestrials? You yourself aren't such a stranger to the question.

WITTGENSTEIN: I'm even less so; I also caught ghosts in my aviary.

I was dumbfounded. I had kind of gotten used to the fact that Wittgenstein didn't want to talk about his brothers who had killed themselves. Were they going to show up at my place? One Wittgenstein was okay, but four I had no room for them.

I started to panic, sensing myself more and more lonely, and finding the clinic gloomy.

FD: What to do?

WITTGENSTEIN: Keep cool. When it looks as if there were no room for such a form between other ones you have to look for it in another dimension. If there is no room here, there is room in another dimension.[12]

At that moment, there was a knock at the door. Fearfully, I opened it. It was only a little boy around ten years old. He must have mistaken the door, for the children's service was located on the other side, on the same level. I accompanied him, and found the other waiting room, open and also deserted. I settled him down with some comics, as if everything was normal, telling him not to worry, that his psychotherapist would certainly come. Calmed by that child's presence, I again took up the conversation with Wittgenstein:

FD: In another dimension, you were saying?

WITTGENSTEIN: When I say the orders "Bring me sugar" and "Bring me milk," they make sense, but not the combination "Milk me sugar." That does not mean that the utterance of this combination of words has no effect. And if its effect is that the other person stares at me and gapes, I don't on that account call it the order, given to you, to stare at me, or gape, or to be in a cold sweat, or to chatter your teeth, as you just did right now, even if that was precisely the effect I wanted to produce.[13]

FD: Are you really amused?

WITTGENSTEIN:	Seriously, to say "This combination of words makes no sense" excludes it from the sphere of language and thereby bounds the domain of language. But when one draws a boundary it may be for various kinds of reason. If I surround an area with a fence or a line or otherwise, the purpose may be to prevent someone from getting in or out . . . or it may show where the property of one man ends and that of another man begins; or to jump over it.[14]
FD:	That little game can end very badly: you jump over the line your brother drew on the ground thinking you're playing hopscotch, whereas he lays you out cold, thinking he had drawn the map of the eternal city.

I immediately regretted this allusion. What a blunder! While we were talking, the little boy squeezed his way inside the room. Undoubtedly bored over there, or indeed, having followed me, he was listening behind the door.

THE CHILD:	And when you're afraid, what do you do?
WITTGENSTEIN:	You have to play-act your fear.[15]
FD:	His analyst will soon come. You're not going to demolish his psychotherapy for him.
THE CHILD:	Then, should we play your game?

Taking his scarf, he went around behind me and blindfolded me.

THE CHILD:	Close your eyes; don't cheat.

Then he asked me to name all the objects he touched in the room, which I did with more or less success. My mistakes delighted both of them. I wanted to be upset, but I didn't have time, for the noises were becoming more and more bizarre: squeaks, murmurs, brushing. I said, "Uncle."

THE CHILD:	You're a fool. Don't be afraid. They're ghosts.

I got permission then to take off my blindfold. Heading right toward the window, the child closed the sliding shutters. Then turning on the light, he came back to sit across from me.

THE CHILD:	This is the dream store. We're playing "shopping for dreams." It's your shop.
FD:	Sir, what would you like? I asked him in a very business-like way.
THE CHILD:	A nightmare.

I wrapped it up for him, and he took it from my hands, and put it in my head. Then he bought a revenge dream from me. Then he turned off the light and said in the dark all the bad words and all the insults he knew—which took a lot of time, for his capacity wasn't small. Then, calmed, he said:

THE CHILD:	And if we were selling nice dreams? Would you turn the light on again?

I complied. Returning to my place, I found it was taken. Holding court in my chair, he was jubilant.

THE CHILD:	The ghost came back into your head, like a butterfly. It set itself down on a thought, and it came back in mine, changed into an idea.
FD:	What ghost?
WITTGENSTEIN:	Why not that of his brother who killed himself?
FD:	You know him?
WITTGENSTEIN:	There are words that can be wrung from us,—like a cry. Words can be hard to say: such, for example, as are used to effect a renunciation, or to confess a weakness. Words are also deeds.[16]

With these words he got up and gently left, the little boy on his heels. I followed them into the street, and I caught up with them at the moment when having passed The Porte d'Orleans,* they went down the avenue Maréchal-Leclerc. The noise of the street made conversation difficult. Nevertheless, I asked:

FD:	So, is it going to stop?
WITTGENSTEIN:	It's going to stop now.
FD:	You can't leave like that, without telling me why.
WITTGENSTEIN:	Your mistake, as always, is to look for an explanation . . . where you ought to have said: this language-game is being played.[17]
FD:	Which one? You can't disappear without telling me.

---

* One of the ancient gates of the City of Paris, leading to the southern suburbs, where the clinic was located.

*I saw them both stop, and then, on the sidewalk, they played a clown skit for me, in which Wittgenstein was the white clown and the child was Auguste.**

WITTGENSTEIN: Imagine someone pointing to his cheek with an expression of pain.[18]

The child complied and said:

THE CHILD:	Abracadabra.
WITTGENSTEIN:	What do you mean?
THE CHILD:	I meant "toothache."
WITTGENSTEIN:	How can one mean "toothache" by that word?
THE CHILD:	But, why don't I have the right to say: "By 'Abracadabra' I mean toothache"?
WITTGENSTEIN:	Of course you have the right.
THE CHILD:	And why wouldn't I have the right to say "to want to say" instead of "to mean"?
WITTGENSTEIN:	That's how you say "to mean" in French, isn't it?

*So, had we been playing, as the Philosopher meant, the game of "wanting to say" as "desiring to talk"? They had started off again, side by side, in silence. Having arrived at the Place d'Enfer** (as it was written in an earlier time), they probably considered this square to be the right place, for they headed toward the mouth of the metro, which beckoned to them. Before stepping into it, Wittgenstein turned around again to shout something to me, but the noise of the cars prevented me from understanding. That wasn't so bad. I didn't even know if I was sad.*

After I got home, I again opened Paul's book to dispel that hint of sadness. On the last page Paul had underlined, Socrates concluded: "Well then, our art of midwifery tells us that all of these offspring are wind-eggs and not worth bringing up? . . . And so, Theatetus, if ever in the future you should attempt to conceive or should succeed in conceiving other theories, they will be better ones as a result of this enquiry. And if you remain barren, Theaetetus, you will be less of a burden to those you meet . . ."[19]

---

* In French circuses, the clown named "Auguste," whose companion is the white clown, is the clumsy one. His name is thought to have been derived from the German *"dummer Augustus,"* (meaning "idiot"), once the emperor of Rome.
** Literally "The Place of Hell." That name was changed to *Place Denfert- Rochereau*, in honor of a famous general of the Franco-Prussian War (1870–1871). *D'Enfer* and *Denfert* have the same sound.

Postfaces

Postface by William J. Hurst

Translating La Folie Wittgenstein

Wittgenstein's Folly is my translation of Françoise Davoine's *La Folie Wittgenstein*. The word *"folie"* has several connotations in French, all of which are in play in this book. It refers to "madness," but also to the "folly" of the "fools" or *"sots"* who play a major role in medieval theater and in French Renaissance literature in the political satires called *"sotties."* It was in this register that Erasmus, in his *In Praise of Folly,* had "Folly" speak as a woman. In the eighteenth century, a *Folie* could refer to a large house that an aristocrat had built for his mistress. Then there is "Seward's Folly," which was a popular description of the purchase of Alaska in 1867 by William Seward, the US Secretary of State. On an etymological level, there is also a connection between *"folie"* and *"feuille"* (leaf). A collection of a certain kind of leaves might be referred to as a folio or a book.

Because of these connotations, the title doesn't especially evoke a folly or madness that is Wittgenstein's, but rather the house or place where it comes to reside, during an analysis, in a psychotic transference. It is important to note that its emergence doesn't correspond to a diagnosis of psychosis but rather to a process that unfolds in certain circumstance, most particularly when pieces of history have not been inscribed in the Big History, perhaps for generations. Folly enters into the relation between analyst and analysand and demands to speak.

Françoise Davoine is a psychoanalyst, formed at the *École freudienne de Paris* in the 1970s. During the latter part of that decade, she began making regular visits to the United States, first to the Austen Riggs Center, in Stockbridge, Massachusetts, and then to Chestnut Lodge, and also, by invitation of Jerry and Robby Mohatt, to the Sioux Rosebud Reservation in South Dakota. These geographical transferences moved her into some different traditions, far from her familiar references. Formed in classical literature and sociology, a teacher-researcher member of the Center for the Study of Social Movements (CEMS), founded by Alain Touraine at the *École des Hautes Etudes en Sciences Sociales,* she conceives of "madness" in the context of social relations and history. For anyone familiar with his work, her choice of Wittgenstein as interlocutor in this book is not surprising. The ways through which "language can bewitch the intelligence" do not depend on the individual speaker, nor upon any of their own deficits.

After having studied with Lacan, who gives all the importance to language and to speech, she continued her investigations through Wittgenstein's "language games," which are also "forms of life." According to this conception, one cannot approach a patient, when madness is present, by working solely on the internal world or by limiting oneself to their individual history. It is important to discover their links with the Big History, within which we all must find our place. And so, "folly" becomes, at the same time for analyst and patient, a field of research where events that have been cut out of the Big History can be actualized at a micro-historical level and inscribed in a symbolic register. This work requires relying on the interferences in the analyst's history, starting with those bits of the real from which traumas are made and which can be authenticated by an agreement worked out in the transference. This research is truly a co-research in which what was inaccessible in the exchange between people can finally be named and inscribed in the past.

I met Françoise Davoine in the fall of 2002 at the Austen Riggs Center, in Stock-bridge, Massachusetts. She was there to present a case to the Lacanian Clinical Forum. She and Jean-Max Gaudillière had come frequently to Austen Riggs since the late 1970s, originally at the invitation of William Richardson, a philosopher, a Heidegger scholar and the clinical research director at that time at Austen Riggs, having been invited by Otto Will.

On the morning of her presentation, she approached me to introduce herself and to find out something about me. I was someone she didn't know, and I gathered eventually that she wanted to find out who was in the room and whom she would be talking to. My immediate impression was that she was one of the Lacanians from Québec, and I asked her if this was so. She laughed and said she came from Paris and was the presenter for the day. I was a little embarrassed, but also very pleased that I had met the day's speaker and had a chance to get to know her a little before settling down to listening.

In general, I am not a very good listener at conferences or talks of any kind. I tend to be too critical and dismissive of what often strikes me as inexcusable inconsistencies or mistaken connections among ideas. I was not prepared for what unfolded that day and the next morning. That day's "talk" has stayed with me for a very long time. It was a true dialogue with the room, often involving the group in the search for more precise wording, for theoretical clarifications or for ways to remove ambiguities. But what struck me most forcefully was the practical dimen-sion of Jean-Max Gaudillière's formula: "Trauma speaks to trauma." This struck a nerve that continues to reverberate.

I had read and studied Husserl, Heidegger and phenomenology with Bill Rich-ardson, who had directed by dissertation on Merleau-Ponty. He had recommended that I participate in a clinical meeting of the Lacanian Clinical Forum, which was founded by John Muller and François Peraldi, and which I had attended the previ-ous year. This time, my wife, Elaine, who is also a philosopher and psychoanalyst, was with me, having just joined the group. As I was speaking with Bill during a break, I learned of the existence of a book by Françoise. Bill knew that my wife had done her dissertation on Wittgenstein, and he thought that a project of translating this book into English might interest her.

In the weeks following, I obtained a copy of *La Folie Wittgenstein* and started to translate it. Elaine was no more prepared than I was to translate a book from French into English but since I had worked over many years with French texts, especially those of Merleau-Ponty, I took up the rather unlikely task of translating Françoise's book.

After having finished a few chapters, I sent what I had done to Françoise, without having asked her in advance if she agreed with my intention to work on her book. The following year we began to meet frequently, almost always in the United States on the occasions of Françoise and Jean-Max's frequent visits for various professional and personal reasons. We worked on the text as a team. My wife, the Wittgenstein expert, and the better writer with a very precise ear for the best and clearest way to say something, was a major player in the work of this team. "What can be said at all, can be said clearly," became our governing principle.

So, the three of us, Françoise, Elaine and myself, went over the text of my translation, comparing it line by line, paragraph by paragraph, with the original. At several important junctures, Jean-Max made some incisive and consequential interventions regarding such topics as the various levels of meaning in French, or the most accurate reading of a classical Greek text. When we had a problem with some sentence or phrase I had chosen, Elaine would always find a better or more felicitous way of saying something.

Over time, the three of us came to call these meetings our "laughing sessions," which were often stimulated by some absurd or surreal effects of my translation, where I sometimes took oral expressions too literally, knowing considerably less about conversational French than I knew about the French of the philosophers. One of the most challenging aspects of translating from French to English is the very different conception of time in each language. Discussions of tenses occupied a lot of our time. Another problem area was the translation of humorous remarks or of remarks whose force is dependent on a play on words. In French, this works much better than it does in English, so at times we resorted to a footnote explanation.

So, the translation was the fruit of the work of several and not an individual effort. In a sense, language itself required this, but in another sense, I required it since I could not have situated myself adequately within a French social world without these attempts to create such a world. And so, I wish to express my gratitude to Elaine and Françoise for their help in this work of translation, for which I take full responsibility because the final decision was always mine to make, knowing that other interpretations are possible for certain difficult passages.

My interest in helping to bring this book to publication in English has arisen, not simply from my involvement as the "translator" but also from my engagement with the text as a psychoanalyst and philosopher. I hope that clinicians, thanks to this work, will be able to come closer to the catastrophic areas of their own histories and then to the madness of their patients. From there, they can perhaps discover more efficacious ways of working with patients usually referred to as mentally ill, by permitting the Folly (madness) of History to enter transferences where the unsayable can finally be spoken.

Postface by Ariel Olmert

"I would like to add the following: we really seem to think that our ability to say something to someone goes without saying."

Ludwig Wittgenstein

There is a land, situated somewhere between Person and Proper Noun and that land is called Someone. Someone is not a place you can find on a map. The misinformed traveler that embarks on a journey across this land alone is likely to lose their way. It is therefore prudent to assemble a crew beforehand. This is a book that gives some useful information about this journey.

On occasion, we hear ourselves tell a friend going through a tough time to go and talk to someone. This banal statement is, nevertheless, a gamble. That "Someone" is in fact, a vague figure that we would especially not like to get confused with just anyone. Luckily, this tip—to go and talk to someone—sets things in motion. "Someone" is simultaneously a land, the name of a person and the idea of a journey.

Everyday language plays tricks on "Someone" and exposes them to other dangers. One can be fervently encouraged to "become Someone" quite precisely, that is to say, something. If one does indeed achieve this, one is celebrated for this achievement. In this case, like in others, it can take years to recover. If it's even possible. The problem is complex. Not to mention those—who are the subject of this book—whose ideas are no longer clear. These people can wake up one morning and see the king of Bohemia in the mirror. They can transform into a lawnmower. They can also not be able to do anything at all. "Psychotic," for what it is worth, is the term used to identify these people. In everyday language, the more generous term is "crazy." In its wake, we can also mention: mad, wacky, deranged, demented, insane, lunatic, maniacal or your average schizophrenic; what thirst in the quest for a label! Or, maybe not after all.

Anyhow, go and talk to someone. But, can this someone, also called a psychoanalyst, ask a lawnmower to freely associate? The psychoanalyst would have a mowed lawn. And, if the king of Bohemia laid down on the couch, would it not become a throne? This results in a lengthy psychoanalytical treatment. Hence, the scientific rigor that oversees a lobotomy: as it is impossible to know what is not right in a person's head, let us look inside! This method and associated modern declinations are becoming more and more sophisticated, and their effectiveness is unquestionable. So, let us call them into question. In the soul's bureaucracy, every evil has a prescription, you only have to follow the case file. It is common sense then, for mankind to think that the secret to a personality is swimming under a microscope in a type of bodily fluid. Might as well look for it in a pumpkin.

And then, finally, we find our way back to this archaic thing that we call speech. That thing was used to give helpful advice to go and talk to someone. Yes, this is even possible for sick people that are not really much but can also be many at the same time. *La Folie Wittgenstein*, a book written by a psychoanalyst up against madness, explores a clinical field in which the spoken word, despite its fragmented existence, remains the principal hobbyhorse. This book is therefore a battle that happens to also be about battles. The psychoanalyst's battle with her own biases; her struggles with patients that resist traditional psychoanalytical recipes; and finally, the battles that patients bring from their family histories, sometimes also from History with a capital 'H', to the analyst's office. In addition to language as the main tool, we can add a vision of mankind aiming toward the crossroad where small stories become part of history. The psychoanalytical journey thus implies the composition of archives. We do not rummage through them, we create them. It is a strange exercise in which the psychoanalyst must also bring something to the table. In order to journey through countries erased from the map, the psychoanalyst must emerge from the shadows. That is essentially the subject of this book. Perhaps now is the right moment to discuss its genesis and content.

Originally from the field of literary studies, Françoise Davoine is also a Doctor of Sociology. She arrived at psychoanalysis' door through a series of chance encounters, among which her participation in Jacques Lacan's seminar. Luckily, her use of the French language was not damaged due to this experience. In the early 1970s, she became interested in the analytical approaches to madness being used in England and the USA. She has included in this book an abundance of materials and authors encountered while overseas. She is a clinician within and beyond psychiatric hospitals, and she has led for the past 30 years a research seminar at the EHESS entitled "Madness and the social link" with Jean-Max Gaudillière. Within this context, her experience as a psychoanalyst is renewed through readings of great texts: medieval satirical plays, the works of Hanna Arendt, the adventures of *Don Quichotte*, which she studied in another one of her books, as well as the works of Tristram Shandy, the English successor to Cervantes and Rabelais. And, of course, Wittgenstein.

Wittgenstein speaks out in this book. The conversation the author has with Wittgenstein can cast doubts on her own mental stability. Hallucinating that a person, known to be dead since 1951, is chasing after you while violently spewing philosophical thoughts could have earned the author, in any other circumstance, a place on a closed ward; as a patient, of course. Furthermore, the immense intellectual prestige that surrounds the figure of Wittgenstein could have facilitated the diagnosis of "mystical madness," like those able to speak with Jesus.

This book's understanding of Wittgenstein exists within the context of experience. Moreover, it is one of her patients, "the philosopher," that brought Wittgenstein to her attention. The Wittgenstein with whom she raves, in turn, represents the space or universe in which the psychotic patient and the analyst are not completely removed from one another. This third party, Wittgenstein, already infers to the existence of the land that we visit during a '*folie à deux*'. The challenge is no longer to establish a diagnostic—there is as much madness in the world as there are mad people—but to take note of this connection.

What remains is that Wittgenstein is not any third party. This ghost that haunts Françoise Davoine carries in his suitcase a procession of specters: two world wars, three brothers who committed suicide and the fall of an empire in which the Wittgenstein family was an important player. With this impressive list of catastrophes under his belt, Wittgenstein is not relegated to the role of arbiter in this book. His thoughts and experience add to Françoise Davoine's clinical practice, and in turn, she tactfully addresses this figure with equal weight.

Wittgenstein knows how to push our buttons; it is as if he is trying to make one feel beside oneself. Wordplay here, wordplay there; he keeps repeating this language game of his. In the case of the psychoanalyst that is having a hard time with a patient, Wittgenstein has the gall to say:

> The mechanisms of the spirits are not material mechanisms. . . This patient is disturbing to you because they are using a language game that you are not familiar with. You have to change the way you see things.

It is as if these formulas, "language game" or "change the way you see things," represent a real form of assistance when one finds themself in front of a raving lunatic. Might as well suggest to someone that has just driven their car into a wall to eat organic food. . .

Careful reading is thus essential and may lead to the discovery of new meanings in these seemingly clear formulas. Indeed, it is a process that will position the psychoanalyst outside their own field of reference. If the senseless content and gestures of a mad person create a language game the psychoanalyst is not familiar with, then, there is a chance that they will have something to learn. To wager on the validity of a senseless message is like getting ready to hear extraordinary things. Let us be clear: there is nothing romantic or complaisant about the clinical state of madness. When Wittgenstein challenges the analyst to consider what patients are saying or showing to be a very particular language game, he insists on the fact—it is a fact—that the mad person is always part of a story. Just like the analyst or anyone else for that matter. The madness that unites them both, in one case, the analyst, and in the other case, the mad person, is no longer about quality but about degree. These roles are movable and must be imagined so. With these ideas in mind, which do not need to be proven but, considered under the lens of ethics, madness loses its fascinating and safe status as a mystery and becomes a research tool.

Some stories are more chaotic than others. Other stories are neither named nor recognized, or even commonly included in an official language. These stories can be expressed in many different ways. A young man lies down, mute and lets himself die of starvation; Mrs. Durant goes on about how she is hooked up to a machine whose operators have her enslaved; another woman loiters on the streets and warns mothers passing by that their children will be kidnaped; Théodore perfectly acts out a role from a script that he has never read. Each of these cases pushes a certain button in their own way. If they press this button and no such mechanism is initiated, they find themselves in a logical stalemate. Anyone who has furiously touched every key on a keyboard that has just stopped working has some idea of this sort of stalemate. Is it possible to kindly indicate that the button is a fantasy?

Françoise Davoine explores with patients the possibility of initiating something else with the button. Mrs. Durant, for example, who is—by the way—500 years old, complains that she carried elderly people all night. Those are her words. Françoise Davoine has just lost her grandmother, and naturally, this event is weighing on her conscience. She consequently decides to disclose this to her patient. Could it be that it was her elderly grandmother that was being carried? This question does not have an answer, but Mrs. Durant certainly seems to feel better once the question is asked. There is no sense in asking whether it really was that elderly person that Mrs. Durant carried all night. Between the patient's delirium and the circumstance evoked by the analyst, there are no causal factors. The essential being that the analyst's story created an application for Mrs. Durant's delusion. The button finally set off things in motion. Moving forward, we learn that when she was little and confined to a hospital during the war, Mrs. Durant's specialty was transporting sick people. As the world around her went raving mad, she developed a necessary skill that would later define her life in a hospital ward.

Let us take another more audacious example. Casimir, a man who spends his time watching women from the apartment building opposite his undress, requests that his analyst acknowledge his pregnancy. Indeed, to hear her say that he, Casimir, is pregnant. Then, a week later, the analyst discovered that she was, herself, pregnant. Casimir heard her talk about her pregnancy on the phone while in the waiting room. The telephone call was the striptease that sanctioned his insistence on the pregnancy. It was also a way to extend his usual voyeurism to other horizons. We then learn of a city that was bombarded: women experienced the unthinkable; his grandmother fled holding the cradle of her deceased eldest daughter. Casimir, the grandchild, held on to this story that was not repressed, only indescribable. His inability to vocalize this story led him to voyeurism. Between his story and the analyst's, one could have furtively caught a glimpse of an entire village that was erased from the map.

Of course, there is not any assurance that these types of stories can be told. Guarantees are made for banks, not psychanalysts. Moreover, if one had to wait to become pregnant for a psychotic transfer to take place, many male psychoanalysts would feel discouraged. In short, Françoise Davoine does not transform her clinical experiences into recipes, she simply points to an important fact: the convergence of many points of view is vital when trying to bring language to the foreground. A nonsensical language game, confined to itself, has two dimensions. The circumstances that add a third is not in and of itself important, but it certainly opens onto new possible horizons. We could start a vegetable garden there.

Based on these discoveries, Françoise Davoine slowly begins to refer to Wittgenstein. What about his language games? Who are these strange inhabitants from the pages of *Philosophical Investigations*? Sometimes they only speak through orders, content with this reduced form of language. We encounter a person who thinks that another person is suffering, all the while asking whether this person is an automaton. It is an inquiry of things less than happy. In time, the reader is invited to answer a questionnaire: are their books really theirs? And what about their body? Then, the philosopher asks other peculiar questions: what is left of a man's name after the man in question has been destroyed?

Respectably lined up one after the other, Wittgenstein's *Investigations* also tell a story. Written in German from the early 1930s until the after-war period, every page is an echo of his era. This era, however long ago it may seem, waits patiently in the wings, and when least expected, it makes its appearance center stage to remind us that it never did fade to black. Hence, in her conversations with Wittgenstein, Françoise Davoine takes a risk by acknowledging these ghosts. Yet, she does so gently and respectfully. The last chapter of her book is a moving example of Wittgenstein within his historical context: we see the Viennese philosopher exit the psychoanalyst's office with a child; they both step onto the street and disappear. It is up to the reader to form an idea of how the term 'historic' is attributed at that moment. In any event, this reading of Wittgenstein already gives an idea of the mental freedom that Françoise Davoine allows during her inquiry into clinical madness.

Another form of freedom: this book does not include jargon. As Françoise Davoine's exploration advances, she constructs her own vocabulary, and just like when we learn a language, she sometimes stutters. This tells us a lot about this book's fundamental position: in the field of madness, many things are possible, but nothing is a given. When psychoanalytical vocabulary makes her think, she does not hesitate to use it. When it abruptly calls a term into question, she painfully learns to unlearn it. In one breath, she calls upon aboriginal Medicine-men as well as battles in Zen, and this among many other things. The field of madness is therefore explored as a cyclical process involving all those who dip their feet. No participant in this dance, whether mad person, psychoanalyst, philosopher, Far-east elder or the author herself, sanctions or disapproves of this approach in an authoritative way. This leaves a lot of legroom for a character we have not yet evoked, the reader.

In his brief preface of *Philosophical Investigations*, Wittgenstein invites the reader to "develop personal thoughts." Like the rest of his preface, this phrase suggests that this valuable research is a sketch and can only be accomplished through a bond. *La Folie Wittgenstein* forms, in its own way, a multi-layer body. Just like at the beginning of our foreword, we imagined the reading of this book like a journey across a territory, a land. We called it "someone" to illustrate a wavering individual making the journey, and to suggest the prospect of a proper noun.

When he gave his *Lecture on Ethics,* Wittgenstein's audience must have been puzzled. The heart of the conference consisted in demonstrating the impossibility of all statements on ethics. But the philosopher ventured to give a personal example of what he could call, for lack of better words, *his* experience of ethics. In his opinion, the sentence that could describe this experience was the following: "I wonder at the existence of the world." Indeed, *La Folie Wittgenstein* preserves, in the therapeutic field of madness, this ability to feel wonder.

Notes

Chapter 1

1 Ludwig Wittgenstein, *The Blue and the Brown Books* (New York: Harper and Row, 1965), 14. This is a paperback edition of this work, which was originally published in the United States by Harper and Row in 1958, and by Basil Blackwell in Great Britain, also in 1958. Future citations will use the abbreviation BB. FD takes many of Wittgenstein's remarks directly from passages in his published works. She often employs literary license in altering them as she weaves them into the dialogue of this book. Sources of Wittgenstein's remarks (whether uttered by him, or recalled by someone else), when they are taken from his own works, will be cited in endnotes.

2 Ludwig Wittgenstein, *Tractatus Logico-Philosophicus* (New York and London: Routledge and Kegan Paul, 2002), # 4.1212. This is a reprint of a 2001 Routledge Classics edition. The English edition was first published in 1922, and this present translation in 1962. Although the statement that appears in *Wittgenstein's Folly* is logically equivalent to Wittgenstein's actual remark: "What *can* be shown *cannot* be said," it does not refer to the logical form of the proposition, which cannot be said, but rather to the facts that gave rise to the particular language game, and which remain outside the language game itself. It also refers to the grammar of statements within the language game, which can only be shown through examples. Most significantly, it refers to the unimaginable, the unnamable, and the Real (in the Lacanian sense), which cannot be said, but can only be shown.

3 Wittgenstein, BB, 66.

4 Helen Swick Perry, *Psychiatrist of America: The Life of Harry Stack Sullivan* (Cambridge, MA and London: Harvard University Press, 1982), 32.

5 Ludwig Wittgenstein, *Philosophical Investigations*, Third Edition (London: Basil Blackwell, 2001), ¶41. Blackwell published the first edition of this work in 1953. Future citations will use the abbreviation PI. References to Part I of the *Philosophical Investigations* will be by paragraph number only. Part II references will be made to the page number. I believe that with this present reference (¶ 41), FD has linked Wittgenstein's famous remark at the end of the *Tractatus* (7) *"Wovon man nicht sprechen kann, darüber muss man schweigen"* ("What we cannot speak about we must pass over in silence" with his statement in the *Investigations* that "the tool with the name "N" is broken." The matter will receive further clarification in Chapter 8, "When the Tool with the Name "N" is Broken."

6 Wittgenstein, BB, 68.

7 Wittgenstein, BB, 50–51.

8 Wittgenstein, BB, 19. The translator of Wittgenstein's *The Blue and Brown Books* uses the word "wish" for the German "*Wunsch*." This is also true of the translation of the

Philosophical Investigations. The tradition in France, particularly since Lacan's reading of Freud, has been largely in favor of translating the German "*Wunsch*" with the French "*désir*." In this translation, the French preference will be used throughout, so that in place of "wish" and "wishing," as they appear in English translations of Wittgenstein's texts, the words "desire" and "desiring" will be used.

9 Wittgenstein, BB, 4.
10 Wittgenstein, BB, 27.
11 Wittgenstein, BB, 22; Wittgenstein, PI, ¶s 437–441.
12 Wittgenstein, BB, 22.
13 Wittgenstein, PI, ¶440.
14 Wittgenstein, BB, 38.
15 Wittgenstein, PI, ¶441.
16 Wittgenstein, PI, ¶437.
17 Wittgenstein, PI, ¶467.
18 Maurice O'Connor Drury, *The Danger of Words and Writings on Witt genstein* (Bristol and England: Thoemmes Press, 1993), 154.

Chapter 2

1 Wittgenstein, PI, Part II, 161.
2 Sigmund Freud, *Beyond the Pleasure Principle* (1920), Vol. XVIII of the *Standard Edition of the Complete Psychological Works of Sigmund Freud* (London: The Hogarth Press, 1991), 14–15. FD's references to *Essays in Psychoanalysis* are in fact to a publication—*Essais de psychanalyse* (Paris: Petite bibliothèque Payot, 1972)—that reproduced in French translation four works of Freud, including *Beyond the Pleasure Principle*. Three of these works, including *Beyond the Pleasure Principle*, date from the 1920s. The other, "Thoughts on Death in Time of War," was composed in 1915. There is no collection of Freud's works in French translation comparable to the *Gesammelte Werke* or to the Standard Edition. In *Wittgenstein's Folly* Freud references will be to the Standard Edition, in order to accommodate the English language reader.
3 Freud, *Beyond the Pleasure Principle*, 16.
4 Max Schur, MD, *Freud Living and Dying* (New York: International Universities Press, 1972), 359–360. Freud's grandson Heinele died in 1923 at the age of 4 ½ years. Binswanger did not know about the death of Heinele when he wrote to Freud in 1926 to tell him of the death of his own son, at the age of eight years. The letter evoked in Freud memories of his grandson's death and of the onset of his own cancer. He wrote that the secret of his own indifference to his cancer lay in his total lack of joy in living as a result of his grandson's death. His grief at the death of his grandson seems to have been intertwined with the emotional upheaval created by the cancer.
5 Wittgenstein, PI, ¶659.
6 Wittgenstein, PI, ¶462.
7 Wittgenstein, PI, ¶517.
8 Wittgenstein, PI, ¶462.
9 Wittgenstein, PI, ¶442.
10 Wittgenstein, PI, ¶631.
11 Wittgenstein PI, ¶518, a passage taken from Plato's *Theaetetus*, 189.
12 Wittgenstein, BB, 57.
13 Wittgenstein, BB, 22–23.
14 Wittgenstein, BB, 23.
15 Wittgenstein, BB, 22.
16 Wittgenstein, BB, 22.
17 Wittgenstein, PI, ¶476.

18 Wittgenstein, BB, 23.
19 Wittgenstein, PI, ¶148.
20 The Brothers Grimm, *Fairy Tales* (New York: Alfred A. Knopf, 1992) , 348–359.
21 Wittgenstein, PI, ¶471.
22 Wittgenstein, PI, ¶596.
23 Wittgenstein, BB, 175.
24 Wittgenstein, PI, Part II, 189.
25 Wittgenstein, BB, 9.
26 Wittgenstein, BB, 9.
27 Wittgenstein, BB, 10.
28 Wittgenstein, BB, 10.
29 Drury, *The Danger of Words*, 154.

Chapter 3

 1 Ludwig Wittgenstein, "Notes for Lectures on 'Private Experience' and 'Sense Data.'" *The Philosophical Review*, Vol. 77, No. 3 (July 1968), 275–320.
 2 Ludwig Wittgenstein, *Remarks on Frazer's Golden Bough*, edited by Rush Rhees. English translation by A.C. Miles. Revised by Rush Rhees (London and England: The Brynmill Press Ltd), 1–18.
 3 Wittgenstein, PI, ¶38.
 4 Wittgenstein, PI, ¶283.
 5 Wittgenstein, PI, Preface, x.
 6 Wittgenstein, PI, Preface, x.
 7 Wittgenstein, PI, Preface, xi.
 8 Wittgenstein, PI, ¶15, ¶26.
 9 Wittgenstein, BB, 28.
10 Wittgenstein, "Notes for Lectures on 'Private Experience'," 283.
11 Wittgenstein, PI, ¶1, ¶10.
12 Wittgenstein, BB, 56.
13 Wittgenstein, PI, ¶11.
14 This statement is a condensation of numerous remarks by Wittgenstein in the opening pages of the *Blue Book* and in various places of the PI, such as page 186.
15 Wittgenstein, PI, ¶19.
16 Wittgenstein, PI, ¶19.
17 Wittgenstein, PI, ¶21.
18 Wittgenstein, PI, ¶7.
19 Wittgenstein, PI, ¶657.
20 Wittgenstein, PI, ¶654.
21 Wittgenstein, PI, ¶23.

Chapter 4

 1 Mary Barnes and Joseph Berke, *Two Accounts of a Journey through Madness* (New York: Other Press, 2002).
 2 Charles Perrault, "Blue Beard," in *The Blue Fairy Book*, edited by An drew Lang (New York: Dover Publications Inc., 1965), 293–294. This book is a paperback edition of a book that was originally published in New York by Longmans, Green, and Co., circa 1889.
 3 Jacques Lacan, "On a Question Prior to Any Possible Treatment of Psychosis," in Écrits, A *Selection*, translated by Bruce Fink (New York: W.W. Norton & Co., 2002), 211.

4 Lacan, "On a Question Prior . . . ," 211.
5 Cf. Jean Bethke Elstain, *Jane Addams and the Dream of American De mocracy: A Life* (New York: Basic Books, 2002).
6 École *de Chicago, Naissance de l'ecologie urbaine* (Paris: Aubier, 1979), 335. Cf. Robert E. Park and Ernest W. Burgess, *The City* (Chicago: University of Chicago Press, 1967). This book was originally published in 1925.
7 Perry, *Psychiatrist of America*, 251ff.

Chapter 5

1 Beulah Parker, *A Mingled Yarn: Chronicle of a Troubled Family* (New Haven: Yale University Press, 1972), 339.
2 Wittgenstein, PI, ¶260.
3 Frieda Fromm-Reichmann, *Psychoanalysis and Psychotherapy: Selected Papers of Frieda Fromm-Reichmann,* edited by Dexter M. Bullard (Chicago: University of Chicago Press, 1959), 126.
4 Fromm-Reichmann, *Selected Papers of Frieda Fromm-Reichmann*, 126.
5 Fromm-Reichmann, *Selected Papers of Frieda Fromm-Reichmann*, 126.
6 Fromm-Reichmann, *Selected Papers of Frieda Fromm-Reichmann*, 126.
7 Wittgenstein, PI, ¶30.
8 Wittgenstein, PI, ¶363.
9 Wittgenstein, PI, ¶28.
10 Wittgenstein, PI, ¶29.

Chapter 6

1 Bill Watterson, *Calvin and Hobbes: Weirdos from Another Planet* (Lon don: Sphere Books Limited, 1980), 127.
2 Wittgenstein, PI, ¶31.
3 Wittgenstein, PI, ¶29.
4 Wittgenstein, PI, ¶29.
5 Jacques Lacan, *The Seminar of Jacques Lacan, Book VII, The Ethics of Psychoanalysis, 1959–1960*, translated by Dennis Porter (New York: Norton, 1992), 270–283.
6 Ludwig Wittgenstein, *Lectures and Conversations on Aesthetics, Psychology and Religious Belief: Conversations on Freud* (Berkeley: University of California Press, 1997), 51.
7 Wittgenstein, *Lectures and Conversations*, 51–52.
8 Wittgenstein, PI, ¶32.

Chapter 7

1 Wittgenstein, PI, 166.
2 Wittgenstein, PI, ¶ 34.
3 *Entretiens de Lin-Tsi*, translated from the Chinese, with commentary by Paul Demiéville (Paris: Fayard, 1972), 25. In the text I have translated "*Entretiens*" by "Sayings."
4 *Entretiens*, 23–25, 126–129.
5 *Entretiens*, ¶19, 113.
6 *Entretiens*, ¶40, 166.
7 *Entretiens*, 118.
8 *Entretiens*, 16.
9 *Entretiens*, 16.

10 Wittgenstein, PI, ¶109.
11 Wittgenstein, PI, ¶35.

Chapter 8

1 Wittgenstein, PI, ¶ 41.
2 Wittgenstein, PI, ¶ 41.
3 Wittgenstein, PI, ¶ 42.
4 Wittgenstein, PI, ¶ 41.
5 Wittgenstein, PI, ¶ 35.
6 *Entretiens*, 140–141.
7 *Entretiens*, 31.
8 *Entretiens*, 117.
9 Jacques Lacan, "The Function and Field of Speech and Language in Psychoanalysis," in Écrits: *A Selection*, 101.

Chapter 9

1 Lawrence S. Kubie, MD, *The Riggs Story: The Development of the Aus ten Riggs Center for the Study and Treatment of the Neuroses* (New York: Paul B. Hoeber, Inc., Medical Division of Harper, 1960). This is a good source for the early history of Austen Riggs Center, including a brief biography of Austen Riggs.
2 Lacan, *The Ethics of Psychoanalysis*, 243–287.
3 William Faulkner, *Absalom, Absalom!* (New York: Vintage International, 1990). This book was originally published in 1936 by Random House. The edition cited follows the text as corrected in 1986.
4 Martin Cooperman, MD, "Some Observations Regarding Psychoana lytic Psychother- apy in a Hospital Setting." *The Psychiatric Hospital*, Vol. 14, No. 1 (1983), 21–28, 23–24.
5 Wittgenstein, PI, ¶109.
6 Cooperman, "Some Observations . . . ," 22–23.
7 Ludwig Wittgenstein, "Lecture on Ethics." *Philosophical Review*, Vol. 74, No. 1 (Janu- ary 1965), 3–12.
8 Wittgenstein, "Lecture on Ethics," 6–7.
9 Wittgenstein, "Lecture on Ethics," 6–7.
10 Wittgenstein, *Lectures and Conversations*, 63.
11 Wittgenstein, *Lectures and Conversations*, 70.
12 Wittgenstein, *Lectures and Conversations*, 70.

Chapter 10

1 Brian McGuinness, *Wittgenstein: A Life—Young Ludwig 1889–1921* (Berkeley: Univer- sity of California Press, 1988), 26.
2 Wittgenstein, *Lectures and Conversations*, 66–67.
3 Wittgenstein, PI, ¶37.
4 Wittgenstein, PI, ¶38.
5 Wittgenstein, PI, ¶46. The Theaetetus, 201e–202c. I have translated FD's French trans- lation of the Greek, rather than using the English translation of Wittgenstein's German.
6 Wittgenstein, PI, ¶39. "Nothung" is referred to in Wittgenstein's German text; "Excali- bur" is used in the English translation.
7 Wittgenstein, PI, ¶40.

8 Wittgenstein, PI, ¶44.
9 Wittgenstein, *Lectures and Conversations*, 69.
10 Donald W. Winnicott, *Therapeutic Consultations in Child Psychiatry* (New York: Basic Books, 1971).
11 Donald W. Winnicott, *Playing and Reality* (New York: Routledge, 1971), 121–123.
13 Winnicott, *Playing*, 89–94.
14 Passe sans porte (Wou-men-kouan), translated and annotated by Ma sumi Shibata (Paris: Editions traditionnelles, 1979), 152.

Chapter 11

1 Wittgenstein, *Remarks*, 13e.
2 Marcel Mauss, *The Gift: The Form and Reason for Exchange in Archaic Societies*, translated by W.D. Halls, forward by Mary Douglas (New York: Norton, 2000). This book was first published in English in 1954.
3 Wittgenstein, *Remarks*, 10e.
4 Wittgenstein, *Remarks*, 5e.
5 Wittgenstein, *Remarks*, 8e.
6 Wittgenstein, *Remarks*, 10e.
7 Wittgenstein, PI, ¶ 50.
8 Wittgenstein, PI, ¶ 55.
9 Wittgenstein, *Remarks*, 7e.

Chapter 12

1 Wittgenstein, PI, ¶ 158.
2 Wittgenstein, PI, ¶ 144.
3 Wittgenstein, PI, ¶ 65.
4 Wittgenstein, PI, ¶ 88.
5 Wittgenstein, PI, ¶ 66.
6 Wittgenstein, PI, ¶ 51.
7 Wittgenstein, PI, ¶ 123.
8 Wittgenstein, PI, ¶ 255.
9 Wittgenstein, PI, ¶ 122.
10 Harry Stack Sullivan, *Schizophrenia as a Human Process* (New York: Norton, 1974), 224–225. Introduction and Commentaries by Helen Swick Perry.
11 Sullivan, *Schizophrenia*, 184. This is taken from a quotation that was included in the mimeographed Proceedings of a Conference. It was cited by Helen Swick Perry in her commentary on this part of the book.
12 Sullivan, *Schizophrenia*, 220.
13 Harry Stack Sullivan, *The Fusion of Psychiatry and Social Science* (New York: Norton, 1971), 220, 108.
14 Sullivan, *Fusion*, 202.
15 Sullivan, *Schizophrenia*, 167.
16 Wittgenstein, PI, ¶ 103.
17 Wittgenstein, PI, ¶ 97.
18 Wittgenstein, PI, ¶ 103.
19 Wittgenstein, PI, ¶ 107.
20 Sullivan, *Schizophrenia*, 198.
21 Sullivan, *Schizophrenia*, 259.
22 Wittgenstein, PI, ¶ 120.
23 Wittgenstein, PI, ¶¶ 126.

24 Wittgenstein, PI, ¶ 164.
25 Sullivan, *Schizophrenia*, 148.
26 Wittgenstein, PI, ¶ 129.
27 Sullivan, *Schizophrenia*, 220.
28 Wittgenstein, PI, ¶ 67.
29 Wittgenstein, PI, ¶ 79.
30 Wittgenstein, PI, ¶ 106.
31 Sullivan, *Schizophrenia*, 224.

Chapter 13

1 Sullivan, *Schizophrenia*, 159.
2 Sullivan, *Schizophrenia*, 218–219.
3 Wittgenstein, PI, ¶ 136.
4 Sullivan, *Schizophrenia*, 163, 187.
5 Sullivan, *Schizophrenia*, 145.
6 Sullivan, *Schizophrenia*, 141.
7 Sullivan, *Schizophrenia*, 186.
8 Sullivan, *Schizophrenia*, 144.
9 Sullivan, *Schizophrenia*, 144.
10 Sullivan, *Schizophrenia*, 169.
11 Sullivan, *Schizophrenia*, 200.
12 Sullivan, *Schizophrenia*, 198.
13 Sullivan, *Schizophrenia*, 104.
14 Sullivan, *Schizophrenia*, 218.
15 Wittgenstein, PI, ¶ 420.
16 Sullivan, *Schizophrenia*, 199.
17 Wittgenstein, PI, ¶ 80.
18 Wittgenstein, PI, ¶ 84.
19 Wittgenstein, PI, ¶ 84.
20 Wittgenstein, PI, ¶ 88.
21 Wittgenstein, PI, ¶ 173.
22 Wittgenstein, PI, ¶ 160.
23 Wittgenstein, PI, ¶ 160.
24 Wittgenstein, PI, ¶ 119.

Chapter 14

1 Wittgenstein, PI, ¶ 309.
2 Wittgenstein, PI, ¶ 133.
3 Wittgenstein, PI, ¶ 255.
4 Wittgenstein, PI, ¶ 125.
5 Wittgenstein, PI, ¶ 144.
6 Wittgenstein, PI, ¶ 132.
7 Wittgenstein, "Notes for Lectures on 'Private Experience'," 287, foot note 11.
8 Wittgenstein, PI, ¶ 176.

Chapter 15

1 Wittgenstein, PI, ¶ 195.
2 Wittgenstein, PI, ¶'s 138, 139.

3 Wittgenstein, PI, ¶ 154.
4 Wittgenstein, PI, ¶'s 146, 150.
5 Wittgenstein, PI, ¶ 199.
6 Wittgenstein, PI, ¶ 189.
7 Wittgenstein, PI, ¶ 210.
8 Wittgenstein, PI, ¶ 241.
9 Wittgenstein, PI, ¶ 241.
10 Wittgenstein, PI, ¶ 235.
11 Wittgenstein, PI, ¶ 201.
12 Wittgenstein, PI, ¶ 193.
13 Wittgenstein, PI, ¶ 201.
14 Wittgenstein, PI, ¶ 201.
15 Wittgenstein, PI, ¶ 193.
16 Wittgenstein, PI, ¶ 193.
17 Harold Searles, "The Effort to Drive the Other Person Crazy—An Ele ment in the Aeti-
    ology and Psychotherapy of Schizophrenia," in *Collected Papers on Schizophrenia and
    Related Subjects* (Madison: International Universities Press, 1965), 254–283.
18 Wittgenstein, PI, ¶ 202.
19 Joseph Needham, *La science chinoise et l'Occident* (Paris: le Seuil, 1977), 112. Cf. Jo-
    seph Needham, *Science and Civilisation in China*, edited by Lu Gwei-Djen and Nathan
    Sivin (Cambridge: Cambridge University Press, 2000). This book was originally pub-
    lished in 1956.
20 Wittgenstein, PI, ¶ 160.
21 Wittgenstein, PI, ¶ 206.
22 Wittgenstein, PI, ¶ 221.
23 Wittgenstein, PI, ¶ 220.
24 Wittgenstein, PI, ¶ 245.

Chapter 16

1 Wittgenstein, PI, ¶198.
2 Wittgenstein, "Notes for Lectures," 306.
3 Wittgenstein, "Notes for Lectures," 275.
4 Wittgenstein, "Notes for Lectures," 275.
5 Wittgenstein, "Notes for Lectures," 277.
6 Wittgenstein, "Notes for Lectures," 314.
7 Wittgenstein, PI, ¶268.
8 Wittgenstein, PI, ¶279.
9 Wittgenstein, "Notes for Lectures," 314.
10 Wittgenstein, PI, ¶249.
11 Wittgenstein, "Notes for Lectures," 282.
12 Wittgenstein, "Notes for Lectures," 282.
13 Wittgenstein, PI, ¶253.
14 Fromm-Reichmann, *Psychoanalysis and Psychotherapy*, 126.

Chapter 17

1 Adapted from Virgil, *The Aeneid*, VII, 312: *"Flectere si nequeo superos, Acheronta
   movebo."* (If I cannot sway the gods above, I will move the world below). Cited by
   Freud as an epigraph to *The Interpretation of Dreams*.
2 Sigmund Freud, "Negation" (1925), *The Standard Edition of the Com plete Works of
   Sigmund Freud*, Volume XIX (London: The Hogarth Press, 1991), 239.

3 Donald W. Winnicott, "Fear of Breakdown." *International Psychoanalytic Review*, Vol. I (1974), 103.
4 Sigmund Freud, *Delusions and Dreams in Jensen's Gradiva* (1907), SE, IX (London: The Hogarth Press, 1991), 48.
5 Sigmund Freud, "Negation" (1925), SE, XIX (London: The Hogarth Press, 1991), 238.
6 Freud, "Negation," 237.
7 Freud, "Negation," 237–238.
8 Freud, "Negation," 237.
9 Freud, "Negation," 239.
10 Sigmund Freud, "The 'Uncanny'," (1919) SE, XVII (London: Hogarth Press, 1991), 248.
11 Wittgenstein, PI, ¶248.
12 Wittgenstein, PI, ¶253.
13 Wittgenstein, PI, ¶256.

Chapter 18

1 Wittgenstein, PI, ¶257.
2 Wittgenstein, PI, ¶256.
3 Wittgenstein, PI, ¶257.
4 Wittgenstein, PI, ¶257.
5 Wittgenstein, PI, ¶257.
6 Wittgenstein, PI, ¶257.
7 Wittgenstein, PI, ¶258.
8 Wittgenstein, PI, ¶258.
9 Wittgenstein, PI, ¶258.
10 Wittgenstein, PI, ¶259.
11 Plato, *Theatetus*, 202, a, b, c.
12 Wittgenstein, PI, ¶262.
13 Marcel Duchamp, *Duchamp du signe*. Écrits. (Paris: Flammarion, 1975), 48.
14 Wittgenstein, PI, ¶271.
15 Wittgenstein, "Notes on Sense Data," 317.
16 Wittgenstein, "Notes on Sense Data," 306.
17 McGuinness, *Wittgenstein: A Life*, 157–158.
18 Wittgenstein, "Notes on Sense Data," 306.

Chapter 19

1 Wittgenstein, PI, 189.
2 DuChamp, *Duchamp du signe*, 154.
3 Wittgenstein, PI, ¶265.
4 Wittgenstein, PI, ¶266.
5 Marcel Proust, *In Search of Lost Time* Vol. VI, *Time Regained*, translated by Andreas Mayor, and Terence Kilmartin, revised by D.J. Enright (New York: The Modern Library, 2003), 266–268.
6 Wittgenstein, PI, ¶270.
7 Sigmund Freud, Carl Gustav Jung, *Correspondance*, t. I, letter du 16 avril 1909 (Paris: Gallimard, coll. "Connaissance de l'inconscient," 1975), 295.
8 Perry, *Psychiatrist of America*, 419.
9 Wittgenstein, PI, ¶302.
10 Fromm-Reichmann, *Psychoanalysis and Psychotherapy*, 126.
11 Wittgenstein, PI, ¶288.

12 Wittgenstein, PI, ¶283.
13 Helen Swick Perry, *Psychiatrist of America*, 166.
14 Wittgenstein, PI, ¶288.

Chapter 20

1 Wittgenstein, PI, ¶296.
2 Wittgenstein, PI, ¶298.
3 Wittgenstein, PI, ¶304.
4 Wittgenstein, PI, ¶307.
5 Wittgenstein, PI, ¶283.
6 Wittgenstein, PI, ¶293.
7 Wittgenstein, PI, ¶293.
8 Wittgenstein, PI, ¶293.
9 Wittgenstein, PI, ¶293.
10 Wittgenstein, PI, ¶293.
11 Raymond Devos, *Sens dessus dessous. Sketches. La protection des espaces vides* (Paris: Stock, 1976), 124.

Chapter 21

1 Wittgenstein, PI, ¶339.
2 Wittgenstein, PI, ¶348.
3 Wittgenstein, PI, ¶348.
4 Wittgenstein, PI, ¶350.
5 Wittgenstein, PI, ¶342. Mr. Ballard's reminiscences were recorded by William James in *The Principles of Psychology*, Volume One (New York: Dover, 1950), 266–269.
6 Wittgenstein, PI, ¶342.
7 Wittgenstein, PI, ¶344.
8 Wittgenstein, PI, ¶344.
9 Wittgenstein, PI, ¶344.
10 Wittgenstein, PI, ¶329.
11 Wittgenstein, PI, ¶344.
12 Wittgenstein, PI, ¶346.
13 Wittgenstein, PI, ¶20.
14 Konrad Lorentz, *Il parlait avec les mammifères, les oiseaux et les poissons* (Paris: Flammarion, 1970).
15 Vicky Hearne, *Calling Animals by Name* (New York: Alfred A. Knopf, 1986).
16 Wittgenstein, PI, ¶354.

Chapter 22

1 Wittgenstein, PI, ¶339.
2 Harry Stack Sullivan, *Conceptions of Modern Psychiatry* (New York: Norton, 1971), 261–263.
3 Sullivan, *Conceptions of Modern Psychiatry*, xii.
4 Harry Stack Sullivan, *The Fusion of Psychiatry and Social Science. The Illusion of Personal Identity*, 119.
5 Sullivan, *The Fusion of Psychiatry and Social Science*, 198.

Chapter 23

1   Erasme, *Éloge de la folie*, traduction par Pierre de Nolhac (Paris: Garnier-Flammarion, 1964). Cf. Desiderius Erasmus, *Praise of Folly*, translated by Betty Radice (New York: Penguin Classics, 1994).
2   Henry Ey, *Manuel de psychiatrie* (Paris: Masson, 1967), 258.
3   René Descartes, "First Meditation," in *Meditationes de prima philosophia/Mediations on First Philosophy*, A Bilingual Edition, edited and translated and indexed by George Heffernan (Notre Dame and Indiana: University of Notre Dame Press, 1990), 97
4   Jacques Lacan, *The Four Fundamental Concepts of Psychoanalysis*, edited by Jacques-Alain Miller and translated from the French by Alan Sheridan (New York: Norton, 1977), 225.
5   Wittgenstein, PI, ¶349.
6   Wittgenstein, PI, ¶354.
7   Descartes, *Meditationes*, "Third Meditation," 123.
8   Wittgenstein, PI, ¶355.
9   Wittgenstein, PI, ¶358.
10 Wittgenstein, PI, ¶358.
11 Denis Diderot, *Entretien entre d'Alembert et Diderot, La Rêve de d'Alem bert* (Paris: Gallimard, « Bibliothèque de la Pléiade », 1958), 910.
12 Diderot, *Entretien, La Rêve,* 913.
13 Wittgenstein, PI, ¶359.
14 Wittgenstein, PI, ¶360.
15 Wittgenstein, PI, ¶360.
16 Wittgenstein, PI, ¶368.
17 Wittgenstein, PI, ¶368.
18 Henry James, *"Les Impressionnistes,"* dans *Le Journal de l'impressionnisme,* Skira (Paris: Flammarion, 1985), 163. Cf. Henry James, "The Impressionists," in *The Painter's Eye: Notes and Essays on the Pictorial Arts by Henry James*, edited by John L. Sweeney (London: Rupert Hart- Davis, 1956), 114.
19 Wittgenstein, PI, ¶386.
20 Wittgenstein, PI, ¶381.
21 Wittgenstein, PI, ¶390.
22 Descartes, *Meditationes*, "Third Meditation," 119.
23 Wittgenstein, PI, ¶390.
24 Descartres, *Meditationes*, "Second Meditation," 113.
25 Wittgenstein, PI, ¶391.
26 Wittgenstein, PI, ¶391.

Chapter 24

1   Wittgenstein, PI, ¶393.
2   Wittgenstein, PI, ¶393.
3   Wittgenstein, PI, ¶394.
4   Antonin Artaud, *Oeuvres complètes*, t. IV, *le Théâtre et son double* (Paris: Gallimard 1964). Cf. *Antonin Artaud: Selected Writings*, edited by Susan Sontag and translated by Helen Weaver (Berkeley: University of California Press, 1988).
5   Wittgenstein, PI, ¶398.
6   Wittgenstein, PI, ¶398.
7   *Aeschlyus, Agamnenon* in *The Complete Plays, Volume I: Oresteia: Agamemnon, Libation Bearers, Eumenides*, translated by Carl R. Mueller, introduction by Hugh Denard (Hanover and New Hampshire, 2002), 115.

8 Aeschlyus, *The Complete Plays, Agamemnon*, 120.
9 Wittgenstein, PI, ¶400.
10 Wittgenstein, *Tractatus*, Proposition 7.
11 Jacques Lacan, Seminar VII, *The Ethics of Psychoanalysis*, translated by Dennis Porter (New York: W.W. Norton& Company), 43–70.
12 Sophocles, *Antigone in The Oedipus Cycle: Oedipus Rex, Oedipus at Colonus, Antigone*, translated by Dudley Fitts and Robert Fitzgerald (New York: Harcourt Brace and Company, 2002).
13 Wittgenstein, PI, ¶398.

Chapter 25

1 Wittgenstein, PI, ¶404.
2 Wittgenstein, PI, ¶404.
3 Wittgenstein, PI, ¶404.
4 Wittgenstein, PI, ¶404.
5 Wittgenstein, PI, ¶404.
6 Wittgenstein, PI, ¶406.
7 Wittgenstein, PI, ¶407.
8 Wittgenstein, PI, ¶409.
9 Diderot, *Rêve de D'Alembert*, 128.
10 Diderot, *Rêve de D'Alembert*, 913.
11 Descartes, *Meditationes*, "Sixth Meditation," 201.
12 Descartes, *Meditationes*, "Sixth Meditation," 207.
13 Descartes, *Meditationes*, "Sixth Meditation," 207.
14 Descartes, *Meditationes*, "Sixth Meditation," 209.
15 Descartes, *Meditationes*, "Sixth Meditation," 207–209.
16 Descartes, *Meditationes*, "Sixth Meditation," 207.
17 Descartes, *Meditationes*, "Sixth Meditation," 211.
18 Descartes, *Meditationes*, "Sixth Meditation," 211.
19 Descartes, *Meditationes*, "Sixth Meditation,' 211.
20 Wittgenstein, PI, ¶411.
21 Wittgenstein, PI, ¶411.
22 Wittgenstein, PI, ¶411.
23 Wittgenstein, PI, ¶410.
24 Wittgenstein, PI, ¶420.
25 Wittgenstein, PI, ¶420.
26 Wittgenstein, PI, ¶420.
27 Wittgenstein, PI, ¶415.

Chapter 26

1 Wittgenstein, PI, ¶182.
2 Wittgenstein, PI, ¶412.
3 Wittgenstein, PI, ¶416.
4 Wittgenstein, PI, ¶414.
5 Jean-Jacques Rousseau, *les Rêveries du promeneur solititaire, Deuxieme promenade* (Paris: Gallimard, "Bibliothèque de la Pléiade," 1959), 1005. Cf. *The Reveries of the Solitary Walker*, "Second Walk," translated by Peter France (Toronto: Penguin, 2004), 35ff.
6 Wittgenstein, PI, ¶423.

7 Wittgenstein, PI, ¶426.
8 Heinrich von Kleist, *Anecdotes et petits écrits. Sur le théâtre marionettes* (Paris: Petite bibliothèque Payot, 1981). Cf. Heinrich von Kleist, "The Puppet Theater," in *Selected Writings*, edited and translated by David Constantine (Indianapolis: Hackett Publishing Co., 2001), 411–416.
9 Kleist, *Anecdotes*, 101.
10 Kleist, *Anecdotes*, 101.
11 Kleist, *Anecdotes*, 101.
12 Kleist, *Anecdotes*, 101.
13 Lin Tsi, *Entretiens de Lin Tsi*, 142.
14 Lin Tsi, *Entretiens de Lin Tsi*, 44.

Chapter 27

1 Plato, *Theaetetus*, 165b.
2 Plato, *Theaetetus*, 186d.
3 Plato, *Theaetetus*, 191c.
4 *Nô et Kyôgen*, t. I, présentés et traduits par René Sieffert (Paris: POF, 1979), 15.
5 Plato, *Theaetetus*, 188e.
6 Plato, *Theaetetus*, 194c–e.
7 Hao Wang, *Reflections on Kurt Gödel* (Cambridge, MA: MIT Press), 1988.
8 Plato, *Theaetetus*, 198 a–b.
9 Wittgenstein, PI, 571.
10 Wittgenstein, PI, 572.
11 Wittgenstein, PI, 193.
12 Wittgenstein, PI, 171.
13 Wittgenstein, PI, 498.
14 Wittgenstein, PI, 499.
15 Wittgenstein, PI, 161.
16 Wittgenstein, PI, 546.
17 Wittgenstein, PI, 654.
18 Wittgenstein, PI, 665.

Index

For Product Safety Concerns and Information please contact our EU
representative GPSR@taylorandfrancis.com
Taylor & Francis Verlag GmbH, Kaufingerstraße 24, 80331 München, Germany

www.ingramcontent.com/pod-product-compliance
Lightning Source LLC
Chambersburg PA
CBHW050641280326
41932CB00015B/2733

* 9 7 8 1 0 3 2 5 6 8 6 7 6 *